# Emergency!

## Crisis in the Cockpit

Stanley Stewart

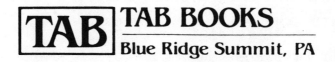

## TAB BOOKS
Blue Ridge Summit, PA

*'One thorn of experience is worth a whole wilderness of warning.'*
James Russel Lowell

FIRST TAB EDITION
FIRST TAB PRINTING

© 1991, 1989 by **Stanley Stewart**.
Published by **TAB Books**.
TAB Books is a division of McGraw-Hill, Inc.

First published in the UK in 1989 by
Airlife Publishing Ltd.

**Library of Congress Cataloging-in-Publication Data**

Stewart, Stanley.
   Emergency! : crisis in the cockpit / by Stanley Stewart.
     p.   cm.
   Includes bibliographical references and index.
   ISBN 0-8306-6499-8     ISBN 0-8306-3499-1
   1. Transport planes—Piloting.  2. Air travel.  I. Title.
TL710.S663  1991
629.132'5216—dc20           91-8735
                              CIP

TAB Books offers software for sale. For information and a catalog, please contact TAB Software Department, Blue Ridge Summit, PA 17294-0850.

# Contents

# Acknowledgements

Much help, assistance and advice was received from many people during the writing of this book and the author is deeply indebted to all those who so kindly contributed. Without the generous support of those involved in the incidents, and others in the aviation industry, this book would not have been possible. To all those who so kindly helped, the author would like to express his heartfelt thanks. **Pacific Search**: Captain Gordon Vette and Captain Jay Prochnow; **Bermuda Tangle**: Captain Steve Thompson, with assistance from Senior Engineer Officer Dave Hoyle (Tristar Flight Engineer Instructor); **To Take-off or Not to Take-off . . .**: Captain Wayne Sagar, with assistance from Senior Engineer Officer Simon Robinson (747 Flight Engineer); **The Windsor Incident**: Captain Bryce McCormick; **Don't be Fuelish**: Captain Bob Pearson and First Officer Maurice Quintal; **The Blackest Day**: Captain Pat Levix; **Ice Cool**: Captain Tom Hart; **Roll Out the Barrel**: Captain Harvey 'Hoot' Gibson and Mr Harold F. Marthinsen, Director ALPA Accident Investigation Department; **Strange Encounter**: Captain Eric Moody, Senior First Officer Roger Greaves, Senior Engineer Officer Barry Townley-Freeman, with assistance from Senior First Officer Frank Avery (747 Assistant Instructor).

I would also like to thank Captain Harry Orlady of NASA's San Francisco office of the Air Safety Reporting System for his help in tracing individuals and, last but not least, two ladies for their excellent work: Andrea Metcalfe for her careful reading and correcting of the manuscript and Sara Phillips for her conscientious work in transferring the manuscript to the word processor.

Any errors remaining are, of course, entirely my own.

# Introduction

Flying is one of the safest forms of modern transport and, as a means of travelling quickly over long distances, its role is unsurpassed. The passenger of today is transported with amazing ease from one side of the globe to the other, with the problems of the earth being left far below. For present day flight crew, however, it is another world, with the view from the flight deck offering a different sight. Aircrew are only too well aware of the hostile nature of their working environment and, armed with such knowledge, are both ready and able to overcome the difficulties.

Aircraft frequently cross great empty oceans, vast featureless deserts, immense ice wastelands and enormous desolate regions in complete safety in spite of the adverse conditions of the terrain below. Aircrew are trained for all contingencies, and survival equipment for sea, ice and desert is carried aboard. On a journey half way round the world many areas of conflict may be crossed without a single sound of the calamity below being heard, the loudest report in the cabin being the pop of a champagne cork. Such danger zones can be traversed or circumvented in safety when approached with vigilance and care.

Natural disasters, civil strife and famine also prove of little effect for the high-flying traveller, although for staff and crew at transit stations the problems may be enormous. In the skies of starving Africa, passengers sitting miles above the horror indulge their tastes in international cuisine. Cosseted by eager airlines, the modern traveller is borne, with diligence and care, in genuine security over the trouble spots of the earth. Journeys over half the world are now so commonplace and scheduled arrivals so frequent that delays of an hour or so can annoy passengers. To arrive, say, a few hours late in Auckland after a 12,000 mile trip from London can be quite unacceptable to some. Yet if the same passengers stopped only for one moment to think of such a journey, they could not fail to be impressed by the accomplishment. The world may be shrinking, but it is not quite as small as we are led to believe. It is still a hazardous place for the unwary and even short flights are rarely as simple as they seem.

In spite of advanced technology and the magic of computers, the movement of something as big as a Boeing 747 from one side of the world to the other is an operation of complex proportions. Anyone who has contemplated driving their automobile in a foreign country will immediately recognise the problems; the difficulties in operating a big jet worldwide are immense; overflying rights, landing permission, insurance arrangements, fuel payments, cargo and passenger quotas are but a few of the challenges, all of which have to be negotiated between governments and often between countries barely talking to each other. The capital equipment required to service a large international airline operation is enormous: aircraft, offices, sales shops, hangars, terminal buildings and a plethora of expensive vehicles from mobile steps to push-back trucks. With air fares over long distances still comparatively low in respect of present-day incomes, it is a wonder that airlines make any profit at all. That they do and, in some cases, manage quite handsome returns in the face of fierce competition, is a great credit to the managers who run these large and costly outfits.

The fact that airlines function successfully throughout the globe is due to the dedicated and hardworking people within the industry who make the system work, in spite of the problems. Managers, office staff, sales persons, accountants, engineers, maintenance personnel, traffic supervisors, the backroom people of the world's airlines, all make a significant contribution, as well as the aircrews at the sharp end of the operation. For passengers, the smooth, comfortable and effortless transition from one place to another is not accomplished without a great deal of exertion from all concerned. Much of the effort is, of course, unobserved by the travelling public, not least the skills of the flight crew in flying the aircraft from departure to destination. It is an esoteric world where few of even the most well travelled of passengers have been permitted to enter.

The airline pilot's job today is essentially one of operations director and systems manager, but even on the most sophisticated of electronic flight decks the human contribution is significant. In spite of the advances in computers and electronics, machines can do no reasoning for themselves and creative thinking is still a necessary facet of the job. Aircraft computers can do only so much and modern electronic capabilities are not quite as fantastic as the public is led to believe. Malfunctions do occur and there are many traps for the unwary. Flight crews, of course, are alert to the problems, but are sometimes too eager to assure passengers by telling them how easy it has all become. Basic airmanship (i.e. the collective practical application of training, skill, experience and professional judgement) is still required to be exercised by all flight crews at all times.

All aircraft computers are required to be programmed before flight for each journey and the autopilot, when engaged, has to be instructed on every move. Automatic guidance of a 747, for example, down a narrow radio beam to accomplish an automatic landing in almost blind, foggy conditions with 400 people on board is not a task to be taken lightly. The automatics have to be very carefully monitored for malfunctions and the autopilot has to be told what to do at each stage of the approach. In the fog, of course, the wind is calm and the air still, and in such circumstances automatic landings can be effective. When the wind is blustery and conditions bumpy, however, especially with a strong cross-wind on landing, the autopilot cannot cope and the pilot has to take over and land the aircraft.

On most flights, crew operation is routine with standard procedures being followed but, of course, circumstances do change, even when flying repeatedly on the same route. Take-off and landing delays, work at airports, equipment malfunctions, re-routeings, adverse weather and so on, all present difficulties. Flight crews, however, not only have to perform the routine well, a highly skilled procedure in itself, but have to cope with any emergency which may arise. When severe weather strikes, systems malfunction, engines fail or aircraft fires erupt, it is sometimes only the skill of the flight crew which lies between safety and disaster. Flight crews have at all times to be alert to every situation. When a major emergency occurs decisions are made, sometimes in a split second, which can affect the safety of the aircraft and perhaps many hundreds of lives. Here the captain comes into his own and the training of the flight crew is put to the test.

Airline crews are well trained, highly motivated and dedicated professionals. Although mistakes are sometimes made and accidents occasionally happen, the high level of safety evident in the airline industry is a testament to the excellent standard maintained by all concerned. Too much publicity these days is given to the rare demise of an aircraft, with little being known of the incidents which, owing to aircrew professionalism, end safely and well. Many of the events told within this book are known in aviation circles, with only a few outside, and most of those involved remain unsung heroes. *Emergency* outlines a number of dramatic incidents and reveals crew procedures during the difficulties, inviting the reader into the exclusive environment of the flight deck to observe the operations.

The author, Stan Stewart, has flown for over twenty years and has operated heavy jets in British Airways for eighteen years. A graduate engineer, 747 pilot and aviation writer, he is uniquely qualified to write on aviation matters. *Emergency* is a celebration of the skills and abilities of pilots and flight engineers throughout the world, and the following chapters can be left to speak for themselves.

# Chapter 1
# Pacific Search

The vast Pacific Ocean is bounded by five continents and covers an area of seventy million square miles. Its deep waters stretch from the shores of Asia and Australia to the coastlines of North and South America, and to Antarctica in the south. Along the line of the equator from Indonesia to Equador the distance across the waves is over eight thousand nautical miles (nm).

The name, Pacific, belies the temperamental nature of the ocean, and on occasions storms of great ferocity lash the region. Even large modern airliners have to treat the area with caution, for all but very long range aircraft must island-hop to overcome the immense distances. Fortunately, the surface of the Pacific is dotted with thousands of islands, although they are mostly very small and widely scattered. The only regular flights to close the enormous Pacific gap are the 747SP (Special Performance) non-stop services of United Airlines and Qantas from Sydney to Los Angeles, a journey of 7,475 miles which takes thirteen-and-a-half hours to complete.

Aboard modern passenger jets, electronic navigation equipment, adequate fuel reserves and skilled crews have transformed flights between far-off islands to safe, routine and everyday events. For the light aircraft pilot, however, the Pacific still presents an awesome barrier. The journeys from island to distant island are long and tedious, with flight at slow speed. Navigation over the featureless stretches of sea is difficult, and any error or malfunction in locating the remote specks of land can prove disastrous. For one pilot venturing alone in a light aircraft across the vast Pacific in 1978, a simple instrument failure led to the aviator becoming hopelessly lost.

In 1978 Jay E. Prochnow was thirty-six years old and a very experienced pilot who had flown in the US Navy. He had also completed a tour of duty in Vietnam. At the time he worked as a delivery pilot for Trans Air of Oakland Airport, California. One assignment he had been given was to fly a Cessna 188 — a light single-engine single-seat aircraft used for crop spraying — from California across the Pacific to a customer in Australia. Such long distance flights, although hazardous for a small machine, are cheaper than inter-continental shipping costs. Extra fuel tanks were fitted to the aircraft for the ordeal. The only sources of navigation, however, apart from chart and compass, were the rather antiquated radio beacons known as non-directional beacons (NDB) scattered amongst the islands of the Pacific.

Although these beacons are relatively inaccurate for the distant plotting of position on a chart, some of the more powerful transmitters have signal ranges in excess of 300 nm over the sea by day and 700 nm by night. These radio beacons transmit a signal, not unlike a broadcast station, and Prochnow's aircraft was fitted with an automatic direction finder (ADF) which could be tuned to a particular NDB and the transmitter identified by its morse code emission. The ADF could then detect the incoming signal and point a needle in the direction of the beacon. The needle direction and compass reading could be utilised to establish the bearing of the aircraft from a distant beacon for plotting a position line on a chart, and three or more bearings could be taken from different beacons to fix the position roughly. At long ranges the needles of the ADF were known to fluctuate wildly, and precise track-keeping was very difficult using such a system. It was sufficiently accurate, however, to guide the aircraft to within range of the destination NDB and the pilot could then home in on the signal by simply following the direction of the needle.

A few days before Christmas, 1978, Prochnow arrived in Pago Pago in the American Samoa Islands, accompanied by a colleague in another Cessna 188 who was flying the same journey. By then they had successfully completed well over half the trip and if all went according to plan they would arrive in Australia in time to return home for Christmas. Two days later the two Cessnas took-off together at 03:30 local time with Prochnow in the lead. Unfortunately the second aircraft's fuel pump shaft sheared at lift-off and Prochnow watched with horror as his colleague was forced to ditch in the sea. Fortunately the downed pilot escaped unhurt. Prochnow returned to land and after a day's rest left on his own with full tanks in the middle of the following night for a now lonely and gruelling trip to tiny Norfolk Island, 1,475 nm away. Cruising at speeds of around 110 knots, the journey would take a minimum of fourteen hours to complete in still wind conditions, but would be nearer fifteen hours flying against the forecast light westerly winds. The flight time would allow a daylight landing in Norfolk in mid-afternoon at about 16:00 local time, giving sufficient leeway for adverse winds. The full tank fuel load gave a total endurance of twenty-two hours at normal cruise speeds, which seemed an adequate reserve for any contingency. If necessary fuel could be conserved by decreasing power a little and by slightly leaning the mixture, i.e. reducing the fuel-to-air ratio, thereby increasing the endurance.

Norfolk Island is situated at 29°S 168°E, about 800 nm off the east coast of Australia. The island lies about 600 nm NNW of Auckland, New Zealand, and 430 nm south of Noumea, New Caledonia. It would not be inaccurate to describe Norfolk Island as a tiny speck of rock lying in the middle of nowhere in a corner of the vast Pacific. There is no land around for over 400 nm in any direction. Although Norfolk Island is Australian territory, for convenience it is enclosed within the Auckland Oceanic Flight Information Region, and all flights in and out of the island airport communicate with the Auckland Air Traffic Control Centre (ATCC).

Prochnow took-off from Samoa in the darkness at about 03:00 local time on 21 December and climbed slowly under the weight of fuel to his cruising altitude of 8,000 ft (2,438 m). He turned due south-west to pick up the direct track of 220° magnetic from Pago Pago to Norfolk Island and settled down for the long flight ahead. With no autopilot to ease the monotony of hand flying, it was going to be a tiring and tedious journey. There would be no chance of a quick nap. He would have to navigate with a map on his knee and plot position while flying the aircraft, and would have to grab snacks from his pack meals whenever he could. The initial routeing lay over the Tonga, or Friendly Islands, then continued on southwest bound about 200 nm south of Fiji. For most of the first part of the route sufficient NDBs were available for reasonably accurate fixing of position and progress was good.

A few hours later the strain of flying through the blackness of the night was eased when dawn broke behind the tail of the Cessna at about 05:15 local, and bathed the ocean in light. Approximately 600 nm from Pago Pago lay the island of Ono-I-Lau, almost directly on route. Prochnow navigated toward the island using the various NDB beacons along the way to plot his track. In due course Ono-I-Lau was sighted and his position was confirmed. Beyond the tiny island stretched a vast area of ocean with the destination still over 850 nm away. Prochnow would now have to traverse several hundred miles of empty sea, without any source of navigation whatsoever except the basic magnetic compass, before picking up the signal of the powerful NDB at Norfolk Island. He could then home in on the beacon over the last two or three hundred miles and be guided to the local airport.

At almost the halfway point of the journey the little Cessna crossed the international date line at 180° E/W longitude, the line at which time is both twelve hours behind GMT and twelve hours ahead of GMT, i.e. at the same time on each side of the line, but on different days. As Prochnow traversed the date line he lost twenty-four hours and jumped one day ahead. The local date was now 22 December 1978 and the local time around 08:00. Approximately eight hours of flying remained.

A further 120 nm along track the small machine crossed the Tropic of Capricorn, the line on a chart marking 23½° South, the most southerly declination of the sun. This day the sun was at its highest point in the southern sky, for 21 December marks the Winter Solstice, the shortest day in the Northern Hemisphere's winter, and the longest day of the summer in the south. Prochnow's trip was well planned, for the maximum amount of daylight would be available for the long flight to Norfolk Island.

After several more hours of flying over the featureless sea the Cessna came within range of the destination radio beacon and the signal was identified by its 'NF' morse coding. The arrows of the ADF pointed directly ahead. Prochnow was now flying within the jurisdiction of the Auckland Oceanic ATCC and had established contact on high frequency (HF) long range radio. His estimated time of arrival (ETA) at Norfolk Island was given as 04:30 GMT, 16:00 local time.

The little Cessna droned on at 8,000 ft (2,438 m) as Prochnow followed the direction of the ADF needle. With the approach of the estimated time of arrival he peered ahead for a glimpse of the tiny island, but the bright sun made forward vision difficult. The ETA came and went with no sign of Norfolk, but the ADF needle still pointed steadfastly ahead. The winds could very well have been stronger then forecast which would easily affect the flight

Captain Gordon Vette.

time, although arrivals were normally within fifteen minutes of ETAs. It was just as well Prochnow had loaded plenty of fuel. He called Auckland and informed them of the situation but as yet felt no cause for alarm. Thirty minutes later the needle still indicated the island lying ahead. The bright sun began to fall in the western sky, further reducing forward visibility as Prochnow's eyes searched eagerly for a sight of the land. He tuned in two distant powerful radio beacons, one on Lord Howe Island and the other at Kaitaia in northern New Zealand, in an attempt to plot his position, but the resultant fix was right off his chart. Something was seriously wrong. On retuning the Norfolk beacon he saw to his horror that the needle now pointed in a completely different direction. In spite of the Norfolk Island NDB being correctly tuned and identified the functioning of the ADF appeared to be seriously amiss and the instrument seemed simply to point at random in any direction. Prochnow rapidly gathered his senses and assessed the situation. He had about seven hours of fuel remaining, perhaps more if he conserved his fuel. What should he do now? Which way should he turn for Norfolk Island? For some time he had been flying in the direction of the ADF needle which pointed where it chose. At this stage he could be sixty miles (ninety-six kilometres) or more adrift from his track to destination. He had no doubt that by now his situation was desperate. Prochnow radioed Auckland declaring an emergency and gave details of his predicament. He was hopelessly lost. Alone in a small aircraft in the middle of the empty Pacific, and with sunset only a few hours away, his chances of being found were very slim indeed. Immediately he began a square search of the area. If, while looking for Norfolk Island, his tanks ran dry he would be faced with ditching at night in the lonely Pacific, a prospect which was not appealing. If he was forced into such a situation his chances of survival would be nil.

At about 17:15 local Fiji time, Flight TE 103, an Air New Zealand DC-10, registration ZK-NZS (Zula Sierra), took off from Nadi airport for Auckland, some three hours' flight time away. The captain, Gordon Vette, a senior pilot with the company, turned the jet due south for New Zealand and climbed the aircraft to its cruising altitude of 33,000 ft (10,060 m). His co-pilot on the flight was First Officer Arthur Dovey and his flight engineer, Gordon Brooks. About twenty minutes later, as the big jet settled at cruise altitude for what was a short hop for the long-range aircraft, news of Prochnow's predicament came through from Nadi on very high frequency (VHF) short-range radio. Further information could be obtained on HF from Auckland ATCC who were handling the Cessna's flight.

By the time contact was established with the Centre, the news from Auckland was bleak, and it was obvious to the crew that the situation was very serious. Prochnow was completely lost and his reserves of fuel were being steadily consumed. Even if help were available immediately it could be a tight-run race for safety. In the busy air and shipping routes of the western world, maritime services and air-sea rescue units would be quickly mobilised to help, but in the remote Pacific it is not such a simple matter. An Orion aircraft of the RNZAF had been placed on standby at Whenuapai Air Base, twenty miles (thirty-two kilometres) north of Auckland, but it would be some hours before it could reach the search area once it became airborne. The Air New Zealand DC-10 would pass about 400 nm due east of Norfolk Island on its route from Fiji to Auckland, but if it proceeded directly to the search area it could be there in about one and a half hours. Since there was very little other aircraft activity in the region, would the crew of the New Zealand jet be able to help?

Captain Vette and his colleagues did not need to be asked twice, and soon the big jet was speeding towards Norfolk on its rescue attempt. By good fortune the DC-10 carried a lot of extra fuel and could remain airborne for some considerable time. In New Zealand aviation fuel is expensive and the jet was 'tankering' fuel to save costs. The flight was also scheduled to proceed to Wellington and the extra fuel load would save refuelling in the transit. But there was more in Prochnow's favour than he might have hoped, for Vette, although a senior captain, was an enthusiastic navigator and still kept his flight navigator's licence current. The DC-10, of course, had sophisticated electronic navigation units on board consisting of three completely separate area inertial navigation systems (AINS), and did not require a navigator, but the DC-8 aircraft in Air New Zealand's fleet at the time were not so electronically equipped. All co-pilots on such fleets were also trained as navigators and performed navigation duties as and when required. Vette used to navigate occasionally on the DC-8 to keep his licence up to date.

The AINS of the DC-10 could navigate with pin-point accuracy and displayed a continuous read-out of the aircraft position at all times. There was no equipment aboard, however, for homing in on the Cessna, and trying to find the light aircraft would be like looking for a needle in a haystack. The radar on the DC-10 flight deck was used only in scanning for weather and could pick out large storm clouds, but would never receive an echo from such a small machine. In this situation the specialist knowledge of the navigator could be put to good use. While the crew continued to co-ordinate the rescue plan with Auckland, Vette turned his attention to the passengers. All on board were expecting a short flight, and since the search could be a lengthy procedure the arrival in Auckland could be quite late. Fortunately there were only eighty-eight passengers. With a life at stake there would be none who could object to the crew's action.

'Ladies and gentlemen,' spoke Captain Vette from the flight deck, 'we've just received news from Auckland of a light aircraft lost in the region of Norfolk Island and since we're the only suitable aircraft in the vicinity we've altered course for the search area to offer assistance. The pilot is in serious danger of ditching and if he lands on the water his chances of survival will be remote. The search could be lengthy, but fortunately we have plenty of fuel. It could mean a rather late arrival in Auckland, however, but with a life at stake I'm sure you understand that all help should be given. If anyone objects, of course,' added Captain Vette jokingly 'we could always leave him to die!'

Meanwhile the DC-10 called Prochnow on a range of HF frequencies and finally managed to establish contact. The Cessna pilot was told of their intentions and that they would do all they could to assist. It was a relieved man who received news that help was on the way for Prochnow was by now three hours overdue on his original arrival estimate. The DC-10 crew were informed that his ADF appeared to be malfunctioning and that only four hours of the Cessna's fuel remained. In spite of his predicament Prochnow spoke on the radio with calmness, and his composed demeanour impressed the listeners. He was a very cool customer indeed.

Amongst the passengers on board the DC-10 was an Air New Zealand first officer, Malcolm Forsyth, like Vette a qualified and still licensed navigator. After the public address (PA) announcement to the passengers he came forward to the flight deck to offer his help. It was amazing that two current navigators should be on board and the good news was transmitted to Prochnow. The two navigators could co-ordinate the search while First Officer (F/O) Dovey and Flight Engineer (F/E) Brooks could fly the DC-10 and monitor the aircraft systems. All crew members would be required at times to operate the radios for a lot of co-ordination work would be required.

As the DC-10 flew southwards Vette questioned Prochnow on all the details of his flight — altitude, airspeed, estimated fuel consumption, estimated fuel remaining, estimated position, if he had any idea — anything they could grasp which might improve the chances of finding him. All communications were being conducted on HF long-range radio, whch is subject to static and background noise, and communications proved difficult. The level of noise in the Cessna cockpit was high and did not help the situation. As the flight continued, Vette still had the needs of his passengers in mind and they were kept fully informed and up to date on the progress of the search.

'When we reach the search area,' added Captain Vette 'you will all be able to help. The more pairs of eyes searching the skies the better the chances of finding the Cessna.'

Vette encouraged his passengers to feel part of the search team and little groups were invited in turn to the flight deck to witness the proceedings.

The next problem facing the DC-10 crew was to try and establish the position of the Cessna. A specialised navigation plotting chart was needed but none was carried on the DC-10. Once again luck was on Prochnow's side, for Vette searched his briefcase and found a spare navigation chart of the region. The Cessna pilot's fortunes were beginning to change. Captain Vette instructed Prochnow to take a series of bearings from what the experienced navigator knew to be powerful NDBs on the north island of New Zealand: Kaitaia on the most northern tip, Tauranga on the coast just north of Rotoru, and Gisborne on the east coast. Although Prochnow's ADF was suspected of being in error, a positive test of the integrity of the equipment was essential. Vette carefully plotted each reading on the chart but the result was nonsense, for it showed the Cessna to be somewhere south of Auckland! There was no doubt now that Prochnow's ADF was malfunctioning and would be useless in the search.

The Cessna's equipment was able to tune and identify radio beacons but unknown to anyone at the time the problem was caused by a most elementary fault. The needle of the ADF had simply become loose on the spindle and pointed totally at random in whichever direction it settled. Also unknown was the fact that the defect had taken the Cessna 200 miles (320 kilometres) to the south-east of

An Air New Zealand DC-10. (John Stroud)

Norfolk Island and that only by some miracle could Prochnow now be saved. That, however, did not take into account the determination of Captain Vette and his crew.

The next attempt at establishing position was made using long range HF direction finding (DF) equipment at Brisbane. The DF system is normally employed using VHF radio. An operator at an airport receives from a flight an incoming radio message from which equipment can detect the direction of the aircraft. This magnetic bearing information is then passed to the pilot for plotting on his chart. It is a useful and accurate method of establishing position. Using HF, DF is a totally different proposition, with radio messages being transmitted for perhaps thousands of miles. Several attempts at obtaining a bearing from the HF station at Brisbane while receiving Prochnow's radio messages gave a rough indication of direction, but a more accurate method of establishing position was required if he was to be found.

The DC-10 and the Cessna were still communicating on the rather difficult HF, but it was expected that shortly the two aircraft would be within VHF range. Prochnow was asked to call repeatedly on the VHF emergency frequency of 121.5 MHz to establish the exact point of contact. Since the maximum range of VHF transmission is of the order of 200 nm, at that juncture the distance of the Cessna from the DC-10 would be known. It would still place Prochnow at the centre of a circle of 200 nm radius, covering an area in excess of 125,000 square miles (323,750 square kilometres), but at least it would be a start. Since the position of the Cessna was unknown, it was considered essential to attempt to establish the relative positions of both aircraft. It could be that Flight TE 103, instead of speeding towards a rescue at Norfolk Island, was flying away from the light aircraft. Once again Vette's expertise was put to the test. The sun was setting low in the sky with the approach of dusk and its direction might just prove useful as a last resort.

'I have an idea,' called Vette over the radio above the noise of the HF static. 'Turn due west and face into the sun. When you are pointing directly at it read me back your compass heading.'

After a few moments came Prochnow's response: 'Heading two seven four degrees,' he radioed.

The large DC-10 also aimed straight for the sun and settled on a heading of 270°. That placed the Cessna, as expected, to the left, i.e. to the south of DC-10 'Zulu Sierra.' But was it east or west of the jet's position? A sextant on each aircraft could have measured the precise angular altitude of the sun above the horizon and the difference in altitudes could have been used to clarify the situation, but without such apparatus it was difficult to judge. Vette, however, recalled that a clenched fist held vertical at arm's length represented about ten degrees above the horizon and a finger a little more than a degree and three-quarters.

'Hold your arm at full length,' Vette instructed Prochnow, 'and measure the distance between the horizon and the centre of the sun using your fist and fingers.'

'That's impossible,' came the quick reply from the Cessna. 'The cockpit is small and with the windshield so close I can't even stretch my arm half-way out!'

It was a short moment of amusement that swiftly passed. As a compromise each agreed to hold his hand about one foot (thirty centimetres) before his eyes and to count the number of fingers.

'I make it almost four fingers,' radioed back Prochnow.

Vette's reading was almost two fingers thick, which placed the Cessna nearer the sun, i.e. to the west of the DC-10. The difference in measurement of about two fingers placed the altitude readings at just over three degrees apart. When a celestial body is observed from two separate points it can be shown mathematically that the difference in measured angular altitudes expressed in units of minutes of arc, is equal to the distance in nautical miles separating the observers' positions. Three degrees is equivalent to 180 minutes of arc which, with the reading a little more than that, placed Prochnow's position approximately 200 nm away. It was now established that the Cessna was to the south and west of the DC-10. If the calculations were correct the two aircraft should be in VHF contact very shortly. A few minutes later F/O Dovey picked up Prochnow's voice on the VHF emergency frequency of 121.5 MHz.

'I've got him,' shouted Dovey. 'He's coming over clearly now on VHF.'

The efforts of the crew were beginning to bear fruit and the co-ordinates of the first point of radio contact were accurately plotted on the navigation chart. At this busy moment in the flight the chief purser, Paul James, was asked to liaise with the passengers and to pass on the good news over the PA. His announcement was greeted with cheers. Vette now instructed Prochnow to turn eastwards towards them with his tail to the sun while Zulu Sierra flew towards the sun. They should now be flying directly at each other and closing the gap more quickly. With the DC-10 flying at a ground speed of 560 knots and the Cessna at 110 knots they should cover the 200 nm separation with ease.

'We'll be directly over Prochnow in eighteen minutes,' declared F/O Forsyth, the DC-8 co-pilot and navigator. Vette concurred. The next problem for the two aircraft was to spot each other, not an easy prospect with the sun low in the sky. Captain Vette had already encouraged his eighty-eight passengers to keep guard at the windows and he now instructed them in proper look-out techniques.

'Move your eyes only one or two inches along the horizon, then stop. Move another inch or so and then stop again, always moving in short bursts. Move down a space then repeat the sequence back across your vision, and so on.'

The Cessna was much lower than the DC-10, and using this method a full square search of the sky in view to each passenger could be made. It might just enable one of them to spot the tiny aircraft.

The DC-10 crew now turned their attention to making their own presence more conspicuous to Prochnow. Dovey turned 'Zulu Sierra' to see if they were forming a vapour trail for the Cessna to spot but nothing was in sight. The Met office in Auckland was contacted and confirmed that in the present conditions the formation of a contrail was unlikely, but it was worth a try. The first officer climbed, then descended the aircraft to different altitudes in an attempt to induce a trail, but to no avail. A few trips previously F/E Brooks recalled witnessing an aircraft dump fuel and how impressed he had been with the sight. Perhaps, suggested

Brooks, if the conditions were right, dumping fuel would leave a bright trail which would help Prochnow spot them more easily. At each wingtip, nozzles pointed rearwards and valves could be opened to allow pumping of fuel overboard at the rate of 2.5 tonnes per minute. Prochnow, in fact, had used the same trick in the Navy as a tanker pilot to help receiver aircraft spot the tanker.

At the rendezvous time Brooks threw open the fuel jettison switches and fuel poured from the nozzles. Two minutes later he shut the valves; five tonnes of fuel had gone!

'Can you see us?' called Vette. 'You should be able to see our fuel dump trail."

Prochnow replied, disappointedly, that nothing was in sight. Perhaps they could try again. A second time Brooks opened the valves and on this occasion dumped fuel for three minutes. Over seven tonnes of fuel spilled into the sky leaving a distinct trail about thirty miles (forty-eight kilometres) long. That made a total of more than twelve tonnes of fuel dumped. With bated breath the DC-10 crew waited for Prochnow's call of a sighting but nothing was heard. The minutes passed and then came Prochnow's voice over the radio.

'It's hopeless,' he said, 'I can't see anything.'

The light was now fading and it was a bitter blow to the searchers that their efforts had been thwarted.

With darkness approaching Prochnow resigned himself to ditching in the Pacific for it now seemed that any attempt at finding him was going to fail. Carefully he prepared the inflatable life raft and emergency food and water supplies for survival at sea, and made sure all sharp objects were removed from his pockets. He had been in the air for nineteen hours and the strain was beginning to tell. He still had about three hours of fuel remaining, perhaps more, since he had been flying at economy cruise for some time with reduced power and leaned mixture, but at almost five hours overdue on his original arrival estimate he could by now be hundreds of miles from Norfolk. Ditching seemed almost a welcome relief to Prochnow as he was so tired and he had to fight to keep himself going.

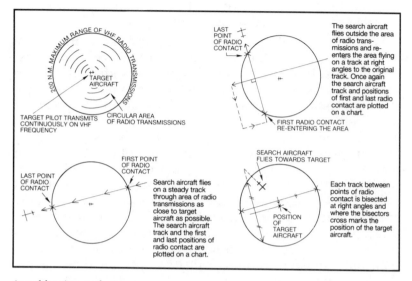

Aural boxing technique.

Vette and his crew were not prepared to give up and a further attempt at establishing position was begun using a technique known as 'aural boxing'. Prochnow would be required to make repeated radio calls, as he did when initially establishing VHF contact, and the points of lost communication and renewed radio contact would be recorded and plotted on the chart. The idea was to fly in a straight line, in this case at first roughly westbound, through the area of the circle of VHF radio transmissions from the Cessna formed by the sweep of the 200 nm radius of the maximum range of Prochnow's radio. The longest line through the circle would, of course, be the 400 nm diameter, taking over forty minutes to traverse, and since the DC-10 was likely to be fairly close to the Cessna, i.e. the centre of the circle, it could be a time-consuming process. The track towards the light aircraft had already been plotted, however, and the point of original radio contact had been marked on the chart, so time could be saved by re-establishing the original track and continuing the traverse. This meant, of course, flying away from Prochnow's estimated position, not an easy decision to make, but since until now all attempts at visual contact had failed it might just be worth a try.

When the traverse was completed and the point of lost VHF contact noted, the plan was then to sweep south-east bound outside the circle of VHF range and then to turn roughly due north to repenetrate the circumference flying at right angles to the original track. Once again the points of radio contact and lost communications would be recorded. The position of the Cessna would then be established by bisecting the lines of traverse and by noting the point at which the bisectors crossed. The Cessna's position was believed, with some justification, to be somewhere southeast of Norfolk Island, so while the 'aural box' method was being applied Prochnow was encouraged to fly in a north-westerly direction to help close the gap. Pin-pointing the Cessna's position would be more difficult with a moving target, but with time and fuel running out it was better than having Prochnow fly round in circles.

Something more immediate was required to try and establish Prochnow's range from Norfolk and once again the navigators conferred as to the best solution. The sun was almost setting over the Cessna and so Prochnow was asked to record the precise GMT time of sunset, i.e. the time at which the upper limb of the sun's circumference dipped below the horizon. Norfolk Island personnel were also asked to record their own GMT time of sunset, which was about 19:00 local, and the two times were compared. A small correction had to be applied to Prochnow's observation, for at 8,000 ft (2,438 m) sunset would be seen a little later than at the same position at sea level. When the calculations were complete the separation in sunset times was found to be twenty-two-and-a-half minutes.

The rising and setting of the sun, of course, results from the spinning earth, with the globe rotating one complete revolution per day, i.e. 360° in twenty-four hours, or 15° per hour, or 1° every four minutes. The earth is also divided into 360° of longitude, 180° to the east and 180° to the west. At a position, therefore, time — which is basically measured by the sun — is related to the longitude of the position, with every 15° of longitude representing one hour. A point 45°

east of the Greenwich Meridian, for example, is also three hours ahead of the time at Greenwich. Prochnow's time was ahead of Norfolk Island by twenty-two-and-a-half minutes which, with an earth rotation of 1° per four minutes, placed him 5.6° east of Norfolk. At about 30°S, 5.6° of longitude represented a range from Norfolk of about 290 nm. At a cruising speed of 110 knots, he could complete the journey in under three hours. Shortly before sunset his fuel remaining was three hours, perhaps more, so he might just be able to make it if only he could be found and pointed in the right direction.

With the sun below the horizon the lone pilot was once again enveloped in darkness. The Cessna droned on through the evening, heading roughly north-west in a desperate attempt to struggle closer to its destination. What Prochnow was feeling inside at that time can only be imagined for outwardly he remained cool. All his radio communications were calm and professional. It is a brave man indeed who can remain so composed when placed in such danger, for death was surely staring him in the face.

At the Auckland Search and Rescue Co-ordination Centre the co-ordinator, Bruce Millar, and his team were becoming increasingly concerned, so the RNZAF Orion on standby at Whenauapai was scrambled to join the search. The Orion would take about two-and-a-half hours to reach the Norfolk Island search area. Meanwhile, Prochnow continued with his series of radio calls on 121.5 MHz as the DC-10 sped away from his estimated position and out of range. As soon as communications were lost the position was plotted and 'Zulu Sierra' manoeuvred to sweep through the audio circle once again at right angles to the original traverse. It was almost an hour before the procedure was completed and the 'aural box' plotted on the chart. Allowing for movement of the Cessna, Prochnow's position was calculated at approximately 30°S 171°E.

'We estimate we'll be overhead your position in about five minutes,' radioed Vette to the Cessna. 'Turn in a circle and look out for our strobe lights.'

The strobes on 'Zulu Sierra' were powerful white flashing anti-collision lights which were so strong they could be seen clearly in daylight. If the Cessna was anywhere nearby surely the lights would be seen. Prochnow peered into the darkness, his hopes rising that at last he was to be found. The estimated time of rendezvous came, but once again the DC-10 was nowhere to be seen. With mounting despair amongst those involved, it had to be admitted that again an attempt at pin-pointing the Cessna's position had failed. Prochnow's spirits must have reached rock bottom. The DC-10 crew seemed to have exhausted all their options and now there was little they could do except sweep the area of the estimated position in the rather weak hope that Prochnow may spot their bright lights.

The crew and passengers of the DC-10 peered desperately into the darkness but there was little chance of one of them spotting the dim lights of the Cessna in the blackness of the night. In a little over an hour the RNZAF Orion would be on

A map showing the relative positions of Auckland, Norfolk Island, Nadi and Pago Pago. The flight paths of the Cessna and DC10 are clearly marked.

station, and with its more sophisticated equipment it was hoped that the Cessna would be found quickly. Prochnow continued to fly north-west, hopefully reducing the gap between himself and Norfolk Island. If the Orion pin-pointed his position swiftly and he was given a precise heading to steer for the airport, he might just make it. Without help of some kind he was doomed, for he would never find the island on his own in such a vast stretch of sea. Prochnow and the DC-10 crew had functioned well as a team and they had all worked hard in the search. Having given of their best it seemed a gross injustice that the Cessna remained unfound. Prochnow had been in the air for twenty-and-a-half hours and he was exhausted with the flying and the concentration. The strain on him was enormous. What was needed now, more than anything, was luck.

'A light!' shouted Prochnow over the radio. 'I see a bright light on the surface. I don't care what it is, I'm going for it.' Any ship nearby would increase his chances of survival in a ditching.

'Aim straight for it and read me back your heading,' instructed Vette, 'but make sure it's not a star low on the horizon.'

Prochnow reported his heading as 310°. As the Cessna flew closer to the source of the light he was able to give a description of the vessel.

'It appears to be a tall structure riding on a platform,' informed Prochnow. 'There are two or three lights on it.'

'Sounds like an oil rig,' said Dovey to the others on the DC-10 flight deck. Prochnow then reported seeing two tugs towing the vessel and all agreed it had to be an oil rig.

'Circle overhead and flash your lights to attract attention,' suggested Vette. 'We'll contact Auckland and obtain what-ever information we can.'

The co-ordination centre was called on HF with a request for the marine division, part of the search organisation, to radio details of any oil rig platform being towed in the area. A few agonising minutes passed in waiting as the information was obtained, then back came the facts requested. It was identified as the *Penrod*, an oil rig being towed from

New Zealand to Singapore, and its position was given as 31°S,179°21'E. That established Prochnow's position as over 600 nm due east of Norfolk. He hadn't a chance. It also meant that the Cessna's position was hundreds of miles from where it had been placed by the navigator's estimates. Their methods had been rough and ready and only approximate fixes of position had been possible, but they were surprised that their calculations had been so far out. The Cessna was radioed with the bad news.

'You are too far east to make Norfolk on your available fuel,' informed Vette. 'It looks like you are going to have to ditch, but don't do anything till we get there. We can switch on our landing lights and brighten the area to help in your rescue when you go in.'

Dovey fed the co-ordinates of the *Penrod*'s position into the AINS and the big jet banked and flew towards the rig. Prochnow had already come to the same conclusion that ditching was inevitable, and in his mind was rehearsing procedures for the hundredth time. The rig had also spotted the Cessna circling overhead, flashing its lights, and the tugs had stopped their engines and hoved to. It was obvious that the light aircraft was in trouble and a boat had been launched in anticipation of ditching. The *Penrod* was now fully illuminated and the rig was ablaze with lights.

'It looks like a giant Christmas tree,' reported Prochnow.

In preparation for the ditching he lowered the Cessna's nose to inspect the sea.

'I'm going down now to take a look at the surface,' he called.

Prochnow gently descended the light aircraft towards the ocean but what he found when he skimmed over the sea made his heart sink. There was a huge swell running, with waves fifteen to twenty ft feet (five to six m) high. In the wake of the current flowing past the rig's platform the surface was a little flatter, but hardly suitable for ditching. If the Cessna struck the top of a wave it could easily flip over and trap Prochnow in the sinking machine. If the little aircraft slammed into the side of a giant wave it would almost certainly break up on impact. Neither prospect was very appealing, yet Prochnow's best chance now was to put the Cessna down on the sea while he still had some fuel left. He could then use the engine power to control his rate of descent. If he landed as close to the *Penrod* as possible there was just a chance that the aircraft would remain upright and in one piece and that the rig's boat could rescue him.

'The surface looks bad,' reported Prochnow. 'I don't like it at all.' There was a touch of anxiety in his voice now but his approach was still very professional. Under the circumstances he remained remarkably cool.

The DC-10 sped on towards the rig's reported position but it soon became obvious that something was amiss. Instead of Prochnow's radio calls becoming clearer his transmissions were beginning to fade. 'Zulu Sierra' was flying away from the Cessna!'

'There's something wrong with the rig's position,' radioed Vette to the search and rescue centre. 'Can you pass us a frequency so we can speak to him directly?'

Soon Vette was dialling the *Penrod*'s frequency of 119.1 MHz and contact was quickly established. Yes, they confirmed, a light aircraft was circling in the vicinity and they had launched a boat to rescue the pilot if he ditched.

'Can you confirm your position,' asked Vette. 'We have it as 31°S,179°21'E.' Moments later the source of the problem was revealed; the centre in Auckland had mistakenly read a nine for a zero and one digit had been incorrectly transmitted. It was a simple mistake that anyone could have made, but one which altered the entire aspect of the scene. The correct position of the *Penrod* was 31°S,170°21'E, and it didn't require the navigators to plot it on a chart to realise that the Cessna was much closer to Norfolk than the rig's incorrect position had first indicated. The new position of the *Penrod* was punched into the AINS, and as 'Zulu Sierra' turned back towards the target the Cessna was called with the good news.

'You may not have to ditch,' announced Vette. 'You are nearer Norfolk than we thought.'

The previous estimates of Prochnow's positions calculated by the navigators had, in fact, been remarkably accurate under the circumstances, and it had only been by the greatest of misfortunes that the two aircraft had failed to make visual contact and that Prochnow had been unable to spot the DC-10's powerful strobe lights. On retracing the steps on the chart it appeared that the fuel dumping had taken place directly over the top of the Cessna. It was possible that the fading light conditions had obscured the fuel trail from view. It was also very close to the aural box position adjusted for progress and the position line earlier indicated from Brisbane on HF.

A measurement by Forsyth from the chart revealed Prochnow to be only 150 nm from his destination, about one hour and twenty minutes' flying time away at the Cessna's cruising speed. Prochnow had now been in the air for about twenty-one-and-a-half hours, and only half an hour of fuel remained of his original endurance estimate. The Cessna had been flying at economy cruise for some time so as much as an hour's fuel could have been saved. That would give Prochnow the one-and-a-half hours' endurance he needed for Norfolk. Whether to make a go for it or to stay put was Prochnow's decision alone, and not an easy choice to make. If the Cessna ran out of fuel on the way Prochnow would be in a worse situation that he was now. He would have to glide alone in the dark into the ocean swell with very little chance of survival.

The DC-10 flew at speed towards the *Penrod* with growing anxiety amongst the crew. It was now a desperate race against time.

'What's your estimate of remaining fuel?' enquired Vette.

'I've got about one quarter of one tank left,' suggested Prochnow. Maybe about ten gallons (forty-five litres).' The Cessna's fuel consumption was eight gallons (thirty-six litres)) an hour, giving a remaining endurance of about one-and-a-quarter hours. It would be touch and go but he might just be able to make land.

The DC-10 had by now descended to 10,000 ft (3,050 m) to improve the chances of sighting the Cessna and already the bright lights of the *Penrod* rig could be seen ahead.

'We reckon you might just be able to make it,' announced Vette. 'What do you think?'

Prochnow took another look at the black and heaving sea

and didn't need to be asked twice. 'I'll go for it,' he said. 'Give me a heading and I'm off.'

'Steer 294° magnetic,' instructed Vette. 'We'll be with you shortly and we'll accompany you on the way.'

With a mixture of fear and hope in his heart Prochnow turned the little Cessna away from the friendly lights of the rig and back into the black night. F/O Dovey slowed the DC-10 to its minimum cruise speed of about 200 knots and turned slightly right to leave the *Penrod* on their left. Just then they spotted the little aircraft.

'The Cessna's been found!' announced Chief Purser James to the passengers. A great cheer rose from the cabin. While approaching the rig, the tiny Cessna could be seen from the flight deck, ahead and to the left, climbing away on its assigned heading. Prochnow was wisely gaining height to increase his gliding range in the event of the engine cutting with fuel starvation. The Cessna was difficult to see, even with its landing lights on, but this was a moment Captain Vette wished to share with his passengers.

'Ladies and gentlemen, if you look out of the left windows, about seventy degrees to the left and below, you'll see something very interesting. It's difficult to spot, but if you look carefully you'll see the dim lights of the Cessna.' Another cheer rose from the cabin. Eighty-eight pairs of eyes, with hands cupped at temples to shade the view, peered into the night for a sight of their quarry. It was a most satisfying moment for all.

The DC-10 sped past the tiny aircraft and Prochnow could clearly see the lights of the big jet above him and to his right.

'We'll set a course for Norfolk,' suggested Vette. 'Follow our strobe lights, and if you lose sight let us know. We'll then double back if needs be and pick you up again.'

The DC-10 remained just sufficiently clear to prevent its jet wash striking the Cessna, and Prochnow tucked himself in behind and followed the airliner's path. Vette was also able to inform the light aircraft pilot that news had just been received of the RNZAF Orion's imminent arrival, and it would shepherd him home for the last miles to Norfolk. The drama was not over for Prochnow, however, for there was still a chance that the episode could end in disaster. With the passing of each mile the chances of reaching his destination improved, but with the consumption of each unit of gasoline so did the risk of running out of fuel. It was a most anxious period of the flight. Prochnow had now been in the air for twenty-two hours and had reached the extent of his original estimated fuel endurance. He was now living on borrowed time and saved fuel, and at 100 nm from Norfolk he still had one hour to go. Prochnow held on as best he could and steadfastly followed the bright strobe lights of the DC-10 which could still be seen ahead.

'You are going to make it,' encouraged Vette. 'Just be sure you use all of your available fuel. Check every tank in turn and run each one dry.'

The RNZAF had caught up with the search by now, and as the Cessna pilot looked to his left he saw the Orion formate off his left wingtip. It was still going to be a close-run race, but at least help was at hand.

At fifty nm to Norfolk, 'Zulu Sierra's' strobe lights remained in Prochnow's sight as the DC-10 turned over the island. The Cessna hugged the side of the Orion. If a last minute ditching resulted, the Air Force crew were ready to aid his recovery. There was little more now that Vette could do and, with the DC-10 crew's tasks completed, the big jet turned for Auckland while the Orion oversaw the home-coming of their charge. Anxiously they listened on the radio for news. At last the Cessna, accompanied by the Orion, came into view at Norfolk, and after twenty-three hours in the air Prochnow approached the airport and turned onto short finals. At least now he was over dry land. Five minutes later, with virtually dry tanks, he touched down on the runway at the local Norfolk time of midnight, a relieved and happy man to be back on solid ground. The Cessna was eight hours late on arrival and twenty-two hours of fuel had been stretched to twenty-three hours and five minutes.

'The Cessna has landed,' announced Captain Vette to his passengers. 'He is safe at last.' The apology which followed for the delay was drowned by cheering and clapping from the cabin.

Vette and his crew, however, still had to complete the work on their own flight so, with the search satisfactorily concluded, they settled down for the one-hour journey remaining to Auckland. As the airliner sped on course, Prochnow called 'Zulu Sierra' on the radio while taxying in at Norfolk and expressed his sincere thanks for the DC-10 team's effort and for their work in helping to save his life.

'I think it's time to celebrate,' said Vette to his Chief Purser. 'Break open the champagne.' In the cabin, eighty-eight glasses were raised in salute to the gallant rescuers.

The entire search and rescue exercise had been an outstanding episode. The two navigators, Captain Vette and F/O Forsyth, had worked ceaselessly at their task for over three hours, while F/O Dovey and F/E Brooks had operated the aircraft over the period at a continuously high workload. It was an admirable achievement. Captain Vette remarked of his team, 'The fact that they were such exceptional airmen helped a great deal.' Prochnow's efforts were not to be forgotten either, for his calmness and professionalism throughout were a credit to the piloting fraternity.

At 01:29 local New Zealand time the following morning, Flight TE 103 arrived at the gate at Auckland international airport, three hours and fifty-four minutes behind schedule. For once, on a delayed service, no-one complained.

The Guild of Air Pilots and Air Navigators awarded Gordon Vette and Malcolm Forsyth the Johnstone Memorial Trophy in 1980 for outstanding air navigation. McDonnell Douglas, the DC-10's manufacturers, also awarded the two navigators, as well as Arthur Dovey and Gordon Brooks*, a certificate of commendation for displaying 'the highest standards of compassion, judgement and airmanship'.

* Gordon Brooks was killed in the crash at Mount Erebus, Antarctica, in 1979. Gordon Vette went on to write a book of the accident entitled *Impact Erebus*, published in 1983.

# Chapter 2
# The Bermuda Tangle

The island of Bermuda sits at the apex of a triangle of infamous dimensions, with its southerly points loosely touching the tip of Florida to the west and the island of Puerto Rico to the east. Along the line of its base lie the other islands of the Greater Antilles chain: Cuba, Jamaica, Haiti and the Dominican Republic. To the north of Cuba lie the Bahama Islands, with the most westerly islands hardly a stone's throw from Miami on the mainland coast of the United States. The capital of the Bahamas, Nassau, is situated on the northern shore of New Providence, one of the smallest islands of the group.

The area bounded by what is now known as the Bermuda Triangle achieved a certain notoriety when Charles Berlitz published a book on the subject in 1974. The accounts of ships and aircraft lost in strange circumstances are numerous. However these incidents, or the explanations of the events, may be received, there is no doubt that some of the losses are alarming. Reports dating from the mid-nineteenth century tell of some fifty ships and twenty aircraft mysteriously disappearing. Some vessels have been found abandoned, while other craft at sea and in the air have vanished without any distress signal being transmitted. In many cases no wreckage of aircraft or ship has ever been found.

One of the strangest aviation mysteries concerns the incident of US Navy Flight 19 which consisted of five Grumman TBM-3 Avenger torpedo bombers. The Avengers took-off from their base at Fort Lauderdale, just north of Miami on the Florida coast, on 5 December 1954. The flight was under the command of Lieutenant Charles Taylor and was scheduled to fly a long-range navigation exercise, ending back at base. By late afternoon the aircraft were reported missing and were never seen again. A US Navy patrol aircraft, a twin-engined Martin Mariner flying boat, took off from Banana River Air Station with thirteen crew members on board and began a thorough search of the region, but its efforts were also to end in catastrophe. The rescuers' aircraft vanished without trace. In neither case was a distress signal heard, nor at the time, was any wreckage found. In April 1987, the five Avenger bombers were eventually found lying close together at the bottom of the Atlantic.

Accounts of these incidents tend to play on the mysterious side of the disappearances, although logical explanations are available for their occurrence. The lead aircraft flown by Lieutenant Taylor was known to have compass problems and he was also unfamiliar with the area. It is believed he thought his position to be over the Gulf of Mexico when in fact he was over the Atlantic. If he had turned east, away from the setting sun, he would eventually have run out of fuel and would have been forced to ditch. The search aircraft was believed to have exploded in mid-air as a flash in the sky was reported by a ship's crew.

The Bermuda Triangle may now be tarnished with a mystical hue, but the number of incidents recorded within its vicinity are not excessive considering the very heavy traffic of the region. The figures, in fact, are similar to those of other busy air and sea routes. Each year many thousands of ships and aircraft navigate the area without incident and of those who experience difficulty, most successfully overcome their problems. A very few have come closer to danger than their crews would have liked, but with skill, experience and perhaps some luck, they have defied the allegedly mystical powers of the triangle. One such relatively recent incident occurred to a Lockheed L1011 Tristar in 1983.

Miami International Airport is Eastern Air Lines' main base and a large number of flights depart from there to cities all over the US, as well as to destinations throughout the Caribbean. Each day many services criss-cross the southern region of the Bermuda Triangle without incident and the airline has a very good safety record.

On the evening of 4 May 1983, an EAL Tristar, registration

*N334EA*, returned home to roost at Miami and was parked overnight at the company's terminal building. Normal line maintenance procedures were conducted and scheduled work card tasks were completed. Any outstanding mainten- ance log book items were also corrected. Apart from routine maintenance, however, there was also a requirement to conduct a master chip detector check. As early as September 1981, Rolls-Royce, the manufacturers of the three RB211 jets on the Tristar, became concerned over problems being experienced with the engine. Some in-flight failures had occurred necessitating shut-down. The master chip detector is positioned on the left side of the low pressure compressors and consists of a small magnetic probe which protrudes into one of the oil lines of the engine oil system. If any engine components are subject to wear, small metal particles are flushed through the oil lines and are attracted to the magnetic probe of the detector. The original inspection interval of 250 flying hours was reduced to twenty-five flying hours in an attempt to detect at an early stage any adverse engine trends.

An Eastern Airlines Lockheed Tristar L1011. (John Stroud)

The mechanic servicing the Tristar simply removed the chip detector from each engine and placed it in a plastic bag. Fresh detectors were then fitted in place. The amount of metal particles adhering to each detector was coded and recorded and found satisfactory. If larger amounts of metal particles had been discovered the detectors would have been sent to a laboratory for analysis of the contamination.

Early on the morning of 5 May, *N334EA* was prepared to operate Flight 855, a regular Eastern Air Lines scheduled service from Miami to Nassau. The flight time for the 156 nautical mile journey was only thirty-seven minutes. At 08:56 Eastern Daylight Time, Flight 855 departed from runway 27 right at a take-off weight of almost 149 tons, carrying a fuel load of twenty-one tons. On board were 162 passengers, most of whom were vacationers on their way to the Bahamas. In the left-hand seat of the Tristar was Captain Richard Boddy and with him on the flight deck was his co-pilot, Steve Thompson, also a captain, and his flight engineer, Second Officer Dudley Barnes. Captain Boddy was a likeable man who was known to be cool and calm under pressure. He had only been on the Tristar since March and Captain Thompson, a supervisory pilot, was conducting Boddy's second check flight on converting on to the Tristar. Since Boddy was not yet qualified on the type, technically he was only acting as captain and Thompson was in command. In the cabin were seven attendants, supervised by Senior Flight Attendant Shirley Alexiou, bringing the total on board to 172.

The Miami weather on departure was fine with a broken cloud layer at 2,300 ft (700 m) and a visibility of seven miles (11.25 kilometres). The forecast weather for Nassau was good although some scattered rain showers were expected: quite normal for the time of year. As the Tristar began its initial climb, however, a frontal system was passing through Nassau's International Airport and the sky was overcast. The cloud had reduced visibility to four miles (6.5 kilometres) and light rain was falling. If the passage of the front was delayed, weather conditions at their arrival time could deteriorate.

Captain Boddy climbed the aircraft on the westerly

runway direction at 170-180 knots following the Miami 5 departure routeing and at about 500 ft (150 m) turned onto a heading of 250° magnetic. Thompson radioed departure control and *N334EA* was instructed to turn left and to proceed all the way round to the south of the airport on to an easterly heading. At 1,000 ft (305 m) the captain retarded the engines to the climb power setting of 1.40 engine power ratio (EPR) and Flight Engineer Barnes routinely scanned his instruments. Passing 1,500 ft (460 m) Barnes radioed Eastern Air Lines on VHF radio box three with the departure time, then completed the climb check list. Once more the engineer scanned his panel. Boddy accelerated the aircraft, retracting the flaps in sequence, and by 5,000 ft (1,525 m) the Tristar was climbing normally at 250 knots. Out of 10,000 ft (3,050 m), the speed was further increased to 300 knots for the en route climb to the cleared flight level of 230 (23,000 ft or 7,010 m). At 09:01, Thompson called Miami Centre on 127.0 MHz and Flight 855 was cleared on a direct routeing to Nassau. Boddy turned the Tristar slightly right to track 110° and the lightly laden aircraft continued its rapid climb. Passing 18,000 ft (5,485 m) the altimeters were selected to the standard pressure setting of 29.92 inches of mercury.

At 09:08, the autopilot captured level 230 and Boddy adjusted the thrust levers to the cruise power setting of 1.30 EPR to maintain 300 knots. The take-off until level flight had taken only twelve minutes and with New Providence Island fast approaching the aircraft would not remain in the cruise for long. It was a short, busy little flight which kept the crew on their toes.

Permission for descent was requested from Miami and *N334EA* was cleared to 9,000 ft (2,740 m). At 09:10, after cruising for only two minutes, the thrust levers were retarded to flight idle. The nose dipped in descent at eighty miles (130 kilometres) from Nassau and the aircraft decelerated to 280 knots. Thompson changed frequency to Miami Oceanic Control Area (OCA) which would retain radio contact until Flight 855 descended below 6,000 ft (1,830 m). They would then be cleared to Nassau Approach on 121.0 MHz. Meanwhile, Flight Engineer Barnes contacted Nassau

Approach on the other radio to inform them of their imminent arrival.

'Nassau Approach, good morning, Eastern 855 is flight level two zero zero, descending, DME*, seven zero.'

* Distance Measuring Equipment.

'Good morning Eastern 855, I have the zero nine hundred weather for you: cloud ceiling one thousand with a visibility of four miles. To the east and south the cloud base is down to five hundred to eight hundred feet and there are thunderstorms to the north. Wind, three zero zero at three knots, temperature seventy five, altimeter two nine eight nine, and recently there has been some light rain. You're number two for the approach following a light twin which is thirty miles ahead.'

At Nassau Airport the runway in use was 32, 11,000 ft (3,350 m) long. Although, with the light wind, the Tristar could land almost straight in on the opposite direction runway 14, a large thundercloud to the north-west precluded its use. Neither runway approach, however, had an instrument landing system and guidance for final approach to land would have to be a non-precision approach using the VOR radio beacon. As a result the minimum weather conditions for landing at Nassau were stated to be: cloud base no lower than 400 ft (122 m) and visibility no less than one mile (1.6 kilometres). A cold front lay across the island and the large storm cell could be seen ahead on the radar. Because ot the weather and other landing traffic Flight 855 was cleared for a DME arc approach to runway 32. The procedure was lengthy and involved flying an arc of ten miles (16 kilometres) radius from the airport all the way round to the south-east before turning onto final approach. There was no approach radar available and, with the weather close to limits, and deteriorating, it would not be an easy approach for Boddy to fly.

Flight Engineer Barnes continued to scan his control panel when able but his duties kept him busy. He quickly completed the landing data card then read through the descent and in-range check lists. He then radioed the EAL company office at Nassau with the estimated arrival time and with some routine passenger details. Suddenly, as

the Tristar descended through 15,000 ft (4,570 m), Captain
Boddy noticed the oil low pressure warning light for number
two engine illuminate on the pilot's centre panel. He called
out to the flight engineer. Barnes had not scanned his
instruments for about five minutes as he completed his
tasks, but the oil quantity and pressure gauges were
positioned in the centre of his panel at just below eye level so
were easy to check. Throughout the flight the oil quantity
gauges had remained steady at eighteen quarts (seventeen
litres), which was a normal reading, although the full level is
twenty-one quarts (twenty litres). Numbers one and three oil
pressure gauges showed in the green, or normal, range and
the oil quantity indicators measured fifteen quarts (fourteen
litres). Fluctuations of up to three quarts (2.8 litres) were not
unusual and did not give cause for concern, but the number
two readings were a different matter. Only eight quarts
(7.5 litres) were indicated as remaining in the number two
tail engine and the oil pressure was oscillating between
fifteen and twenty-five lb/sq in (psi) (1.05-1.4 kg/cm$^2$). The
minimum acceptable normal operating pressure was thirty
psi (2.1 kg/cm$^2$).

Flight Engineer Barnes had never before had oil pressure
trouble on the Tristar, but there was no doubt that he had a
problem now. If the engine continued to run in this low oil
condition it would not be long before it seized and Captain
Boddy had little choice but to call for it to be shut down. The
flight engineer initiated a precautionary engine shut-down
by closing number two thrust lever and by selecting the fuel
ignition switch to cut off to disconnect the fuel supply. As
the engine ran down the captain called for the auxiliary
power unit (APU) in the tail to be started. This was normal
practice on the Tristar with one engine failed and the APU
would help supply the systems normally powered by
number two engine. N334EA was light and the flight could
be continued on two engines without difficulty.

The weather at Nassau, however, was posing a problem.
Rain was beginning to fall again and at times the visibility
was dropping to as low as a quarter of a mile (400 metres),
well below the minimum one mile (1.6 kilometres) permitted.
Flying an approach on two engines in poor weather without

radar is not recommended and it could be some time before conditions improved. Even if the weather cleared quickly, the light twin ahead would still delay their arrival. The time was now 09:15 and the range to Nassau fifty miles (eighty kilometres), with Miami just over 100 miles (160 kilometres) away. With the low visibility at destination it might be quicker and more prudent to return home. Weather conditions there were fine and there was also good engineering cover. If a major problem existed with number two engine it would be easier to repair it at base. The crew quickly conferred over their predicament and the captain made the sensible decision to return to Miami. They would be back on the ground there in, at the most, about thirty minutes.

Captain Boddy advanced numbers one and three thrust levers to 1.35 EPR and held the aircraft level at 12,000 ft (3,660 m) while Thompson called Miami OCA.

'Miami, Eastern 855, we have lost number two engine and we've stopped the descent at twelve thousand. We'd like reclearance to return to Miami.'

'Roger, Eastern 855, you're cleared to make a one eighty on to a heading of two nine zero and maintain twelve thousand. For further clearance contact Miami Centre on one two seven point zero.'

At 09:17, Flight 855 commenced a left turn at 300 knots, level at 12,000 feet, back towards Miami. The flight engineer called the company at Nassau on VHF 3 to say they were returning and Captain Boddy informed Senior Flight Attendant Alexiou of the bad news. Whilst turning through north, Thompson re-established contact with Miami Centre. The controller was ready to receive Flight 855 but did not yet have the Tristar back on his radar scope.

'Eastern 855, just continue on the to heading,' replied Miami. 'We'll have you back on radar shortly. Did you want any higher altitude?'

'Affirmative. We'd like to go up, ah . . . say, ah, oh, nineteen to twenty-one thousand.'

'Okay, Eastern 855. Ah what are you in, a left turn now?'

'Yes, sir.'

'Eastern 855, climb to flight level two zero zero for now.'

'Twenty thousand, roger.'

Once again the flight engineer was kept busy with his tasks as he completed the engine shut-down check list and the secondary items required to tidy his panel.

'Okay, 855, I have you back in radar here, leaving about one three six . . . Proceed on two seven zero heading . . . radar vectors towards Biscayne.'

'Okay, two seven zero, heading back to, ah, Biscayne, roger.'

'And any problem that we should know about?'

'We've, ah, we've had precautionary shutdown on number two engine.'

'Okay, you need any special handling?'

'Negative, sir.'

'Okay.'

As *N334EA* climbed through 15,000 ft (4,570 m), Captain Boddy faced a further problem, and the flight began to go seriously wrong. The low oil pressure light for number three engine also suddenly illuminated. With number two engine already shut down and number three engine now giving trouble, the crew were less than happy with the circumstances. The routine flight was turning out to be anything but routine. Boddy eased the power back slightly on number three engine to see if that would help, and reduced the rate of ascent. Almost immediately, before the crew could assess the situation they saw to their horror the number one engine low oil pressure light illuminate as well. Barnes quickly scanned his instruments; the oil pressures on both operating engines were low and dropping and all the oil quantity gauges indicated zero. The busy little flight of only ten minutes ago was turning into a major emergency. But this couldn't be right; the oil indicators had to be mis-reading. It was surely impossible for all three engines to lose all their oil in a similar fashion. No; it had to be an electrical fault causing incorrect indications. There was little point in going higher for the time being until everything was checked out, so Boddy levelled off at 16,000 ft (4,880 m), still flying at 300 knots, while Thompson radioed Miami with details of their problem.

'And Miami Centre, Eastern, ah 855, we have, ah, some rather serious indications of all three oil pressures on all three engines, ah, ah, down to zero. We believe it to be faulty indications, ah, since the chances of all three engines having zero oil pressure and zero quantity is almost nil. However, that is our indication in the cockpit at the present time.'

'Okay, fine. Why don't you turn right about fifteen degrees. We'll give you direct to Miami. Maintain flight level twenty thousand, or whatever altitude you wanna maintain, and we're just gonna have the emergency equipment standing by anyway for ya.'

'Proceed direct to Miami Airport. Roger, sir.'

While Thompson spoke on the number two radio box, Barnes switched VHF 3 to the Miami Technical Centre frequency and explained the situation. Could a common electrical source affect the engine instruments, he asked? Captain Boddy butted in.

'The low oil pressure and zero oil quantity for the three

Captain Steve Thompson.

engines seems a faulty indication since the likelihood of simultaneous oil exhaustion in all three engines is one in a million, I would think.'

The maintenance personnel at Miami referred to the appropriate manuals and soon came up with a possible cause for the malfunction. The number two AC electrical busbar was the common source for the oil quantity gauges and the problem might lie in that department. The flight engineer quickly checked the relevant circuit breakers but could find nothing amiss. The bizarre instrument displays remained a mystery. In spite of the indications, however, the flight seemed to be proceeding satisfactorily and Boddy maintained 16,000 ft while letting the speed drop back to 230 knots. In the meantime, Miami Centre called back requesting the numbers on board and Thompson mistakenly replied that there were 168.

'One hundred and sixty eight, okay. Does that include your crew?' asked Miami.

'Negative, sir, ah, stand by on the crew.'

With one engine shut down and the other two displaying alarming indications, the number of crew on board was the last thing on their minds. The Miami controller, of course, was thinking ahead and was concerned that the situation might deteriorate. If the rescue services were required for Flight 855 it would be useful to know the numbers involved. With no reply from Thompson on the number of crew, Miami repeated the request.

'Well, we've got three in the cockpit,' said Thompson. 'We'll have to count in the back and we'll give that to you in just a minute, sir.'

'Okay.'

'We have seven in the back.'

'Seven in the back, okay. Eastern 855, you can descend and maintain twelve, one-two, thousand at your discretion.'

Thompson had no time to reply to the descent clearance to 12,000 ft, for in an instant the course of events took a turn for the worse. At 09:33, without further warning, number three engine failed with a loud bang causing the aircraft to judder. It flamed out and combustion ceased. They were now flying on one engine.

'Ah, Eastern . . . number . . . Eastern 855, we've just lost our number two engine, sir.'

In the excitement of the moment Thompson had called that number two engine instead of number three, had failed.

'Okay, losing number two. You still got two turning?'

'Negative. We only have one now and, ah, we're gonna restart our number two engine.'

'Okay, fine. We're listening. Okay, cleared direct. Miami's altimeter two nine eight nine and you can descend at your discretion to any altitude you need. You're clear of traffic.'

'Okay. We need a bearing, ah, we'd like a heading to go to, ah, two seven left.'

'Okay, your position right now is seventy miles south-east of Miami. You're about fourteen minutes out, heading two eight five, two eighty-five, for Miami.'

'Two eighty-five, okay.'

'And you can plan a straight-in two seven left. We're telling Approach about it right now. Equipment will be standing by.'

'Roger.'

As number three engine failed, Flight 855 was about seventy nautical miles from Miami, and Captain Boddy began a gentle descent while letting the speed drop back slowly. To save weight with only one engine operating, Barnes started dumping some of the seventeen tons of fuel on board. It would take approximately five to ten minutes to dump about ten tons of fuel which would just leave sufficient for landing. At 15,000 ft (4,570 m) the number one engine power was increased to 1.40 EPR and, with the speed stabilised at 225 knots, the Tristar continued on a gradual descent at 600 ft (180 m) per minute. The aircraft was becoming lighter and could keep flying, albeit with difficulty, on one engine. The crew completed the single engine operating check list, which basically rearranged the power sources of the back-up systems. All secondary systems were appropriately distributed between the one remaining engine and the APU which was still running satisfactorily. The island of Bimini passed beneath Flight 855, but it remained out of sight under a low cloud cover. A 4,000 ft (1,220 m) runway was available at Bimini Airport for light aircraft.

The weather was good and, with Miami Airport nearby, the crew felt they could make it. There was, however, no doubt now that the engine instruments were reading correctly and that all the power plants had been starved of oil. How long would number one engine survive? The flight crew were not about to wait to find out and they began the drill to start number two engine which had been shut down earlier in the flight. The in-flight start sequence was not a simple exercise and each step was carefully undertaken from the check list. The number two engine instruments were checked to indicate the engine was turning and not seized, the thrust lever was checked closed and the tank pumps were checked on. The engine in-flight start table was entered with the aircraft altitude of about 14,000 ft (4,270 m) and a speed of 225 knots and the conditions were confirmed as lying in the middle of the in-flight start envelope for engine start using the windmilling effect of the airflow. Unfortunately the table was entered in the wrong way, with speed on the altitude scale and vice versa, and the indication that a windmilling start was possible was not correct. For such a procedure a speed of 285 knots was required and in the present circumstances a start could only be achieved using the engine starter motor. Having incorrectly checked the details the windmilling air start switch was selected to on to supply ignition. Nothing happened; the engine refused to start. The situation was becoming desperate and the captain gave the order to prepare for ditching.

The flight engineer now turned his attention to the ditching check list: the flight crew donned their life jackets, the aircraft systems were tidied up by appropriate switching, the seat belt and no smoking signs were switched on and in the cockpit the crew checked their seats and harnesses were secure. Barnes now called Senior Flight Attendant Alexiou to the flight deck and instructed her to initiate ditching procedures. Alexiou informed the other flight attendants of the situation and they returned to their stations and quickly made preparations to brief the passengers. The senior flight attendant announced to the passengers the captain's intention to land on water, repeating the instructions for the use of life vests which had been given, as required by law, before departure. On the ground few people listen to emergency briefings and it was deemed prudent to repeat the exercise. Many passengers were already aware that problems were being encountered and some now became hysterical. A handful were close to panic.

On the Tristar there are eight exits for evacuation, but on Flight 855 only seven attendants, so helpers were requested from the able-bodied passengers. It would have been a relatively simple exercise to instruct the volunteers how to open a door on coming to a stop on the water and that the slide/raft would then inflate automatically, but unfortunately no-one came forward. Some flight attendants also had to assist with the donning of life vests and had to give individual instruction to a few people. At least eight passengers inflated their life vests, in spite of instructions to the contrary, so if an evacuation became necessary their movements would be restricted. The passengers were also instructed to remove sharp objects, spectacles, high heels, etc, and to place their seat backs upright. They were shown the brace position for impact and told, when announced, to lean forward and grasp their ankles. They were instructed to remain seated until the aircraft had come to a halt and which exits to use for evacuation. The flight attendants then had to secure the cabin and to stow all loose objects. They were kept very busy at their tasks and, being unsure of how much time remained, were under a lot of pressure.

As the activity on the Tristar continued, Miami Centre called Flight 855 asking, politely, if they were not busy could they pass the quantity of fuel on board. The information might also prove useful to the rescuers. The flight crew were occupied with the emergency and Thompson missed the call.

'Say again, sir.'

'If you're not busy,' repeated Miami, 'we need fuel on board.'

'Okay, we have, ah, thirty-six thou.'*

* 36,000 lb : 16,400 kg

'Roger, Eastern 855, you're cleared to six, or any altitude you need. Advise.'

'We'll advise.'

'And Eastern 855, if you can, can you give me a status report how you're doing?'

'We're doing okay.'

'Okay, Eastern 855 your position now fifty-nine miles south-east of Miami Airport. Turn left about five degrees. You're about thirteen minutes out at your speed.'

'Roger.'

At 09:33, while approaching 12,000 ft (3,660 m) over the ocean, the inevitable happened. As abruptly as number one engine failed, number three engine also flamed out and began to run down.

'We're losing another engine. We've lost our third engine right now!'

'Okay, have you got the other one started?' asked Miami.

'Not yet.'

'Do you have any of them turning?'

'Negative.'

The big Tristar jet was now fifty-five miles (eighty-eight kilometres) from Miami and was gliding without engine power. The rate of descent increased to 1,600 ft (488m) per minute with the speed constant at 225 knots. Fortunately, the APU continued to function, pressurising the hydraulic systems via pneumatic pumps and supplying electrical power, so all the controls remained in operation and the aircraft could glide satisfactorily in this condition.

The engines windmilled in silence in the airflow, and it was obvious now that oil starvation had been the cause of failure. But why had three good engines similarly run out of oil? Unknown to the crew, the fault lay in the maintenance procedures which had been undertaken during the previous night. The master chip detectors on each engine had been removed for analysis of the deposits and placed in plastic bags. Replacement chip detectors were normally acquired from a cabinet in the foreman's office, but in the early hours of 5 May none were available. These chip detectors were usually fitted with two oil sealant 'O' rings (see diagram). Three chip detectors were drawn from the stock room, but none had the oil rings fitted, a fact which escaped the mechanic's attention. A 'serviceable parts' tag attached to the transparent plastic package containing each fresh chip

Master chip detector magnetic probe and position of the 'O' ring seals. (NTSB)

detector served to support the illusion that 'O' ring seals were fitted. Working by feel in dark conditions when fitting the replacement chip detectors reduced the chance of the mechanics discovering the error. To check for leaks all three engines were turned for about ten seconds and no drips were noticed. It was only established later than a minimum of thirty seconds of engine motoring was required to induce leaking if oil seals were omitted. The work was duly signed off and the aircraft was released for service with the chip detector 'O' rings missing.

In the morning, when *N334EA*'s engines were started and the oil systems pressurised, oil had begun to leak rapidly from the chip detector installations. After only a short period of flight, the engines were almost out of oil, and number two engine's remaining oil had been saved only by shutting it down. The power increase on numbers one and three engines on the climb back to Miami had probably increased the rate of oil loss in these engines and serious damage had resulted. The bearings had become molten and the movement of assemblies had resulted in the drive to the fuel pump being disconnected, stopping the engines. The engines had flamed out due to the lack of fuel but had that not happened they would have eventually seized anyway.

As the ditching drill was completed on the flight deck, Flight Engineer Barnes announced on the PA that ditching was imminent and the passengers assumed the brace position. A second attempt to restart number two engine was initiated. Meanwhile the rescue services were already in the air and on their way. As early as 09:28, the Coast Guard had been notified of the emergency by Miami and immediately a Falconjet and a helicopter had taken off from Opa-Locka Coast Guard station.

'The Coast Guard is coming out towards you now,' informed Miami.

'Roger.'

'Keep me advised of your intentions and we'll keep you on here as long as we can. Approach is also watching you at the same time. You're about twenty miles west of Bimini right now. And it looks like you're gonna have to ditch; just keep us advised. We should be able to hear you at least down to twenty-five hundred feet.'

'Yeah.'

Had the short runway at Bimini been in view as they had flown overhead they might have tried to make it back for an emergency landing, but with the island obscured by low cloud they didn't stand a chance.

At 09:35, Flight 855 approached 10,000 ft (3,050 m) with about six minutes' gliding time remaining. The fuel dumping had now been completed and the aircraft weighed about 135 tons. The second attempt to start number two engine proved in vain and ditching seemed inevitable, but at least the conditions were fine: good daylight visibility, fair weather and a calm sea. A gentle breeze was blowing and the water temperature near the coast was a comfortable 79°F. The crew had been well trained in ditching procedures and all those in the cabin were prepared for the worst. Captain Boddy would touch down on the sea with the landing gear retracted, landing flap set and with the aircraft nose pitched up at 12°. It had been calculated that on impact in that configuration the wing engines, flaps and horizontal stabiliser would probably be torn off. Even sustaining such damage, the

Tristar was still expected to remain afloat for at least twenty to twenty-five minutes. Although the event would be risky and an unpleasant experience for the passengers and crew, there was every likelihood that the ditching would be successful. Danger could be averted only if number two engine started, but so far it had resolutely refused to function. There was little hope of engines number one or three re-starting, but anything was worth a try. With time fast running out an in-flight start was attempted on each wing engine.

As *N334EA* continued inexorably on its descent towards the ocean, Miami called with the latest radar position report. 'Eastern 855 you're forty-nine miles south-east of Miami right now, twelve minutes out at your speed.'

'Okay, we don't believe we can make land, ah . . .'

'Okay, we've got all the help we can coming out as fast as we can.'

The Coast Guard aircraft was now close to the scene and the rescue pilot was listening out on the frequency. He interrupted the exchange.

'We're a Falconjet coming off the beach at, ah, flying out of Opa-Locka,' called the Coast Guard to Flight 855. 'Ah, what's your position, sir?'

Miami Centre had both aircraft on radar and required only a positive identification of the Falconjet to co-ordinate efforts.

'Okay, I'll tell you what,' suggested the Miami controller. 'Coast Guard, just give me an ident. I'll give you a position in relation to yourself. What code are you squawking?'

'Squawking one two seven seven.'

'Okay, squawk ident. Okay, I see you out there. He is one o'clock. Your position twenty miles. I'll vector you to him. I have you radar contact.'

'Roger, sir. Okay, we'll be turning to about a heading of one one zero.'

'Okay, one one zero. Let's make it a one two zero. We'll intercept closer.'

'Roger, that, one two zero. And, ah, what's the altitude?'

'Right now seventy-nine hundred and he's descending slowly.'

'Roger, were climbing through twenty-five hundred.'

'Roger. Try heading one three five Coast Guard, one three five.'

'One three five.'

'He's twelve o'clock, ten miles Coast Guard.'

'Roger that.'

'Coast Guard's gonna be right next to you here pretty soon, Eastern 855,' reassured the Miami controller.

'Okay, ah. Ah, say his altitude again, sir,' asked the Falconjet pilot.

'Eastern is sixty-nine hundred descending.'

'Roger, we're thirty-two hundred climbing.'

'Ah, roger.'

Another two aircraft already airborne from US Coast Guard Air Station Clearwater, a helicopter and a C-130, were now also diverted to assist in the operation. Three more Coast Guard choppers and another Falconjet were also scrambled and at sea a Coast Guard cutter and five other patrol vessels were standing by. A USAF helicopter and a C-130 were preparing to take off from their base at Homestead. It was an impressive rescue team that was being assembled, but it was just as well, for there was every indication that their services would be required.

A map showing the relative positions of Miami and Nassau with the flight path of the Lockheed L1011 Tristar indicated.

At 09:37 the Tristar passed 7,000 ft (2,130 m), still flying at 225 knots, with about only four minutes' gliding time remaining. The attempts to start numbers one and three engines had failed and ditching seemed imminent. Boddy asked for guidance to land on the water as near to the shore as possible.

'Heading direct to closest land point, please,' radioed Thompson.

'Okay,' replied Miami, 'just as straight in is about the best you can do right now, Eastern 855, the way it looks here. Are you over land now, Coast Guard?'

'Ah, negative, sir. We're off shore about, ah, about fifteen miles.'

'Okay, Eastern is a ten eleven ah, turn further right another ten degrees. He's out there about twelve o'clock, be crossing left to right about seven miles.'

'Roger, just for your information there's a small scud, ah, thin layer, at about, ah, oh, four thousand feet.'

'Okay, suggest you stay down. He's fifty-two hundred descending, 855, suggest a heading of about another twenty degrees to the right.'

On N334EA's flight deck the crew tried a third and final attempt to start number two engine. The unsuccessful windmilling start technique was abandoned and a full engine start procedure using the starter motor was implemented. It was a last effort before committing themselves to ditching. At the same moment the Coast Guard aircraft caught sight of the Tristar.

'We have him,' called the Falconjet pilot.

As Flight Engineer Barnes persevered with the in-flight drills, Miami continued to guide the rescue aircraft to its quarry.

'Eastern's forty-seven hundred descending, Coast Guard. He's about eleven-thirty, four or five miles.'

'Ah we have him at twelve-thirty, sir.'

'Okay, twelve-thirty. Keep him in sight. I'm gonna stop talking. Advise Approach what you have to do.'

'Ah, negative, sir. He just went into the clouds.'

'Okay, he's forty-four hundred feet. No traffic that I can see underneath you.'

'Roger that.'

'Okay, I'll tell you what,' continued Miami. 'If you want to turn to a heading of one eight zero now we'll bring you in behind heading one eight, make it one nine zero.'

'Roger, one nine zero.'

'He's forty-one hundred descending. Turn right heading two hundred degrees, Coast Guard.'

'Two zero zero.'

At 09:39, the last item of the in-flight start check was completed with the selection of the start switch to on. Shortly Boddy would ask for the full 33° flap setting and in just over two minutes they would hit the sea. Suddenly, as they had almost given up hope, number two engine ignited and began to run up. Slowly its speed increased to idle and the power remained steady. It had started! The Tristar was just passing 4,000 ft (1,220 m) and was still twenty-two miles (thirty-five kilometres) from Miami, but now they were in with a chance.

'We have an engine going now and we believe we can make the airport.'

'Okay, you say you have one of them turning, Eastern?'

'That's affirmative.'

'Okay, the Coast Guard's gonna come in behind ya. He's behind ya right now. Coast Guard 277, turn right heading two five zero.'

'Two five zero, turning.'

Captain Boddy opened up number two thrust lever to about 1.30 EPR for thirty seconds and the power held. He then increased the power to 1.50 EPR and at 3,000 ft (914 m) he managed to arrest the rate of descent. The immediate problems were now over but the flight crew still had to complete a one-engine approach and landing, a far from simple task on a big jet. If the approach was improperly handled they would be back in trouble. And for how long would number two engine continue to function? It had been shut down by crew action earlier in the flight so still had some oil left, but the captain was only too well aware that the oil would not last for long. If the engine flamed out on the approach over land they would be in a worse position. Runway 30 offered the fastest time to touchdown but no descent path signal was available from the instrument landing system (ILS) and its absence would further complicate the approach. The flight path to runway 30 also tracked a long distance over land. Runway 27L, on the other hand, had both centre line and approach path ILS signals functioning and the approach, mostly over water, gave a better chance of ditching if the remaining engine failed.

The Tristar crew completed the check list items of the one engine approach, switching half the fuel pumps off to reduce the electrical load, depressurising the aircraft and supplying all the pneumatic functions from the APU. Such an arrangement permitted maximum power availability from the one remaining engine. Meanwhile the Miami controller continued his dialogue.

'What are your flight conditions now, Eastern?'

'In the clear.'

'Okay, Coast Guard, you should have him in sight out there. You make your right turn from twelve o'clock a mile and a half.'

'Roger, sir, we have him.'

'Okay, I'm gonna stop talking, Eastern. You're cleared a straight-n, contact Approach if you can. Don't talk if you don't have to.'

'Cleared for a straight-in. We want 27 left. Ah, are we about pretty good for that?'

'Ah, just go on in. We're waiting for ya.'

'And this is the Coast Guard. Ah, we've lost him in the scud again.'

'Okay, you're coming in behind him, about a mile behind him. He's at three thousand now. He's gonna be 27 left.'

'Roger.'

'Okay, Coast Guard, you have him in sight?'

'Ah, negative, sir.'

'Okay, turn right, heading, ah, three zero zero degrees. He's looking, he's picking away from you, he's about three thousand.'

'We don't see him.'

'Okay. And he's holding two three zero knots. He's looking in pretty good shape.'

'Okay, we're at two four zero knots now and we'll follow

him all the way into the airport, if that's okay with you.'

'Okay, we'll tell Approach you're gonna be right behind him. Change to one two six eight five, that's one twenty-six eighty-five. That's Miami Approach, and tell them you're behind the Eastern.'

'Roger, we have a visual now.'

'Okay, very good.'

At 09:43, Flight 855 intercepted the instrument landing system for runway 27 left at a height of 3,000 ft (914 m) and at a distance of just under ten miles (sixteen kilometres) from the threshold. Boddy eased back on the power on number two engine and let the speed fall off gradually as he descended on the glide path. He called for the flaps to be set to 10° and the landing gear to be selected down.

'Well, we believe we've got it made,' radioed Thompson.

'Fantastic,' shouted the Miami controller.

'Of course, we're cleared to land?' added the captain, tongue in cheek.

At 1,000 ft (300 m) Boddy was satisfied with the situation and committed the aircraft to land. The passengers were still crouching in the brace position so Captain Thompson quickly informed them on the PA that they were about to land at Miami. It was a very relieved group of passengers and flight attendants who heard the announcement.

'Eastern 855, you need not acknowledge if you're still on the frequency,' radioed Miami. 'On landing call point nine.'

'Okay, sir, sure thank you for your help.'

'Certainly.'

At 09:46, the Tristar touched down safely on 27 left at Miami and the tension of the emergency drained from all on board. The landing was only just in time, for the oil quantity left in number two engine was less than had remained in engines number one and three when they had failed and it was very close to stopping. As the Tristar rolled down the runway it seemed the emergency was over, but there were more problems to come. The controller radioed to say that number one engine was smoking and there appeared to be a serious risk of fire. The fuel ignition switches had been left on in the forlorn hope of achieving a start-up and on the roll-out the windmilling engine was still pumping fuel. On slowing, the fuel residue began to smoke in the hot engine. Quickly the number one engine fire bottles were discharged to dampen any flames. On stopping the aircraft, Boddy received a further warning from ground personnel that number three engine was also smoking badly. The number three engine fire bottles were likewise discharged and the fire services, which were standing by, also doused the wing engines with water and foam. Eventually the smoke dispersed and the risk of fire was averted. Captain Boddy called for a tug to tow the aircraft to the terminal but when informed there would be a fifteen minute delay he decided to taxy using number two engine. Boddy opened up the number two thrust lever but there was insufficient power to move the aircraft, even with the lever pushed right to the stop. Within moments the power began to drop and number two engine failed. It had been very close indeed!

The round trip had only taken fifty minutes but had seemed to the passengers like hours. The crew had done a magnificent job in extremely difficult circumstances and their skill and composure had saved the day. They were lucky too, of course, for if number two engine had not re-started they would have been faced with a ditching. And if it had seized on the approach over land the situation would have been much worse. But there was more. The decision to return to Miami had also been opportune for if the flight had continued to Nassau, on the lengthy approach the engine would probably have failed before landing. If the short runway at Bimini had been visible the crew might have attempted a powerless, or deadstick, landing with possibly disastrous results. And, more significantly, if the in-flight start table had been entered correctly and the number two engine had been started earlier it would undoubtedly have failed before touchdown at Miami.

Flight 855 had defied the Bermuda Triangle and at the last moment had slipped from its grasp. Had all three engines failed simultaneously in a more remote part of the triangle, however, it might have been a different story. The Tristar could have been forced to ditch with little or no warning and if the landing had been on a stormy sea the aircraft could have sunk quickly in deep waters. The incident could well have been another Bermuda mystery. Fortunately it ended safely and Captain Boddy also passed his flight check!

The flight crew were each presented with an Award for Outstanding Airmanship from the American Airline Pilots' Association.

# Chapter 3
# To Take-off or Not to Take-off . . .

Pre-flight checks and procedures before the departure of a big jet are numerous and complex and about forty minutes are required to prepare something as large as a Boeing 747 for flight. The calculation of speeds for take-off form an integral part of the preparations and all particulars of aircraft weight, weather and runway details are carefully checked. The speeds important to pilots on take-off are assigned the letter 'V' for velocity and are designated V1, VR and V2. V1 is the go or no-go decision speed. In the event of an emergency occurring before V1, sufficient runway is available for stopping, but after V1 the aircraft is committed to take-off.

The second speed of interest to pilots is VR, or V rotate, which is the speed at which the pilot raises, or rotates, the aircraft nose to a predetermined pitch angle. As a result, lift from the wings is increased and the aircraft climbs into the air.

The third important speed is V2 which, after take-off, is the minimum safe climb-out speed required in the event of an engine failing at V1, the worst possible moment. The normal climb-out speed is V2 plus ten knots.

A performance manual is carried on all flight decks and contains the relevant runway pages and technical details required for take-off calculations. Each runway page lists maximum take-off weights for various conditions and is constructed with runway length, gradient and airport elevation in mind. The list is entered with wind component and temperature and a maximum permitted take-off weight for the prevailing conditions is obtained. The maximum structural take-off weight of the Boeing 747 100 series, using Pratt and Whitney JT9D-3 engines (known as the dash

three), was about 323 tons, but short runways, high airports
or hot days can all take their toll. On occasions, even using
full power, the weight may have to be reduced by carrying a
lower payload or less fuel. Even at sea level, a shorter
runway or higher temperature can reduce the permitted
maximum take-off weight considerably. Where the take-off
is close to the maximum permitted in these conditions, even
a slight change of wind or temperature can be critical. A one
degree centigrade rise, for example, can result in a reduction
of two tons from the permitted maximum take-off weight. In
such situations the take-off calculations have to be conducted
with diligence and care.

On 30 July 1971, a Pan American Airlines (PAA) Boeing
747, appropriately registered N747PA, landed at San Francisco
International Airport, California, at 13:58 Pacific Daylight
Time (PDT: GMT −7). The aircraft was the flagship of the 747
fleet and was named 'Clipper America.' The big jet was
operating Flight PA 845, a regular, scheduled service
originating in Los Angeles, California, and transitting San
Francisco en route to Tokyo in Japan. Flight 845 took off from
Los Angeles at 13:11 PDT for the short forty-five minute hop
to San Francisco, and after a one hour stop-over was
scheduled to depart for the ten hours forty minutes sector to
Tokyo at 15:00 PDT. A fresh crew was to take over for the
long Pacific flight and an extra co-pilot and flight engineer
were to be carried to accommodate the extended duty day.

At just after 14:00, Captain Calvin Dyer and his flight crew
of First Officer Paul Oakes, Second Officer Wayne Sager,
first Flight Engineer Winfred Horne and second Flight
Engineer Roderic Proctor, assembled in the operations room
for the flight briefing. The crew were very experienced with
the captain and both flight engineers having each accrued
flying times in excess of 20,000 hours, but none of the five
cockpit personnel had operated the Boeing 747 for longer
than eighteen months. In fact, the inaugural commercial
Boeing 747 service from New York to London had been
flown by Pan Am only at the beginning of the previous year
on 22 January 1970.

The duty dispatcher presented Captain Dyer and his crew
with the paperwork for the flight: destination, diversion and

en route weather, fuel requirements, air traffic control flight plan, flight logs, notices to airmen (NOTAMS) and take-off information. All the relevant details were outlined by the dispatcher and using a wind of 300° at fifteen knots, a temperature of 66°F (19°C), and a pressure setting of 29.99 inches of mercury, the take-off speeds were calculated for runway 28L, the longest runway at the airport. The actual take-off weight was 321.8 tons and was only just inside the maximum permitted take-off weight on 28L in the present conditions of 323 tons. The preferential noise abatement departure runway was OIR, but the dispatcher had opted for the longer 28L because of the aircraft's heavy weight. San Francisco Airport is situated on the western shore of San Francisco Bay and flights taking-off from the northerly runways were conveniently routed out over the water, while those landing on the westerly runways also approached over the bay.

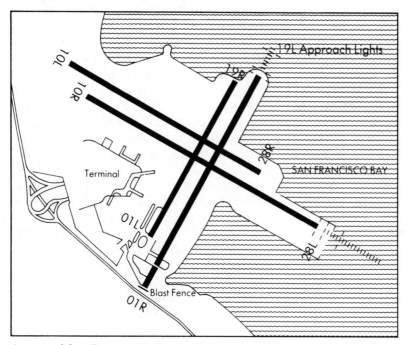

A map of San Francisco airport showing the location of the runway 19L approach lights.

The fuel requirement for the trip was 133.5 tons, close to the maximum possible of about 140 tons. Captain Dyer, in fact, had requested that the tanks be topped up for the long flight if the load dropped, but otherwise no more could be carried. Using standard 10° flap setting for take-off, the speeds of V1, 156 knots; VR, 164 knots; and V2, 171 knots were obtained. Normal operations were not possible without the use of 10° flap and the extra lift available more than compensated for any drag on the take-off run. In more critical conditions, flap 20° could be used on certain occasions further to improve lift. Runway 28L was 10,600 ft long (3,230 m) but on departure most of the runway would be used up before lift-off and the take-off run time would be of the order of fifty seconds.

Captain Dyer and his colleagues boarded N747PA at about 14:30 and began their pre-flight checks. As part of the procedures the take-off speeds were marked on the airspeed indicators using small, movable white plastic bugs on the rims of the two instruments. One hundred and ninety-nine passengers were travelling to Tokyo on Flight 845 and with five in the cockpit and fourteen stewardesses in the cabin, the total on the aircraft amounted to 218 people.

When boarding was completed, the engines were started in sequence, and almost precisely on time Flight 845 pushed back from the San Francisco gate at 15:01. During the process of push back, the first officer monitored the automatic terminal information service (ATIS) on 113.7 MHz, which broadcast weather and airport advisory material, and he soon became aware of a problem with runway 28L. The current ATIS, information 'X-ray,' had been valid from 14:02 and stated: 'Weather, clear; visibility 15 miles; temperature 66°F; wind 300° at 15 knots; altimeter 29.99. Landing runway 28R, departure runways one. Notice to airmen: runway 28L is closed; the first 1,000 feet of runway OIR is closed.' Unknown to the crew, the runway had been closed for repair since 08:30 because of break-up of the surface at the intersection with taxyway 'golf.' By misfortune, the dispatcher who had briefed the crew had been absent earlier to attend a company medical check, and on his return after lunch had not been apprised of the circumstances. He had been left unaware of the closure of the runway. The situation had been compounded by the omission of this information from the previous ATIS, 'whiskey,' which had been valid from 12:30.

In four consecutive ATIS broadcasts since 08:36 the non-availability of 28L had been announced, and it was unfortunate that by an oversight it had been omitted at the moment of the dispatcher's return. The exclusion was corrected in ATIS 'X-ray' which had been transmitted from 14:02, after the briefing of Flight 845's crew had begun. In addition, the information that the first 1,000 ft (300 m) of runway OIR was closed was also included in 'X-ray,' the first ATIS of the day to disclose this detail. The dispatcher had checked the feasibility of take-off from the shorter, 9,500 ft (2,895 m) OIR preferential runway and had found it possible, although more critical, and had opted for the longer 28L. The wind was also more favourable on this runway. Some delays could occur using the non-assigned runway but that would be acceptable under the circumstances. Now that the crew knew 28L was closed, they opted for take-off from the arrival runway 28R. Further delays would be inevitable using this runway because of landing traffic.

At 15:11, First Officer Oakes radioed the tower for taxy clearance using Pan Am's call sign, Clipper, and was instructed to proceed to the threshold of OIR.

'Negative,' replied Oakes, 'we require 28R.'

'OK, taxy to 28R.'

'Clipper 845, taxy 28R, and just confirm that 28L is closed.'

'That's affirmative.'

Oakes now contacted Pan American Operations (Panops) on the company frequency, stating that they had established 28L was closed and were planning 28R. Could the dispatcher check along with them the take-off details for the new runway? This message was received by the assistant dispatcher who simply informed the duty flight dispatcher responsible for PA 845 that a request had been received for a runway change. The duty dispatcher assumed radio control and, unaware of the specific choice of 28R, began discussing the feasibility of using OIR which had been checked earlier and found satisfactory.

'Take-off from OIR is possible using a zero wind component.'

'OK,' replied Oakes, 'but according to the ATIS the first 1,000 feet of OIR is closed.'

'It's not restricted as far as I can tell but, standby, I'll check it out.'

The dispatcher now listened for the first time to information 'X-ray' and afterwards contacted the tower controller by telephone to obtain confirmation of the details. The controller verified the closure, but added that the first 1,000 ft portion of runway OIR which was now shut to all traffic was not available to Boeing 747 aircraft at any time because of 'blast over-run'. He made reference to a statement issued by the airport authority on 11 February 1971. A highway ran to the south of the OIR threshold and a blast fence which had been constructed along the perimeter was too low to afford adequate protection from such a large jet. The jet efflux from the powerful engines of the Boeing 747 simply passed over the top. Even when a big fanjet engine is running at idle, a man can be blown over by jet blast within 150 ft (forty-five m) of the jet pipe, and at full power any vehicles proceeding along the freeway would be at risk.

This restriction to departing big jets from OIR had been issued as a Notice to Airmen (NOTAM) as early as 10 February 1970 by the airport authority and applied to all high thrust-line type aircraft. 'Take-off power was not at any time to be used until reaching the displaced threshold marker due to jet blast on the freeway.' Oakland Federal Aviation Administration Flight Safety Station (FAA FSS), who were responsible for dissemination of this information, did not consider the detail to meet the criteria of a NOTAM and downgraded the notice to an Airmen Advisory (AIRAD). AIRADs were accorded a more restricted and local circulation.

Early in 1970, the San Francisco Airport ATIS had originally broadcast a reminder of the take-off power restriction to Boeing 747 and other aircraft but had not done so for some time. To confuse the situation, the Boeing 747 restriction was rescinded on 16 April 1970 and reinstated on 11 February 1971. It was this last notice to which the tower controller had referred in his discussion with the dispatcher, but once again the detail had been issued by the Oakland FAA as an AIRAD and not as a NOTAM. Pan Am, in keeping with other aviation organisations, did not possess the teletype circuit required to receive AIRADs.

The airport authority became aware of the problem at an early date and made available a telephone number for airlines to call to obtain current information. Airline personnel, however, tended to use this facility only in unusual circumstances and normally relied on NOTAM and ATIS information. As a result, the dispatchers were not aware of the Boeing 747 take-off restriction on OIR, and never had been. They only became aware of the facts when confirming with the tower the details broadcast on the ATIS regarding the closure of the first 1,000 ft of the runway up to the displaced threshold. A trailer with flags had been placed on the centre-line of OIR about 500 ft (150 m) from the end and barricades had been erected across the taxiway to the original threshold to indicate closure. The first access open to the runway was taxiway 'M,' situated about 200 ft (sixty m) north of the displaced threshold which was marked by painted lines on the runway surface. All aircraft, therefore, irrespective of size, were compelled to depart from this point.

At 15:17 the dispatcher radioed PA845 with the information.

'Talked to tower: the 1,000 feet they were talking about that's closed is actually overrun. You couldn't start from that point in any event because of thrust damage. Start at the painted threshold and you still have 9,500 feet plus clearway ahead of you and under these circumstances the page using 3A power shows no take-off limitation at your gross, over.'

'We don't have those charts in our particular manual,' replied Oakes, 'we only have the dash 3.'

Although the aircraft was powered by upgraded 3A engines, only dash 3 engine details were available to the cockpit crew. The 3A charts were held only in the dispatch office. Because of the critical nature of the departure maximum available power would be required. It would also be necessary to use 'wet' take-off thrust, whereby a system would be activated to inject water into the engine to increase power. A flap 20° setting would be needed as well.

The 'clearway' the dispatcher referred to in his communication with the crew was, in fact, the flat expanse of San Francisco Bay which stretched to the north of OIR. The lack of obstructions on the departure path could be used in the calculations to improve the maximum permitted take-off weight from the runway. The only structure beyond the end of OIR was the approach light system for landing on the opposite direction 19L runway. The structure on which the lights were placed was constructed of 2 x 2 in (fifty mm) angle iron, and a maintenance walkway with a safety rail ran along the entire length of the system. The approach lights and walkway stood proud of the water surface by sixteen ft (4.9m) at the highest point, only five ft (1.5 m) above the runway which was eleven ft (3.35 m) elevation at the northern end. To add to the problem, however, the inclusion of the clearway computation in the take-off calculations also required special charts which were only available in operations and were not held on board Flight 845. Departure from OIR without a weight restriction, therefore, required the use of flap 20°, 3A 'wet' engine power and clearway computations, none of which could be calculated on the flight deck. The crew had to rely on the dispatchers to complete the work satisfactorily and to pass the results over the radio. After a final check of the details, the take-off speeds for runway OIR using flap 20° were radioed to Flight 845: V1, 149 knots; VR, 157 knots; and V2, 162 knots. First Officer Oakes copied down the figures and selected the flaps to 20°.

Although the flight dispatchers appeared to have overlooked the original runway change request to 28R, the crew were still contemplating its use. In 1971 the length of 28R was promulgated as 9,700 ft (2,956 m), but it was known that there was uncertainty regarding this figure. The actual length available was, in fact, 9,500 ft (2,896 m), the same as the noise abatement preferential northerly runway, and a flap 20° take-off was also required for departure. Runway 28R, however, was favoured by the wind which by that time had backed to a westerly direction at twenty knots. This shift in the wind had placed OIR outside the FAA recommended crosswind limits for a noise abatement preferential runway although this factor alone did not preclude its use.

The assistant tower controller on duty at the time was aware of the problem, but also knew of the complaints of noise from the public that would be received by the airport authority if a switch was made to 28R. Also, landing on the northerly runways was prohibited because of the proximity of the built-up area. With 28L closed, only one runway would be available for departure and arrival for the entire airport if a change to 28R for take-offs was implemented. Serious delays would result, and under the circumstances it was felt prudent to retain OIR for departures.

If Captain Dyer still preferred take-off from 28R, the chance to exercise his choice was fast receding. Flight 845 had been taxying and holding for over fifteen minutes while trying to sort out the confusion and precious fuel reserves were being consumed. If Dyer insisted on the use of 28R, further, inevitable and possibly lengthy delays could result. In their present position on the airport they were also blocking the progress of other aircraft and a decision had to be made quickly. The flight dispatcher had already confirmed the suitability of OIR for take-off with no delays expected on that runway. The calculations had been completed and the speeds passed to the aircraft, so to avoid further inconvenience the captain opted for the northerly departure. At 15:19, taxy clearance to the displaced threshold of OIR was received and Flight 845 proceeded on its way.

Captain Dyer and his crew continued with the before take-off checks, aware of some of the problems using OIR, but not all. The temperature remained the same at 66°F (19°C), but the wind had changed to a less favourable quarter with the speed increasing in strength. Initial calculations had been based on a wind component of zero, but the crew were now presented with a slight tail wind. Even under the most relaxed circumstances the maximum permitted tail wind of the Boeing 747 was only ten knots. The take-off limitations of OIR had been improved by use of the clearway — the area of water to the north of the runway — but unknown to the crew and the dispatchers the clearway did not meet FAA criteria in spite of the relevant charts being available in the manuals.

The height of the opposite direction 19L approach light system, standing proud of the runway by only five ft (1.5 m) at its highest point, *did* constitute an obstruction and negated the use of a clearway in the calculations. Barges were also known to cross the take-off zone. But there was more. A further, more serious and insidious error lurked within the manuals. The page for OIR clearly stated the length of the runway to be 9,500 ft, but this was highly misleading. The total distance of the runway *was* 9,500 ft, but the displaced threshold lay 1,100 ft (335 m) from the beginning of the runway and only 8,400 ft (2,560 m) was available for take-off for Boeing 747 aircraft. It appeared from the chart that 9,500 ft was available from the displaced threshold. The dispatchers had only just been made aware by the tower controller of the Boeing 747 take-off restriction precluding use of the runway surface south of the displaced threshold, but there was no indication that this had not been taken into account in the charts. The airport authority had properly disseminated the details and it was not unreasonable to assume that any runway restrictions appropriate to the Boeing 747 had been considered in the manuals for the aircraft type. The airline, however, had never received the information. Captain Dyer and his crew had been assured by the dispatchers of the adequacy of OIR, but unknown to anyone involved in Flight 845's departure, the big jet was about to depart from a runway which had a take-off run 1,100 ft less than stated.

As *N747PA* taxied towards the OIR threshold, the crew continued with the before take-off checks. The 20° flap setting and the stabiliser trim were checked, the flight instruments were confirmed operating satisfactorily, the flying controls were tested and the fuel and hydraulic systems were arranged for departure. The take-off speeds pertaining to the flap 10° take-off on 28L had been set on the airspeed indicators with the white plastic bugs during the engine start check which had been completed before push back. It was now necessary to set the lower take-off speeds relating to the flap 20° requirements, but in the confusion the crew omitted to reset the bugs. Confirmation of the bugged take-off speeds did not re-appear on the check list after the initial setting during the engine start check and no reminder was available to prompt the crew. VR remained at the original speed of 164 knots instead of the correct 157 knots, and more runway would be needed to gain the higher speed. It now appeared the trap was well and truly set.

Although, by any standards, a departure on OIR under the present circumstances was unacceptable, there *was* sufficient runway to complete the take-off. A rejected take-off at V1 could not be accommodated on the length available for there was insufficient stopping distance, but there was just enough runway for a take-off run. It would be close, very close indeed, but it was possible. In fact, the distance required for Flight 845 to accelerate to lift off by rotating at the flap 20° speed of 157 knots was only 7,400 ft (2,255 m), well inside the 8,400 ft (2,560 m) available. Rotating at the higher, incorrect speed of 164 knots, also with flap 20° set, required 8,400 feet, right on the limit; an extremely critical but not impossible situation. The position of the aircraft at the start of the run, the rate of application of power, the rotation technique and any slight change of wind would all play a part and any one might tip the balance. It would be touch and go.

Flight 845 now approached runway OIR unaware of the insidious danger of the situation. Captain Dyer stopped by the side of the runway and checked the departure routeing which had been issued earlier as a San Francisco 3. After take-off from runway OIR the big jet was to turn on to a heading of 030° magnetic for radar vectors to the assigned route. A few moments later the tower controller radioed the instruction to continue.

'Cleared into position on runway OIR to hold.'

Entering the runway from taxyway 'M' required a back-track to the displaced threshold. Dyer taxied the aircraft beyond the take-off point and turned to face north with the nosewheel sitting on the painted line. Every foot would count on the take-off run and this start position was in the 747's favour. The last of the before take-off checks was completed and Flight 845 was ready to go. The tower controller frequently called out the wind velocity to departing aircraft as a check and at 15:26 the information was relayed to Dyer.

'Clipper 845, the wind's two seven zero at twenty two.'

Two minutes later, at 15:28, the instruction to depart was issued by the tower. 'Clipper 845, cleared for take-off. The wind two six zero at twenty.'

The wind had backed a further 10° to 260° and resulted in a tail wind in excess of three knots. It seemed an insignificant amount blowing the jet down the runway, but under the critical conditions it could just tip the balance. It would be desperately close.

Captain Dyer opened up the thrust levers with his right hand to 1.1 engine pressure ratio (EPR) while his left hand rested on the nose wheel steering tiller.

'Power stable,' called F/E Horn.

Captain Dyer quickly released the brakes and steadily advanced the thrust levers close to maximum power. The big jet leapt forward and began to accelerate rapidly.

'Set full power,' called Dyer.

F/E Horne finely adjusted the levers to the maximum setting while Captain Dyer's hand rested gently on top. As the airspeed indicators became effective the co-pilot checked both instruments and the needles were seen to move. At eighty knots the rudder became fully effective and at the call of 'eighty knots' from F/O Oakes, the captain transferred his left hand from the nose wheel tiller to the control column and continued to steer with rudder. The co-pilot released his hold on the wheel.

'I have control,' confirmed Dyer.

A good degree of right rudder was required against the effect of the cross-wind as the captain steered the 747 down the runway with delicate movements of the rudder pedals. The captain's right hand still rested on the thrust levers ready to close them in the event of a rejected take-off while his left hand grasped the control column and held down the windward wing. The control felt uncomfortably crossed with right rudder and left aileron selected. F/O Oakes and F/E Horne scanned the instruments and monitored progress; the aircraft seemed to be accelerating normally. At the bugged speed of 156 knots the first officer called out 'Vee one.' The aircraft was now committed to take-off and the captain moved his right hand from the thrust levers to the control column. Both hands now carefully held the wheel and the flight engineer assumed control of the throttles. The aircraft continued to accelerate and reached 157 knots, the correct VR speed for flap 20° at which rotation should have occurred. A further four seconds and another 1,000 ft (300 m) of runway would be needed to achieve the bugged VR speed of 164 knots. By now, however, the increase in speed seemed to be agonisingly slow . . . 158 knots . . . 159 . . . 160 . . . and the end of the runway was rapidly looming. The crew were seriously alarmed by the situation and the co-pilot began to sense that they were not going to make it. Five men held their breaths as the runway end rushed towards them.

'Rotate,' Oakes yelled to his captain.

The shout was uttered not because the bugged rotation speed of 164 knots had been reached but because the end of the runway was 'coming up at a very rapid speed'. At 15:29 and a speed of 161 knots Dyer pulled back steadily on the control column. The aircraft was now above the flap 20° speed required for take-off of 157 knots and would fly satisfactorily, but the moments to lift off seemed an eternity. At fifty-two seconds on the take-off run, as the speed edged through 165 knots, the end of the runway flashed beneath the nose. The main wheels still touched the asphalt surface. A fraction of a second later the landing gear left the paved runway and for a moment the 747 seemed to be airborne safely. Climb was neglible but the aircraft did not sink. Dyer continued to rotate to the required nose-up attitude. Eagerly the machine clawed for height and seemed to hang in the air.

Just as all seemed well the flight crew were suddenly alerted by a slight jolt which belied the danger of the situation. With the upwards rotation of the nose the rear section of the 747 had lowered and, unknown to the crew, the landing gear had smashed into the approach lights of 19L. Serious damage was being sustained. At just after rotation, the speed rose to 175 knots but with the impact it dropped to 160 knots. Desperately Dyer fought to save the big jet's life.

The Boeing 747's landing gear comprises sixteen wheels set in four bogies of four wheels each. Two bogies extend from the belly of the fuselage, known as the body gears, while the other two extend from the wing roots and are known as the wing gears. The body gears are positioned inboard and aft of the wing gears. On impact with the approach light structure the right body gear struck the first platform of the system and was forced backwards and upwards through the fuselage and into the cargo compartment. The right rear wing spar was completely severed and seriously affected the load bearing capacity of the wing. A large area of the cabin floor above was raised about one to two ft (thirty-sixty cm) and six passenger seats in the middle were dislodged by the floor bulge. Fortunately the seats were unoccupied. The left body gear also hit the first light platform and piling and went progressively deeper into the pier striking the second and third platforms on its way. It was half severed with the sequence of impacts and dangled uselessly from the aircraft with two wheels ripped from its bogie. The bulkhead to which the left body landing gear was mounted broke loose and the number one hydraulic system line fractured. Fluid spilled from the break and all control surfaces supplied by the number one hydraulic system failed.

At a point 300 ft (ninety-one m) along the lighting system, just past the third platform, the underside of the rear fuselage came into contact with the structure. The tail of the big jet dragged through the lighting system and large pieces of the two-by-two angle iron and parts of the handrail on the walkway pierced the fuselage skin. Angle iron sections and handrail lengths lanced the aircraft like giant spears. Seven pieces of steel, mostly handrail sections, shot deeply into the rear of the aircraft as debris scattered in all directions. All the metal spears entered the fuselage on the right, except one length which penetrated the aircraft skin just below door five left, shot through the tail section and exited at the tail cone. On the right side, another piece, fifteen ft (4.5 m) in length, also entered the tail section, piercing the fuselage just forward to door five right and becoming lodged in the tail cone below the auxiliary power unit. Two long sections, sixteen-and-a-half and seventeen ft (five and 5.2 m) long

Runway 19L approach light structure damage. Note the twisted angle iron sections.

became jammed in the fuselage side at the base of the centre cargo door and trailed bent and twisted in the airflow.

Of the three remaining metal lengths, all penetrated the passenger area causing extensive damage. One handrail section, like a lethal missile, streaked right through the rear section of the cabin. It punctured the skin just aft of the centre cargo door, passed through the cargo compartment and entered the cabin under seat 54F. It then shot through the aft cabin partition, through the three rear right-hand toilets, pierced the rear pressure bulkhead (an umbrella-shaped dome which plugs the end of the pressurised cabin), and exited the fuselage close to the tail fin, just below the lower rudder. The two other metal pieces, one a thirteen ft (four m) section of angle iron, pierced the fuselage just forward of the centre cargo door and tore a large hole in the skin. The projectiles then ripped through the cargo hold and punctured the cabin floor. The thirteen ft angle iron piece impaled the empty 'F' seats at rows 45, 46, 47 and 48, and remained embedded in the seats. Fortunately this cabin penetration, like the incident described above, caused no injuries to aircraft occupants, but the trajectory of the third, smaller seven ft (2.1 m) length was not so favourable. It struck the cabin floor below seat 'G' at row 46 with great force and continued through the same seat of rows 47 and 48. A passenger seated in 47G received a bad leg injury below the knee and another passenger in 48G had his left arm cut and crushed. The handrail length then smashed through the overhead hat racks and the ceiling above row 52, knocking sections of the ceiling panelling on to the seats. It then punctured the fuselage roof in the middle and became embedded in the centre of the tail fin. It was by the greatest of good fortune that so many seats were unoccupied in the damaged areas and that no one was killed.

The tail of the Boeing 747 continued to plough through the structure. As handrail and angle sections lanced the fuselage, wood and metal debris flew at random with great force causing serious damage to other aircraft sections. The inboard trailing edge flaps, the left and right horizontal stabilisers and the right elevator were all struck. Flying fragments caused severe structural damage to the stabiliser, and the hydraulic lines of numbers three and four systems were severed. One missile penetrated the right stabiliser and passed into the right elevator, only narrowly missing the line for the number two hydraulic system. Within a matter of seconds, with the number one system already fractured, the big jet had lost three of its four hydraulic systems and had come within four in. (10 cm) of all the aircraft flying controls being completely disabled.

Now with only number two hydraulic system functioning the Boeing 747 was left with a minimum of flying controls: the left outboard and right inboard ailerons, the right inboard elevator and the lower rudder. It would fly in this condition but handling would be quite different and control response would be slow and sluggish. It would not be easy to control. The fuselage tail continued to trail in the approach light pier and with only one hydraulic system operating, Flight 845 was close to disaster. With great skill Captain Dyer wrestled to save the stricken machine. At a point about twenty ft (six m) beyond the sixth light platform the big jet at last broke free from the tangled metal and eased slowly into the air. Oakes quickly checked the altimeters and was relieved finally to call 'positive climb'. Dyer climbed away at the achieved speed of 160 knots. The take-off had been a close run event and the aircraft had been badly damaged but now they were back from the brink of disaster and were climbing safely.

The flight engineer quickly checked the extent of the damage. From his panel he could see that the hydraulics were in a bad way and the hydraulic pressures of systems one, three and four were dropping rapidly. The hydraulic fluid quantity indications were also decreasing.

'We're losing hydraulic systems one, three and four,' called Horne.

Immediately he selected the air-driven pumps to off and depressurised the engine-driven pumps. With the aircraft settled in the climb the landing gear would normally have been selected up but with serious hydraulic problems and possible gear damage it was left extended. At this stage the crew were still unaware of the destruction caused by the impact.

Once more, Flight Engineer Horne checked the hydraulic systems and found one, three and four still leaking, so he switched the engine pumps to off.

'I've had to shut down one, three and four hydraulic systems, captain, so we're down to number two hydraulic system only.'

Dyer could feel the aircraft was handling in a sluggish manner but he climbed at a steady 160 knots and held the aircraft close to the runway heading as it flew out over the bay. At 1,000 ft (300 m) he gently eased forward on the control column to increase speed to 165 knots and continued striving for a safe height. Suddenly the cabin crew in-flight director appeared on the flight deck and informed the captain of the serious damage that had been sustained. Long pieces of metal were sticking through the cabin and two passengers had been hurt. Captain Dyer sent back the second officer and number two flight engineer to assess the damage and to report on the condition of the injured cabin occupants. Dyer maintained control of the stricken aircraft and continued to check out the effectiveness of the flying controls. Flight Engineer Horne returned to the check list to confirm which services would be available and which secondary systems would have to be employed.

The immediate problem was the lack of hydraulic power from numbers one and four systems to raise the trailing edge flaps. The leading edge flaps operated using pneumatic power and would retract and extend as scheduled with movement of the trailing edge flaps. The normally hydraulically powered trailing edge flaps, however, would have to be raised using the secondary electrical system. It would take time to bring in the flaps in this manner, but it was essential to retract them to accelerate to a safe flying speed. Dyer would also be unable to raise the landing gear, but since, under the circumstances, it was sensible to leave it extended that difficulty was eliminated. Normal and secondary braking systems were also lost but that was not a problem for the moment. Fortunately the reserve brakes were still available from number two system and the source could be opened up just before landing. Flight Engineer Horne quickly checked through the major systems that had been lost and read them out to his captain.

'Okay,' replied Dyer. 'Let's have the alternate trailing edge flap check list.'

Horne opened the book at the required page and stood by for the drill. At 15:32 Captain Dyer decreased the ascent and began accelerating. The flight engineer called out the appropriate drill while First Officer Oakes selected the trailing edge flap alternate switch to arm. He then placed the alternate trailing edge flap switches to up and, fortunately, the flaps began to run in. After a few minutes the drill was completed.

The Boeing 747 was now flying with clean wings but with the damaged landing gear still extended. Captain Dyer levelled off and flew the aircraft between 2,500 and 3,000 ft (760-910m) at about 280 knots while the crew continued to assess the situation. With the aircraft safely airborne the next concern of the crew was to get it back down again without incident. The most sensible course of action was to land back at San Francisco as soon as possible and plans were made accordingly.

Meanwhile, in the cabin, passengers were moved forward

from the damage area and an announcement was made calling for medical assistance. Two doctors came forward and, with the aid of one of the stewardesses who was a nurse, administered to the injured. There was little they could do except stem the bleeding and make the passengers comfortable.

N747PA was much too heavy for an immediate landing and arrangements were made to dump fuel to reduce the weight to a structurally safe level. The 747 still weighed about 320 tons and the weight would have to be decreased to below the maximum permitted landing weight of 265 tons before commencing an approach. Oakes contacted radar control with the request to dump fuel and Flight 845 was vectored on to a westerly heading to steer the aircraft away from the built-up area and out over the Pacific Ocean. Captain Dyer discussed the fuel situation with his flight engineer and decided to discharge eighty tons of fuel. That would bring the aircraft down to a manageable 240 tons and would still leave fifty tons of fuel for the return and landing back at San Francisco.

As the Boeing 747 flew westbound over the Pacific, the two extra flight crew who had been sent aft to check the damage, returned with their report. It appeared from the metal lengths in the cabin that the aircraft had struck the 19L approach light system and there was little doubt that the landing gear was badly damaged in the process. The injured passengers were being attended to by qualified personnel and they were being made as comfortable as possible.

'I think we better get an observer in another aircraft to check out the landing gear,' suggested Dyer.

Oakes called control with the request and immediately the Coast Guard were alerted and Pan Am engineers summoned. The controller also informed the airport authorities who confirmed that the lighting pier at runway 19L was damaged and that a landing gear bogie was lying in the water. Within a short time a US Coast Guard aircraft took off from its base with airline personnel on board and flew in pursuit of the Boeing 747. Radar control vectored the Coast Guard flight on to the tail of N747PA and it flew below the big jet to allow the engineers to inspect the damage.

'The right body gear is missing,' radioed the pilot from the inspection aircraft, 'and the left body gear is hanging down with two wheels missing.'

Some minor damage to the flaps, tailplane and elevator was also reported, but the engineers were able to inform the 747 crew that the nose gear and wing landing gears appeared intact and looked able safely to sustain a landing.

As the Coast Guard aircraft flew off and returned to base, Flight Engineer Horne completed the drill in preparation for fuel dumping. An altitude of 6,000 ft (1,830 m) was the normal minimum height for jettisoning fuel to allow the kerosene to disperse, but dumping at 3,000 ft (915 m) over the ocean would cause little problem if particles rained on the sea. On each wingtip a large nozzle protruded rearwards at the trailing edge from which fuel could be discharged, and powerful pumps could push the fuel overboard at an average of 2.3 tons per minute.

'We're now ready for dumping,' radioed Oakes, 'and we'll need just over thirty minutes to lose the fuel.'

With permission received, Horne opened the appropriate valves and switched on the pumps in sequence. Fuel poured from the wingtips in two powerful streams.

As the kerosene discharged from the aircraft, Dyer spoke to the passengers on the PA system. He explained the structural damage which had been caused and assured the cabin occupants that the aircraft was flying safely and that a return to San Francisco would be commenced as soon as possible. They were dumping fuel to bring the weight down for landing and that would take about thirty minutes. Once the drill was completed they would be ready to commence an approach and they would be back on the ground in about one hour. Dyer also instructed his cabin crew director to prepare the cabin for an emergency landing. The passengers were briefed on crash landing drills and also on ditching procedures in case the aircraft landed in the bay. The use of life jackets was demonstrated and they were donned by all on board. Shoes, pens, combs and other sharp objects were removed, blankets and pillows were issued for protection, and the 'brace' position was demonstrated. The passengers were informed that the aircraft would be evacuated via the slides and groups of cabin occupants were assigned specific exits. With the landing gear so seriously damaged there was a likehood of it collapsing on touch-down and it would be as well to get people out of the aircraft as quickly as possible. There would also be a serious risk of fire, even if the gear held on landing. Amongst the passengers was a positioning crew, 'dead-heading' to Tokyo, and they were commandeered into service to help the operating crew with the preparations.

Meanwhile, on the flight deck, Dyer and his crew rechecked the control availability on the number two hydraulic system and referred to the flying manual for landing with the body gear up.

The fuel dumping took longer than expected and about forty-five minutes was required to reduce the aircraft weight to 240 tons. At the appropriate moment, Flight Engineer Horne switched off the pumps and shut the discharge nozzles to stop the jettisoning while Oakes radioed control that dumping was completed. Flight 845 was radar vectored for landing in a westerly direction and in the clear, daylight conditions Dyer would be able to make a safe visual approach over the bay. The approach and landing checks were completed in good time and as the aircraft slowed the flaps were successfully lowered to the 20° setting using the alternate electrical system.

Approaching the airport from the east at about six miles (9.5 kilometres) and level at 1,900 ft (580 m), the previously closed runway 28L, being the longest, was opened up to receive the stricken aircraft. At 17:07, just over one-and-a-half hours after take-off, N747PA established on the 28L instrument landing system and Dyer stabilised the speed at 145 knots. The flaps were selected to the 30° landing position and the crew were relieved to see them properly set. If the flaps had jammed at one of the earlier stages the touch-down speed would, of necessity, have been fast and the damaged landing gear would not have helped the situation. The threshold reference landing speed was 123 knots, but with the strong twenty-knot headwind the captain would increase this speed by ten knots to touch down at 133 knots. The aircraft seemed to handle satisfactorily, but the crew were greatly concerned about the damaged landing gear. They were more than aware that the gear might not support the aircraft on the ground and if it collapsed under the strain on landing the machine would career along the ground on its belly. The chance of fuel spillage and a major fire developing would be high and the occupants would be in great peril.

Flight 845 was cleared to land and approaching 200 ft (sixty m) Oakes called 'brace, brace' over the PA. The passengers and cabin crew took up their crash landing postures. At the same moment Dyer stretched forward with his right hand and opened up the reserve brakes. Slowly he eased back on the power to reduce to 133 knots, but at the lower speed the effectiveness of the single elevator section was reduced. Also, unknown to the crew, the stabiliser leading edge forward of the inboard elevator was badly damaged, exposing the tailplane spar, and further affected the operation of the remaining elevator. He pulled back on the control column to reduce the rate of descent but the response was extremely sluggish. The captain increased the power for more speed to arrest the sink rate, but his efforts were in vain. The aircraft's momentum carried it downwards and at 17:11, one hour and forty-two minutes after departure, the 747 contacted the right side of the runway with great force about 2,000 ft (610 m) forward of the 28L threshold. N747PA bounced back into the air. Moments later it landed heavily again a short distance from the first point of contact. By great fortune the landing gear held and the aircraft rolled on down the runway.

Captain Dyer immediately pulled the thrust levers to the reverse thrust selection but only number four engine indicated it had gone into reverse condition. Since asymmetric reverse thrust is not permitted the captain did not apply reverse power, which was just as well. As he pushed on the toe brake pedals the brakes locked on. The anti-skid system was defective and six of the eight tyres remaining on the wing landing gears blew out. Flat spots were milled on the wheel rims as the bogies scraped along the ground and a fire erupted on the left wing gear. The aircraft started to veer to the right and had reverse thrust been applied on number four engine only, the 747 would have swung violently.

Dyer tried desperately to hold the aircraft straight using rudder but once again his efforts were thwarted. *N747PA* ran off the right side of the paved surface just before cross taxyway 'L', about 4,000 ft (1,220 m) from the threshold, and ploughed on through the grass. The 747 then ran across OIR, the runway from which it had departed, and came to a halt, 5,300 ft (1,615 m) from the approach end of 28L, on a grass square in the middle of the airport at the intersection of all four runways. Fortunately the fire at the left wing landing gear was extinguished by the dirt and dust as the shredded tyres dug through the earth.

On stopping, Dyer gave the order to evacuate and as Horne shut down the engines Oakes made the call for the passengers to depart. Present day aircraft have emergency evacuation alarms but such systems were not available on earlier models. Immediately the two extra flight crew members left the flight deck and ran down the stairs to help. They arrived in the cabin before the evacuation had commenced and each opened up a door at the front. On opening the doors, the escape slides, positioned in packs on the inside of the doors, automatically deployed. In moments the chutes were inflated but the strong breeze blowing could be felt by the open doors and soon the slides were being caught by the gusts. The aircraft had stopped at an angle to the runway and the left side of the 747 was being exposed to the twenty-knot wind.

As door one left slide deployed the wind lifted the chute and twisted it backwards. It was unavailable for use. The same fate befell the slide at door two left. It flew backwards and flapped across the wing parallel to the fuselage. Evacuation from doors three and four left was not possible owing to further problems. Door three left is an over-wing exit and the escape route is deployed in two portions; one over the wing and another slide section over the trailing edge to the ground. The slide portion failed to deploy because the gas bottle trigger mechanism for inflation situated in the left body gear wheel was damaged on take-off. At door four left the entire slide pack had been dislodged from the door on impact with the lighting pier and was completely useless. At that stage door five left had not been

The Pan Am 747 shortly after landing. The wing gear only is down with the tyres on the left wing gear blown. Only number four engine is in reverse. (Captain Wayne Sager)

opened and in the first forty seconds after stopping no slides on the left, exposed side of the aircraft were usable.

At forty-three seconds after the aircraft came to a halt the first passenger slid down door one right escape route. Door two right chute inflated satisfactorily but the wind blowing below the 747's fuselage lifted it horizontal. One passenger was persuaded to venture on to the slide and his weight brought it to the ground. That exit was then used successfully for escape. Someone on the ground ran round to the door one left escape slide to pull it straight and at fifty-six seconds after stopping passengers began using this exit.

At door three right over-wing exit the escape route deployed satisfactorily, but the door four right slide failed to inflate. Its gas bottle had shifted on impact and the trigger mechanism had misaligned. Door five right was also late in being opened and as yet neither of the two aft slides had been deployed. As a result, only the left most forward door and the three forward doors on the right were being used as escape slides. Since most passengers were seated in the economy section, only a few people departed using these doors. At about one minute after the aircraft stopped, both doors five left and right were opened and normal slide inflation was achieved. Passengers began to evacuate by these doors and cabin occupants near the failed exits in the centre of the aircraft started moving rearwards towards the usable escape slides.

In a matter of seconds the unexpected happened. Devoid of any landing gear support at the aft section of the aircraft, the 747 slowly began to tilt rearwards. No-one knew at the time, not even Boeing, that with body gear support lacking the aircraft could tip backwards. The movement was so slow that few people realised what was happening but eventually it settled on its tail. The nosewheel lifted clear of the ground and N747PA's nose stuck in the air. As the tail dropped, door five left's slide jack-knifed and was jammed below the fuselage. The two most forward chutes slanted almost vertically and a few passengers received back injuries while using the slides in this condition before the exits could be blocked. Escape from the four exits forward of the wings now became impossible. As the front slides became unusable, all five escape routes on the left side were once again rendered inaccessible, although the sill of door five left was only five feet from the ground and a few people simply jumped on to the grass.

On the right side only two doors, the over-wing and aft exits were available for evacuation. The door five right slide

The arrival of the rescue services. Note the door two left slide blown backwards over the wing. (Captain Wayne Sager)

After the event. Note the steepness of the slides at the forward doors and the damage to the wind blown upper deck slide. (Captain Wayne Sager)

was lying at a very shallow angle and people were able to run straight along it on to the ground. In spite of the major problems being encountered, however, the cabin crew accomplished their tasks well and the evacuation of the remaining passengers was completed in good time using the only two doors available. In all, twenty-seven people were hurt departing the aircraft, but fortunately no further outbreaks of fire occurred and all on board escaped to safety.

The incident began as a result of a sequence of errors and omissions by a number of people, including the flight crew, leading to impact with the lighting pier, but with skill a potential disaster had been averted. The accident had been relegated to a minor incident and only two people had been hurt on impact. Captain Dyer and his colleagues may have been partly responsible for their predicament but their misdemeanour should not detract from the professional way in which they and the entire crew handled the emergency.

Firemen stand by. Note the damage to the right leading edge stabiliser just forward of the right inboard elevator, the only elevator control remaining.
(Captain Wayne Sager)

As always, however, they were lucky too. A piece of metal debris had passed only four in. (10 cm) from number two hydraulic system and had it severed the line all flying controls would have been lost. And had the wing folded when the right rear spar separated on initial impact the result would have been inevitable.

# Chapter 4
# The Windsor Incident

'Shall we give it a try?' asked Captain McCormick.

'OK, I'll switch off the hydraulics.'

The instructor turned to the flight engineer's panel and selected the hydraulic pumps to off.

'You're on your own now.'

With hydraulic pressure reduced to zero the flying controls became ineffective and McCormick was left with engine power only to guide the machine. Both men watched the performance with interest and were pleased with the result. The DC-10 'flew' quite well and could be controlled with reasonable success on engine power alone. A bit of practice was all that was required.

Captain Bryce McCormick was a very experienced pilot with 24,000 flying hours to his credit. In the spring of 1972 he was fifty-two years of age and had been with American Airlines since before the end of the war. In his career he had flown a number of aircraft: Convair 240, DC-3, DC-4, DC-6, DC-7 and Boeing 707. In early 1972 McCormick had converted to the DC-10 and by the end of March had completed his ground school, simulator and flying training. In April he recommenced line flying duties on his new aircraft type.

McCormick liked the DC-10 and thought it a fine machine, but his admiration was not entirely without misgivings. The DC-10, like the Lockheed Tristar and Boeing 747, was one of the new generation of 'wide bodied' aircraft which were introduced into service in the early 1970s. These aircraft were not only bigger with more powerful engines and larger passenger capacity, but also incorporated new design concepts. Conservative pilots like McCormick, steeped in traditional values, felt uneasy about accepting some of the

Captain Bryce McCormick.

more radical changes. All jet transport aircraft, for example, have hydraulically operated flying controls, but the three 'wide bodies' had no manual back-up facilities to operate the controls in the event of complete hydraulic failure, unlike the earlier generation Boeing 707 which McCormick had flown.

Back-up systems normally consisted of cables running from the control column which were connected directly to the elevators, ailerons and rudders. With total hydraulic power loss the pilot could, albeit with some difficulty and a lot of muscle, successfully retain control of the aircraft. The 'wide bodies' also employed control cables, but these only fed demands to hydraulic power control units which in turn deflected the control surfaces. Any pilot of one of the newly introduced 'big jets', faced with the unlikely event of total hydraulic power loss, would have no flying controls available to fly the aircraft. What would happen in these circumstances? Could the aircraft be turned, climbed and descended by simply varying the power of the appropriate engines? It was a question that McCormick had pondered on a number of occasions during his DC-10 conversion course and one that he was determined to find out. He now sat in an American Airlines DC-10 flight simulator at their training school at Fort Worth, Texas, and, with the aid of an instructor friend, was experimenting in guiding the aircraft on engines alone.

'It handles pretty well,' commented McCormick.

Both men were pleased with the outcome but not entirely surprised by the success of the exercise. The DC-10, in particular amongst the three 'big jets', has its engines exceptionally well placed for steering by engine power only: one on each side slung in pods below the wings about one third of the way out from the wing roots with the lines of thrust sufficiently far apart for directional control and also directed below the fuselage, and one placed high on the lower half of the tail fin with its line of thrust directed above the fuselage. The Tristar is similar, but the DC-10's highly placed tail engine makes pitch control easier. By using asymmetric power, i.e. by increasing power on one wing engine and decreasing the other, the aircraft could be turned, not unlike the differential steering of a tank by varying the speeds of the tracks. Likewise, the aircraft could be climbed by pitching the nose up using increased power from the low slung wing engines and decreased power of the highly placed tail engine, and vice versa for descent. McCormick spent thirty to forty-five minutes practising the technique and became quite adept at 'flying' the DC-10 simulator in such a manner. By the end of the exercise he could control the simulator from initial climb to approach phase using only the thrust levers without touching the flying control column. McCormick was satisfied with the outcome of the experiment and his success in handling the stricken machine helped allay some of his concern. He was not to realise at that time, however, that in only a few short months his expertise would be put to the test in earnest.

On the morning of 12 June 1972, American Airlines Flight 96 took off from Los Angeles, California, on a scheduled service to New York's La Guardia Airport, routeing via

Detroit Metro, Michigan, and Buffalo in the western tip of New York State. Flight 96, a DC-10-10, registration *N103AA*, was commanded by Captain McCormick, with First Officer R. Paige Whitney as his co-pilot, and Flight Engineer Clayton Burke. In the cabin eight stewardesses were led by Chief Flight Attendant Cydya Smith. The DC-10 departed forty-six minutes late from the American West Coast because of passenger handling difficulties and air traffic control delays. After an uneventful four-hour flight, *N103AA* arrived in Detroit at 18:36 Eastern Standard Time. Of the few passengers aboard, thirty-eight disembarked, while sixteen remained, to be joined by forty others for the next leg. Captain McCormick hoped for a good turn-round time to help make up some of the delay. With only fifty-six passengers travelling on the next sector and little fuel required for the short forty-five minute hop, there was every likelihood of a swift departure.

Soon ground preparations were completed and the passenger doors closed. The two main cargo doors on the right side, situated in the mid-and-forward positions, were checked closed, but the smaller aft bulk cargo hold door on the left side was causing difficulty. It was not the first time that

An American Airlines DC-10. (John Stroud)

problems had occurred in the locking of this door and all
four airlines operating the DC-10 at that time (American,
Continental, National and United) had experienced trouble.
The door was shut by an electric motor and actuator and
was then secured in position by latches being wound on to
spools (see diagram). The door handle operated a locking
mechanism and when placed flush with the door slid locking
pins into place to prevent movement of the latches. Closing
of the handle also shut a small vent door and extinguished
the 'door open' light on the flight deck. In such a condition
the door was safe and would not burst open in flight under
the force of the air in the pressurised cabin.

The problem being encountered with the aft cargo door
was that the actuator being powered by the electric motor
was not driving the latches fully home and it was necessary
on a number of occasions to use a hand crank to complete
closure. McDonnell-Douglas were already aware of the
circumstances and had issued service bulletins recommend-
ing rewiring of the electric motors with heavier gauge wire.
Captain McCormick's aircraft, unfortunately, had not yet

A DC-10 aft cargo door operating mechanism. (NTSB)

Bolts
Sheared

Latch actuator

Incomplete extension
of actuator shaft

Restraining
flange

Actuator shaft

Engagement of
lock pins impossible

Lock pin

Torque tube

Stop

Stop

Link

TORQUE TUBE
BENT

Latch hook

Over-centre achieved
System irreversible
Correct closure

Over-centre not achieved
System reversible
Incorrect closure

LOCK
TUBE

LOCK PIN STOPPED
BY FRONT FACE OF
RESTRAINING
FLANGE

🔴 Fixed points on the structure

→ Direction of forces transmitted
by the latches

*Above:*
DC-10 aft cargo door latch closing system.

*Above:*
The problem of forced closure.

The aft cargo door latch closing system — the problem of forced closure.
(NTSB)

been modified. On the transit in Detroit the ramp service
agent closed the door electrically and listened for the motors
to stop running. Cut-out of the electric motor should have
indicated the correct positioning of the latching mechanism,
but once again problems occurred. The latches were not
driven fully home and the latch linkages were not moved to
the over-centre position (see diagram). Flanges obstructed
movement of the locking pins and prevented the door
handle from being placed flush with the surface. Using a
certain amount of pressure the ramp agent could feel
movement of the handle and simply assumed that the
mechanism was stiff. Eventually he managed to force the
handle into position using his knee and with the lever
properly stowed assumed the locking procedure to be
completed. The latches, however, were still improperly
seated and the door remained unlocked. With the locking
pins jammed against the restraining flanges the forced
closure of the door handle had buckled the locking rods.
The linkage had moved sufficiently, however, to close the
vent door, although in a slightly cocked position, and to

extinguish the 'door open' light on the flight deck. Not surprisingly the ramp agent was unhappy with the circumstances, and he called over a mechanic to examine the vent door which could be viewed through the vent aperture. The mechanic could see the vent door slightly out of position but all the indications appeared normal. The state of the door, however, was anything but normal and was in a most unsafe position. In the cockpit the flight engineer checked the 'door open' light extinguished and could only assume that the door was closed and locked. Captain McCormick and his crew were unaware of any danger.

On Flight 96's departure from Detroit, compressed air would be tapped from the engine compressors to pressurise the cabin for relatively normal breathing for those on board as the aircraft climbed into the thinner air. The aircraft hull and doors were designed to contain the pressurised air in the cabin from bursting outwards into the rarefied atmosphere. To help ease the exertion on the structure, however, cabin pressure is reduced as the aircraft climbs (for example, to an equivalent cabin altitude of 6,000 ft (1,830 m) when cruising at 35,000 ft (10,670 m), but the outwards force is still quite considerable. Would the partially locked aft cargo hold door be able to withstand the strain of several tons of pressure as the cabin pressurised after take-off? If not, and the latches released under the pressure, the door would blow off. The rapid venting of the pressurised air to the atmosphere would cause untold damage and could place the aircraft in great jeopardy.

Meanwhile, unaware of the insidious danger of the situation, the DC-10 crew continued with their departure preparations. As the mechanic inspected the aft cargo door, Whitney called on the radio for departure instructions. The time was just after 19:03.

'Metro clearance delivery from American 96, information "delta", and airways to Buffalo.'

'Delta' was the current weather details transmitted by the automatic terminal information service and indicated the cloud base to be 4,500 ft (1,370 m), the visibility reduced to 1-1½ miles (1.6-2.4 kilometres) in smoke and fog, a southwest wind at six knots, a temperature of 61°F and an altimeter pressure setting of 29.85 inches of mercury. The weather, although not good, would give no problems on departure. Clearance delivery replied instructing American 96 to turn right after take-off on to a heading of 060° for radar vectors to airway Jet 554. The flight was to maintain 4,000 ft (1,220 m) and could expect to be cleared to flight level 250 (25,000 ft, 7,620 m) ten minutes after departure. The departure frequency was given as 118.95 MHz and the squawk, or radar identification code as 0200. Whitney repeated the clearance as read, but the controller corrected himself and re-issued a departure frequency of 118.4 MHz.

In the cockpit the crew completed their pre-start checks. A few minutes' delay ensued as the aft cargo door inspection continued, but finally the door condition was accepted and the all-clear was received on the intercom from the ground engineer. The engine start sequence was commenced and Whitney contacted ground control on 121.9 MHz.

'Ground, American 96, push from gate ten.'

Clearance to push was given, and as the push-back truck revved its engines the DC-10 moved slowly backwards from the gate. The time was 19:11 Eastern Standard Time and the turn-round had been an excellent thirty-five minutes. McCormick was pleased to be making up some time. A few minutes later, with all engines running, Whitney requested permission to taxy and ground quickly replied.

'American 96, taxy to runway three right.'

On the taxy out the take-off performance on runway 03R was checked and the 'before take-off' check list commenced. Approaching the threshold Whitney called the tower on 121.1 MHz.

'American 96,' replied the tower controller, 'into position and hold.'

The DC-10 lined up on the runway and with the anti-skid selected the flight engineer pronounced the checks completed. First Office Whitney was to fly the aircraft on this sector and he stood-by for the take-off. The Captain took over operation of the radio.

'American 96, maintain runway heading and contact departure. Cleared for take-off.'

Whitney opened up the power to the required setting and

the lightly laden big jet rapidly accelerated down the runway. At 19:20 the wheels lifted from the surface and N103AA climbed easily into the air. McCormick established contact with the departure controller.

'American 96, Detroit departure, radar contact. Climb and maintain six thousand.'

'OK,' replied McCormick, 'you want us to climb and maintain six thousand, American 96.'

'Roger, American 96, now turn right heading zero six zero.'

Whitney increased the DC-10's speed and the flaps were selected from the take-off position to up.

'American 96, turn right heading zero nine zero.'

Flight 96 was being carefully radar vectored to pick up the easterly airway Jet 554 en route to Buffalo.

'American 96, turn right heading one one zero. Join Jet five five four when you intercept.'

The DC-10 now entered cloud, and as the aircraft climbed rapidly towards its cleared altitude of 6,000 ft (1,830 m) McCormick replied asking if they were to maintain this height.

'OK, I'll have something higher for ya in just a moment,' replied departure. 'Climb and maintain, ah, flight level two one zero.'

Clearance for further climb arrived just in time for the '1,000 to go' alert tone sounded in the cockpit.

'OK, ah, climb two one zero, American 96,' repeated McCormick. 'We are out of, ah, fifty five hundred now.'

'American 96, call Cleveland Centre now on frequency one two six point four. Good day.'

The US/Canadian border lies lengthwise along the centre of Lake Erie and most of Flight 96's journey would be spent in Canadian airspace. Since the DC-10 was operating between two American airports, however, US controllers continued to direct the flight. N103AA was already over Canadian territory and was now close to the town of Windsor in Ontario.

In the cockpit McCormick quickly selected the Carleton radio beacon on both navigation receivers and set the course indicators to 083°, the Jet 554 airway centre line, to permit interception of the airway. As the DC-10 settled on the heading of 110° Whitney engaged the autopilot, but out of habit kept his hands on the control column. The Cleveland frequency was dialled on the radio box and McCormick called the Centre.

'Good evening, Cleveland Centre, American 96 is out of, ah, seven thousand now for two one zero.'

'American 96, squawk code, ah, one one zero zero and ident. Maintain flight level two three zero, report reaching.'

The DC-10 continued towards Jet 554 and, still in cloud, climbed at the maximum permitted speed below 10,000 ft (3,050 m) of 250 knots to its newly assigned flight level. At 19:24, only four minutes after lift-off, the lightly laden aircraft passed through 10,000 ft. Whitney lowered the nose of the DC-10 using the autopilot vertical speed control to accelerate the machine to the normal climb speed of 340 knots. The aircraft's rate of climb reduced to the 1,000 ft (305 m) per minute selected and the speed began to increase. As the flight approached the top of the weather the cloud thinned and above could be glimpsed the first signs of the sun. A few moments later, passing 11,500 ft (3,500 m), the DC-10 broke from the cloud layer into a bright mid-summer's evening. 'What a beautiful day,' thought Whitney to himself.

N103AA passed over the town of Windsor, situated by the shore of Lake St Clair lying over two miles (3.2 kilometres) below, and continued towards Jet 554 as it headed east-south-east between the Great Lakes of Huron to the north and Erie to the south. At only four-and-a-half minutes after take-off the DC-10 climbed through 11,750 ft (3,580 m) and the increasing speed edged past 260 knots. Captain McCormick looked out into the clear sky and could see far above a giant Boeing 747 flying majestically through the air.

'There goes a big one up there.'

Whitney leaned forward to catch a better view of the other aircraft, still resting his hand gently on the control column. It was a pleasant moment in the trip with the weather and the busy departure behind and a clear flight ahead, but it was a calm which did not last long. Suddenly an enormous 'thud' was heard from the rear of the aircraft and in an instant their

The flight crew: Captain Bryce McCormick (left), First Officer R. Paige
Whitney (centre) and Flight Engineer Clayton Burke (right).
(Captain Bryce McCormick)

peace was shattered. The air 'fogged' and a great rush of air
swept past the flight crew. Dirt and dust flew in their faces
and stung their eyes and skin as if a firecracker had gone off
below their noses. For a moment they were blinded.

'Oh . . .!' someone shouted.

The rudder pedals exploded and smacked at great speed
to the full left rudder position. The captain was resting his
feet on the pedals and his right leg was thrown back against
the seat with extreme force. His right knee was driven to his
chest and his headset was knocked from his ears. First
Officer Whitney, still leaning forward, was thrown violently
rearwards and hit his head as he crashed against his seat. At
the same moment the three thrust levers snapped to flight
idle with the number two (tail) engine throttle hitting the
stop with a loud crack. The aircraft was felt to 'jerk'
momentarily and the autopilot disengaged with the red
disconnect light flashing. McCormick feared a mid-air
collision had occurred and suspected the windshield had
shattered. When his eyes cleared he could see it was still in
place but, disbelievingly, he stretched out his hand to touch
the window.

'What the hell was it, I wonder?' he called.

One of the crew replied with a long whistle. Captain McCormick now noticed a red failure flag on his airspeed indicator and speculated that the radar dome might have blown off. With the aircraft nose cover missing erratic speed indications could be expected. Whitney still maintained his hands on the column but the DC-10 yawed and banked slowly to the right with the nose dropping sharply out of control.

'Let me have it,' yelled the captain as he grabbed the control wheel. Quickly he tried to 'feel out' the controls.

'I think it's going to fly,' reassured Whitney.

At three seconds after the initial explosion an engine fire warning sounded, together with the *beep, beep, beep* of the cabin altitude warning horn. The DC-10 appeared to have suffered an explosive decompression and the intermittent horn indicated that the cabin air pressure had reduced to an equivalent altitude in excess of 10,000 ft (3,050 m). McCormick had no doubt that he had a 'pretty sick airplane' on his hands and the first priority was to keep it in the air. 'Fly the airplane, fly the airplane,' he kept saying to himself. The engine and pressurisation problems could wait.

'We'll pass the fire warning,' he called.

Capain McCormick was an advocate of the theory that he who hesitates, survives. When faced with a sudden emergency he firmly believed that a pilot's first action should be to do nothing — think the problem out, then act. In normal circumstances, with an intermittent horn warning of reduced cabin pressure, the crew would commence an emergency descent, but the captain was reluctant to force the aircraft into a steep dive until the damage could be assessed. If he did drop down quickly he might not be able to recover. Flying at around 12,000 ft (3,660 m) few breathing problems would be experienced, although strictly speaking flight crew should don oxygen masks above 10,000 ft. The engine fire, too, was a serious problem, but a more pressing matter was the need to keep the aircraft flying. There would be little point in extinguishing a fire if the DC-10 tumbled out of control. To the crew their actions felt strange, like moving in slow motion.

'We've hit something,' said the flight engineer.

The co-pilot had been looking out at the time and had not seen anything of another aircraft so thought it more likely to be disintegration of number two engine. That would explain the fire warning and the rudder problem.

'We've lost . . . lost an engine here,' he said.

'Ah, which one is it?' asked the captain.

Flight Engineer Burke could see the problem from the engine instruments.

'Two. Number one is still good . . . and, ah, Captain . . . we'll have to . . . to check this out.'

McCormick could see the aircraft descending towards the cloud tops which lay below at 10,000 ft and he wanted to avoid penetrating the weather until he was sure he had control of the stricken machine. Steadily he heaved back on the control column but the response was very sluggish. The speed had dropped to 220 knots and simultaneously he pushed the three thrust levers forward. The numbers one and three (wing) engines responded but the number two (tail) engine remained in flight idle. The number two throttle could be moved backwards and forwards quite easily and it obviously wasn't attached to anything. Immediately the DC-10 responded to the power increase from the wing engines and the nose pitched up. McCormick only just managed to stay in the clear.

'OK,' said Whitney, 'we apparently . . . master warn ing . . . this board's got an engine fire over here. Yeah, we got two engines, one and three. Do we have, ah, hydraulics?'

'No,' replied McCormick, 'I've got full rudder here.'

The rudder was still jammed with the left pedal fully forward and the captain assumed the condition to be the result of hydraulic failure. The flight engineer checked out the systems, however, and found them satisfactory.

'Hydraulic pressure is OK,' he said.

In the cabin there was just as much confusion as there was in the cockpit, and some of the passengers were hysterical. Chief Flight Attendant Smith rushed forward to the flight deck to check with the captain.

'Is everything all right up here?'

'No,' called McCormick. The co-pilot turned and shock his head. 'You go back to the cabin.'

The DC-10's speed established at 250 knots and Captain McCormick managed, with difficulty, to hold the aircraft clear of cloud at 12,000 ft. While the other two continued to check out the systems he retrieved his headset from the back of the seat and quickly radioed Cleveland Centre declaring an emergency. There was little information he could give as they didn't know what had happened except that they had a serious problem.

'Ah, Centre, this is American Airlines Flight 96, we got an emergency.'

'American 96, roger,' replied Cleveland. 'Returning back to Metro?'

'Ah, negative, I want to get in to an airport that's in the open. Where's one open?'

Having just left Detroit Metro with a visibility of one to one-and-a-half miles in smoke and fog and having climbed through a 6,000 ft thick cloud layer, McCormick was reluctant to return there until he was sure of the integrity of the flight controls. It would be more sensible to avoid flying on instruments if there were control problems and to head somewhere clear of weather. He would make a decision once he had checked out the DC-10's controllability. The aircraft was continuing to fly, albeit with difficulty, but there was no doubt that the controls were severely impaired. The rudder pedals were solidly jammed, with the left pedal fully forward, but with the rudder itself trailing slightly to the right. The effect yawed the aircraft nose to the right and the aircraft flew in an askew condition. The elevators controlling climb and descent were extremely stiff to move and produced a very sluggish response.

McCormick tried to trim out the elevator control column forces by operating the electric stabiliser trim switches, but to no avail. Trimming consists of varying the angle of the tailplane to the airflow to stabilise an aircraft in flight, and as such the variable tailplane is known as the stabiliser. On McCormick's aircraft the stabiliser position indicator remained fixed and the stabiliser did not function. The captain then tried to operate the manual trim control but as he did so the handle came away in his hand. So much for that! There was little McCormick could do now to ease the elevator strain but he felt he could overcome some of the difficulty in pitch control by varying the power of the wing engines. The off-set rudder kept rolling the aircraft to the right, but, with the control wheel turned 45° to the left, it was possible to use the ailerons, which are normally employed to bank the aircraft for a turn, to hold the wings level. In this condition, turning of the aircraft, especially to the right, was a delicate operation and only slow 15° banked turns could be achieved.

In a few moments, by experimenting with the controls, McCormick quickly brought the stricken airliner under control. He sensed now that he could keep the aircraft in the air, but could he land it in such a condition. That was going to be a different problem. Flying the DC-10 on engines was one thing, but guiding a large jet in such a manner on to a 200 ft (sixty m) wide runway was a different matter. Unfortunately there was little choice but to try.

McCormick's thoughts now turned to his passengers whom he suspected would be in some distress. Quickly he picked up the public address (PA) handset to offer reassurance. He had little to tell them but he felt any words of encouragement would be better than none. Trying to hide his own apprehension he spoke as calmly as possible saying that they had a mechanical problem and that they would be returning to land.

'American 96,' called Cleveland Centre, 'start right turn. Heading'll be one seven zero, maintain ten thousand.'

As the stricken aircraft banked slowly to the right, the flight crew pondered the problems which lay ahead. As yet no one had any idea of what had happened. Back in the cabin Chief Flight Attendant Cydya Smith took stock of the situation and began assessing the damage. She knew that the captain would expect a full report as soon as possible. As she proceeded rearwards, comforting and assuring passengers, she was amazed at the destruction she could see towards the rear. At the time of the 'explosion' she had been standing in the service centre preparing coffee and drinks for the passengers. The door of the lift to the lower galley suddenly burst open, narrowly missing her head, and out billowed what appeared to be a 'smoky substance'. She was thrown off balance but managed to steady herself by grabbing a handrail. She felt a sensation of weightlessness which was followed by complete silence. Instantly she thought the aircraft had suffered a depressurisation and quickly checked to see if oxygen masks had dropped in the cabin. They remained in position and she had no difficulty in breathing. (At cabin altitudes above 10,000 ft [3,050 m] the warning horn on the flight deck sounds but it is only at cabin altitudes above 14,000 ft [4,270 m] that passenger oxygen masks drop automatically.) It was then that she rushed forward to the flight deck to check on the situation and on the way had been puzzled to see the captain's hat lying on the floor of the front cabin. In the cockpit she had seen from the expressionless look on the co-pilot's face as he spoke to her that something was seriously wrong so she had returned immediately to the cabin. She then spoke on the PA, instructing the travellers to stay in their seats, not to smoke and to remain calm.

Suddenly Stewardess Carol Stevens grabbed her arm and told her that one of the flight attendants at the back was trapped by the edge of a large hole and that she urgently needed help. Stevens had been sitting with her seat belt still fastened when she heard a 'varoom' type of noise and the cabin had fogged. Air had rushed from front to rear of the aircraft. When the mist cleared she had seen the devastation in the rear section of the cabin. A small lounge bar was situated in this area for the use of economy passengers, but since few people were on board and the sector was short it was considered not worth offering the facility. No one was seated in the area, which was just as well, for the floor had caved in and ceiling panels were hanging down. The bar unit had collapsed and had fallen into the hole on the left side of the aircraft. On the floor and halfway into the cavity lay Stewardess Bea Copeland, prostrate on her side but facing forwards with her head towards the centre. She was trapped by the wreckage and was shouting for help. Stevens had tried to call Cydya Smith to tell her of the girl's predicament but the cabin interphone failed to work. She was hesitant to leave her seat since she assumed the cabin had decompressed and she was expecting an emergency descent. Eventually she noticed some of the other attendants out of their seats so she had run forward to raise the alarm.

On take-off Bea Copeland had been positioned by the aft left exit and had remained in her seat with her seat belt fastened. There were few passengers on board and, with time to spare, she had sat chatting to Stewardess Sandra McConnell who sat by the aft right exit. The bar area was situated immediately forward of the girls' positions. Copeland had only just released her seat belt when suddenly she had been lifted from her seat and thrown to the floor. A ceiling panel had detached and had fallen on her head and debris had trapped her foot. From where she lay she could see down into the cargo hold. The large bar unit had crashed behind her, partially blocking the hole and preventing her from falling further. She had tried to shift the panel covering her head but was unable to move it so she begun calling for help. On the right side Stewardess McConnell had been thrown from her seat with the 'explosion' and had struck the divider position behind the bar. She had landed on the damaged floor and had felt the area around her begin to crumble. From where she lay she could see daylight through the side of the aircraft and she could feel herself slipping slowly into the hole.

Chief Flight Attendant Smith, with Carol Stevens and a male passenger who offered to help, rushed back to assist the trapped stewardesses. One of the other attendants, unaware of the rescue in progress, called the flight deck on the interphone to ask if someone could lend a hand. In the cockpit the flight crew had their own problems, of course, but they seemed to be overcoming the initial difficulties. As Cleveland Radar vectored N103AA southwards for a return to land, the crew quickly rearranged their duties. Until the moment of the incident the co-pilot had been flying the aircraft. The captain had taken control but had continued to operate the radio while the other two inspected the systems. They had checked out the number two engine fire warning and found it to be false. McCormick continued to fly the aircraft while Whitney now took over communications.

'We've got one seven zero heading, sir,' called the co-pilot to Cleveland Control, 'and, ah, maintaining twelve thousand.'

'96, roger, type of emergency?'

Whitney misheard and simply replied, 'Yeah, yes sir.'

'We have a control problem,' McCormick added. 'We have no rudder, got a full jam. We've had something happen, I don't know what it is.'

'American 96, understand . . . cleared to maintain, ah, niner thousand, altimeter two nine eight seven. Be, ah, radar vector back towards the ILS course runway three. You want the equipment standing by?'

Cleveland was suggesting the DC-10 return to Detroit Metro, landing in the same direction as take-off with radar guidance onto the instrument landing system (ILS) for either of the parallel 03 runways.

'OK, sir,' replied Whitney, 'ah, say again the heading and we'll let down slowly to nine thousand.'

'Heading'll be two zero zero . . . two zero zero for American 96. And do you wish the equipment to be standing by?'

'Affirmative.'

'Understand. Full equipment standing by at Metro.'

'Yes, sir.'

The interphone now chimed in the cockpit and Flight Engineer Burke answered. It was the call requesting help for the trapped stewardess. The floor had collapsed, explained the caller, and she was lying by the edge and in need of assistance. Clayton Burke discussed the situation with the captain and since the immediate flying problems seemed to be resolved the flight engineer left his seat to help. Aware of the need to be properly dressed in the cabin he searched for his hat which was missing from the clips on the flight deck door. He looked in the crew wardrobe but it was nowhere to be seen. Unknown to Burke the initial rush of air had blown the crews' hats from the back of the door as it flew open and they lay scattered on the cabin floor. Stewardess Carol McGhee had been sitting strapped in by the front entrance at the time of the incident and had seen the flight deck door burst open and the escape hatch from the downstairs galley shoot up and strike a passenger on the head. A dusty rush of air had gushed from the flight deck together with the flight crews' hats which had flown out at head height as if worn by ghosts bolting from the cockpit. Hence the captain's hat seen by Cydya Smith lying on the floor and the flight engineer's inability to find his own.

At the back of the aircraft Bea Copeland still struggled on her own to free herself from the wreckage. Several times she tried to move the panel covering her head and eventually she managed to push it away. Her shoe was stuck in the debris and she was unable to move it, but with some effort she managed to pull her foot out of the shoe and set herself free. She then began to climb out of the area and as she struggled over the bulkhead was met by Smith and the others. Her rescuers helped her onto the rear lounge seats and then grabbed her hands and pulled her into the economy section. They now looked for McConnell who had been sitting by the aft right exit but they could see no sign of her and feared she had fallen into the hold. Smith called out her name repeatedly, but to no avail.

Map showing the relative locations of Detroit, Windsor, Buffalo and New York. Inset shows the DC10 flight path from Los Angeles.

'Sandy, Sandy, are you OK?'

Suddenly as if from nowhere, she appeared in view. She had managed to pull herself out of the hole and, somewhat dazed, had clambered into a rear toilet. The floor appeared very weak and she had felt that it would have collapsed if she had walked over it. Fortunately those on the scene were now able to help and with some difficulty manoeuvred her over the rear seats and into the cabin area. She was badly shaken, as was Copeland who had been trapped on the other side, but otherwise both girls were unhurt. It had only been a few seconds before that the call for help had been put through to the flight deck so one of the girls now rang to say that the two flight attendants had been rescued. Flight Engineer Burke had only just started to look for his hat when the good news was received, so he simply resumed his seat.

At the back of the aircraft Chief Flight Attendant Smith instructed the stewardesses to move away from the damaged area and to shift all the passengers nearby to forward sections. She then returned to the flight deck to report to the captain. Smith informed McCormick of the destruction at the rear of the cabin and that 'there was a hole in the fuselage in the very aft of the left-hand side'. The situation was worse than any of them had expected and they had done well to keep the aircraft flying. The reason for the DC-10's plight was still a mystery, for the problem with the locking of the left rear cargo door was unknown to the crew.

As the fuselage interior had pressurised on the climb out from Detroit the partially locked latches had been subjected to an increasing force. About five minutes after take-off, as Flight 96 passed through 11,700 ft (3,570 m), the pressure on the door was in excess of five tons. The door's electric actuator bolts had suddenly sheared under the stress and the door latches had sprung. The door had blown open, causing explosive decompression of the aircraft. The door had been torn off by the airstream, damaging the left tailplane in the process. The pressurised cargo air had immediately exhausted to the atmosphere via the gaping hole and the cabin air pressure had placed an undue load on the floor. With insufficient venting in the cabin floor area the floor had simply collapsed, tumbling the bar unit into the gap.

Unfortunately the structural devastation was not the only damage sustained. Through the beams of the cabin floor ran a number of vital control cables, hydraulic pipes, fuel lines and wiring to the empennage control surfaces and the number two engine in the tail fin. Many had either been severed or jammed, or had their operation severely curtailed. Ironically, McCormick's original fears of total hydraulic failure remained unfounded in this circumstance for the three hydraulic system lines, like the fuel line to number two engine, remained intact. They did not run through the collapsed central section of the floor and, with the lines coiled at various points to allow for stretching, had survived the impact of the decompression.

The flying controls at the tail, however, functioned via power control units which, like the number two engine controls, were operated by cables which ran from the flight deck through the central floor section along the entire length of the aircraft. As the pilots manipulated the control columns, or engine thrust levers and fuel controls, the taut and finely adjusted control cables moved in response. When the rear cabin floor collapsed the left rudder cable was broken, allowing the right rudder cable to slacken. The intact right cable was then forced downwards by the fallen floor which had deflected the rudder to the right, jamming it in that position. Three of the elevator control cables were severed and only the right outboard elevator panel remained functioning. The downwards load of the collapsed floor also resulted in the elevator being extremely difficult to operate. The tail engine thrust lever cable and the fuel shut-off valve cable were also broken. Severed wiring had resulted in the spurious number two engine fire warning.

McCormick informed his chief flight attendant that they expected to be landing in about eight to ten minutes and he instructed her to prepare for an emergency landing. Smith enquired if they'd be evacuating via the chutes but since the captain was uncertain of what would happen when they touched down he was unable to say. As the discussion ensued Cleveland Centre called again.

'American 96, you say you believe you hit something?'

'Ah, I don't know, sir,' replied Whitney. 'Just standby

one. Standby one until we assess the situation. We've got here, ah, definite problems.'

McCormick interrupted the exchange.

'OK, now we have got, ah, problems. I got a hole in the cabin, I think we've lost number two engine, we got a jammed full left rudder and we need to, ah, get down and make an approach. I guess Detroit Metro would be best and, ah, can you vector us around?'

McCormick felt the DC-10 to be flying satisfactorily, so Control's earlier suggestion of landing back at Detroit seemed a reasonable course of action.

'American 96, roger,' replied Cleveland. 'Turn further right now, heading'll be two zero zero.'

'OK, two zero zero, American 96.'

'Roger. And that the left, ah, rudder is jammed?'

'Er, it's possible,' continued McCormick. 'We don't know

The collapsed floor at the rear of the cabin. (Captain Bryce McCormick)

what the problem is. We've got a hole in the side of the airplane and we've got a full left rudder here. But we're under control and we're heading, ah, two three zero at the present time, letting down slowly to nine thousand.'

'Roger, two three zero, and continue around the, ah, turn to a heading of two seven five.

'Continue around to two seven five, sir.'

'Can you make a standard rate of descent?' asked Cleveland.

'Ah, negative, we gotta go a little slower.'

'Understand, slow descent. And what about turns?'

'Ah, turn we can give you, ah, is close to fifteen degrees maximum.'

'OK, that'll be fine.'

'I have no rudder control whatsoever, so our turns are gonna have to be very slow and cautious.'

'Understand.'

The crew discussed their predicament further and agreed that with judicious use of engine power the captain could more readily control the descent and turns. It was an amazing and fortunate coincidence that this incident had happened to a pilot who had previously practised such procedures. McCormick was thankful for his earlier experience in the simulator and was glad that he could now put the lessons learned then to good use.

'Thank goodness it's one and three we've got,' said Whitney to his captain.

'American 96,' continued Cleveland, 'descend to five thousand. Say altitude now.'

'Twelve to five,' replied Whitney.

'American 96, if you are able to, squawk code zero two zero zero on your transponder.'

'OK.'

'American 96, altitude now?'

'Ah, eleven thousand two hundred.'

'OK. About two hundred feet per minute, then?'

'Yes, sir.'

American 96, you wanna make a left turn now to a heading of, ah, two four zero.'

'Two four zero on the heading?' questioned Whitney.

'Yes sir. Two four zero, so it can give you, ah, a little more room for descent.'

'Yeah. Give me plenty room to start a long approach.'

As McCormick gingerly descended the stricken aircraft he was able to experiment with the use of engine power to aid control. The attempt seemed to be effective. Number two engine appeared to be inactive but they were uncertain if it had stopped at the time of the decompression or if it was still operating in idle. Whitney and Burke executed the appropriate drill and shut the engine down. What effect it had on the engine was unknown but it seemed to ease the heaviness of the elevators. In the cabin the flight attendants were equally busy with procedures as they prepared the passengers for an emergency landing. Chief Flight Attendant Smith gathered the stewardesses together on her return from reporting to the captain and gave them details of the

Detached ceiling panels expose the roof wiring. (Captain Bryce McCormick)

situation. She then spoke on the PA while the other flight attendants gave a demonstration of the brace position. She instructed the passengers to lean forward when told with their seat belts tightly fastened and to place their heads on cushions on their laps with their arms folded across their heads for protection. She then pointed out the six exit locations they would use, disregarding the two rearmost doors near the damaged area, and instructed them in the use of the emergency escape slides. The passengers were then requested to remove spectacles, pens, combs and other sharp objects which could cause injury and the attendants collected them in plastic bags. Shoes were also taken off to avoid ankle and foot injuries. With the cabin secure and the briefings delivered, Smith returned to the flight deck to inform the captain that her preparations were completed. She also asked McCormick if he would give the 'brace' command on the PA if required.

The return to Detroit was taking a little longer than anticipated and, with just over ten minutes to touchdown, the approach procedures were commenced.

'OK, give me about fifteen degrees on the flaps now,' called McCormick to his co-pilot. 'Watch it carefully.'

'We'll be landing about two ninety two thousand pounds,' added Burke.

It was possible to lower the weight further by dumping fuel overboard but since there was little in the tanks and the aft damage was unknown the thought was discarded. The apprehension on the flight deck could be felt and the air was very tense. At that moment one of the stewardesses popped her head through the cockpit door.

'Do you guys have a problem up here?' she asked.

In the strained atmosphere, with the captain struggling to maintain control, the question seemed quite ridiculous and the crew laughed.

'Yes, we have a problem,' they called.

She asked if the escape slides would be used but the captain said he didn't know and that if necessary he would activate the evacuation signal.

Captain McCormick spoke once more to the passengers on the PA as calmly as possible, assuring them that the aircraft was under control and that they were returning to Detroit. He apologised for the inconvenience and said that American Airlines would do all they could to provide transport to their destinations. The composed and routine tone of his voice had a comforting effect and helped ease the tension in the cabin.

'American 96, Cleveland, call me out of ten thousand.'

'We're out of eight seven for five thousand, right?' replied Whitney.

'American 96, roger. Turn back right now, heading'll be two eight zero.'

'Two eighty. I'm guessing that we're gonna have to have a long turn on the final for the ILS. I have no control on rudder and steering directions.'

'Roger, I'm planning about twenty miles. It'll be enough?'

'Ah, I hope so, thank you. I'll keep you advised.'

'American 96, now cleared to maintain three thousand.'

'Three thousand.'

'American 96, contact Metro Approach now, one two five one five. Good night.'

'Thank you. One two five one five.'

'We've got a nice rate of descent,' commented the co-pilot to McCormick. 'Even if we have to touch down this way we're doing well.'

'American 96, Detroit,' called Metro Approach.

'Loud and clear, sir. And we're through fifty five hundred for three thousand.'

'American 96, turn right heading three six zero, descend and maintain three thousand. Vector for the ILS for three left final approach course. Altimeter two nine eight five. Visibility one and one half. Braking, clear for all types of aircraft.'

'We'll probably have no brakes, ah, so we'll try reverse . . . we're heading north and we're outta forty eight hundred for three thousand.'

'American 96, turn right heading zero two zero. Your position is thirteen miles from the marker. You're cleared for ILS three left approach.'

'Zero two zero, and cleared for ILS three left approach, American 96.'

The left tailplane damage caused by the ejected cargo door.
(Captain Bryce McCormick)

The DC-10 joined the ILS localiser radio signal indicating the extended centre line of runway three left at about eighteen miles (twenty-nine kilometres) from touchdown, thirteen miles (twenty-one kilometres) from the marker beacon positioned at the five miles (eight kilometres) to go point. The aircraft speed was 150 knots with a rate of descent, or sink rate, of 6-700 ft (180-210 m) per minute.

'Well, gimme the gear,' called McCormick.

Whitney leaned forward and selected the landing gear lever to down.

'OK,' said McCormick, 'here we're coming into the ILS. I'm gonna start slowing her down. Give me twenty two on the flaps.'

The aircraft then intercepted the ILS glide path radio signal marking the descent profile at about ten miles (sixteen kilometres) from the threshold, and continued its approach to touchdown.

'All right, we got the green lights,' commented the captain, confirming the landing gear was down and locked.

'American 96,' radioed approach 'you're two and a half miles from the marker, contact tower on one two one point one. Good night.'

'Good night, sir.'

Whitney switched to the tower frequency as the DC-10 neared the marker beacon.

'American 96 is approaching the outer marker inbound.'

'American 96, roger,' replied the tower, 'continue your approach.'

The DC-10 was now only three minutes from touchdown and the atmosphere on the flight deck was very tense.

'American 96, the wind is one two zero at five, cleared to land.'

'American 96,' repeated the co-pilot, 'cleared to land.'

'Give me thirty five on the flaps,' called McCormick.

With full landing flaps set and the landing gear down the sink rate doubled to 1,500 ft (460 m) per minute, the captain had no choice but to increase power to maintain an acceptable descent of 800 ft (240 m) per minute. The speed rose to 165 knots, thirty-five knots faster than the required threshold speed for the aircraft's 130-ton weight. The touchdown would be fast, but if they didn't land too far down the runway the DC-10 should be able to stop in the 10,500 ft (3,200 m) length available. It was necessary to fly the entire approach with the nose yawed five to ten degrees to the right to keep in line with the runway, so what would happen when the wheels touched was anyone's guess. The captain tried to reduce speed a little by pulling back on the power but the sink rate rose dramatically. Whitney was calling out the rates of descent and was alarmed to see it momentarily increase to 1,800 ft (550 m) per minute. McCormick restored the power to regain the approach path and settled for the high landing speed.

'I have no rudder to straighten it out when it hits,' McCormick reminded the others.

The DC-10 crossed the runway threshold at 100 ft (thirty m) and the captain began to pull back slowly on the control column. The movement was so stiff he had to ask his co-pilot to give him a hand. McCormick squeezed on a little more power to lift the nose for a gentle touchdown. The aircraft was flying flat and fast and floated some way down the runway, but eventually the wheels contacted smoothly with the surface at 19:44, twenty-four minutes after take-off. The aircraft landed 1,900 ft (580 m) deep into the runway at a speed of 160 knots, with the nose pointing slightly to the right. McCormick was only just thinking to himself that it had been a good landing when 'all hell broke loose'.

Almost immediately Flight 96 ran towards the right side of the runway and for the first time since the incident the captain felt he had completely lost control. The DC-10 veered off the runway and ploughed through the grass. The spoilers on the wings deployed automatically to impair the lift and help the aircraft settle on the ground while the captain pulled on full reverse power on the wing engines. McCormick shouted at his co-pilot to take control of the thrust levers and the captain grasped the flying controls with both hands,

View from the left side of the fuselage showing the collapsed floor inside and the skin torn by the ejected door. (Captain Bryce McCormick)

holding the wheel left in an effort to keep the wings level. Whitney pulled the left wing engine throttle to maximum reverse power and cancelled the right wing engine reverse in an attempt to guide the machine. The asymmetric reverse power had the desired effect and countered the influence of the trailing right rudder. The swing to the right stopped and the DC-10 paralleled the right side of the runway.

The captain desperately tried to brake using the toe pedals on the rudder bar but with the bar askew to the extreme left it was very difficult to apply. The DC-10 raced on at speed between the runway and the parallel taxyway, digging up the turf in its path. Each time the aircraft met a cross taxyway McCormick tried to ease the strain on the nose wheel by pulling back on the control column, but the landing gear smashed into the hard surfaces with great force. The ground was extremely rough and with the bumpy ride the crew feared that the gear couldn't take much more punishment. If it collapsed now the flight could yet end in disaster.

Gradually the aircraft began to decelerate and the effect of the rudder displacement decreased. Under the influence of the asymmetric reverse thrust, aided by the full left deflection of the rudder bar which steered the nose wheel about ten degrees to the left, the DC-10 slowly eased to the left and back onto the paved surface. Eventually the aircraft came to a halt, severely shaken but still intact apart from the hole at the rear, about 1,700 ft (520 m) from the end of the runway. The left main landing gear and the nose wheel rested on the runway with the right gear still on the grass. McCormick, alarmed by the rough landing and fearful of ruptured fuel lines and the risk of fire, ordered an emergency evacuation. He activated the evacuation signal while the other flight crew carried out the appropriate drills. Quickly Whitney and Burke completed the check list.

'OK,' said the co-pilot, 'now the engines at your discretion.'

'SHUT 'EM DOWN!' called back the captain.

In the cabin the flight attendants rushed to their tasks and using the chutes at the forward six exits evacuated the aircraft in thirty seconds. The last of the travellers were off before the crew had finished their duties in the cockpit and the captain could see his passengers on the left looking up at

him from the far side of the runway. Around the aircraft the
fire trucks were standing by. At the last moment Chief Flight
Attendant Smith called into the flight deck.

'All passengers are off, captain. Goodbye. See you later.'

McCormick quickly left the cockpit and marched down the
aisle of the aircraft to check that all the passengers had
departed. As he passed the first door a fireman yelled at him
to jump but he called back saying he still had things to do.
When he reached door three left he stepped on to the wing
to check for fire but could see that the aircraft was safe. He
thought that number two engine would be damaged but
when he looked up he could see it was intact. Then he
noticed the aft left cargo hold door was missing and the
damage it had caused the tailplane. He stepped back into the
cabin and, joined by his co-pilot and flight engineer walking
down the opposite aisle, the three made their way to the rear
of the aircraft. Only now could the flight crew realise the full
extent of what had happened. They could see the amount of
damage the aircraft had suffered and now appreciated how
well they had done to effect a safe landing. McCormick's
totally professional approach to his job had won the day.
They had been lucky, too, of course, but the entire crew had
done a magnificent job. All passengers had escaped unhurt,
except for a few minor injuries sustained during the
evacuation.

With the immediate danger over the three flight crew took
their time in leaving, but when they returned to the cockpit
to collect their belongings they were unable to find their
hats. Unknown to them, one of the stewardesses had found
the hats lying on the cabin floor and had thrown them in
to a forward toilet. Eventually the hats were discovered
and, with uniforms complete, Captain McCormick and his
colleagues disembarked.

Captain McCormick and the crew received distinguished
service awards from American Airlines and the captain also
received a card for he and his wife to travel first class with
the airline with reserved seats. Only the president of the
company can displace them. McCormick's fellow pilots also
voted him president of the Grey Eagles, an organisation of
senior pilots.

# Chapter 5
# Don't be Fuelish

Weather, followed by fuel, are the two most important factors of any flight, the forecast of the former often deciding the quantity of the latter. In the 'good old days' it was simply a matter of filling the tanks, a procedure which became somewhat modified with the introduction of jets. Even then it was standard practice to carry more than requirements, adding extra for 'mum and the kids' and a 'bit for gran' as well. Fuel was plentiful and cheap and no-one thought much about it. The first oil crisis which began in the 1970s ended that attitude, with fuel prices trebling in three years. Costs to industry and the private individual soared. The United States was hit especially hard, the outcome of the crisis being smaller, more fuel-efficient cars and lower speed limits on the highways. An advertising campaign was introduced across America encouraging people to save fuel, with billboard signs saying, 'Don't be fuelish', being pasted throughout the nation.

Governments of the world encouraged their public to be fuel-conscious and industry searched for any means of saving fuel. Airlines found their fuel bills soared to thirty per cent of operating costs and companies were forced to examine their fuel policies closely. The world's airlines had no alternative source of energy to which they could turn and the only option open to them was to carry less fuel. The minimum legal fuel load requirements for a journey are: sufficient fuel for the flight from A to B, extra fuel for a diversion to C (in case of problems such as bad weather at B), some reserve fuel to cover contingencies, and a little for taxying. A typical London-New York flight for a Boeing 747 would require: eighty tons of fuel for the journey from Heathrow to Kennedy, thirteen tons in case of diversion, say to Boston, four tons of reserve fuel for contingencies, and one ton for taxying. The total fuel requirement would be ninety-eight tons but a flight would normally use only eighty-one tons — trip plus taxying fuel — and would land with seventeen tons still in the tanks.

Any fuel carried over and above the minimum fuel load is referred to as excess fuel. The B747 is a very long-range aircraft and the maximum fuel load which can be carried in the tanks is about 140 tons; a weight equal to a fully laden Boeing 707. The equivalent volume is 39,000 gallons (177,290 litres). On a typical transatlantic journey, therefore, the average flight has forty-two tons spare fuel capacity. The greater the aircraft weight, however, the higher the fuel consumption and the problem for airline accountants is that any excess fuel carried above the minimum requirements has a significant portion (i.e. three per cent per hour) of that quantity used up just to carry the excess. If ten tons of excess fuel are carried on a ten-hour flight, for example, then three tons of that fuel will actually be used carrying itself. Only seven tens will be available for use over the destination. In fact, it has been calculated that to carry regularly the weight

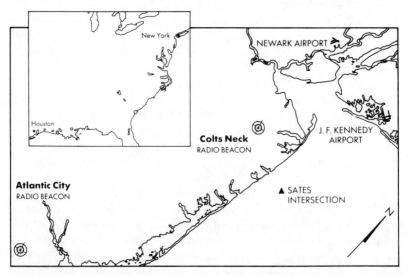

Map showing JF Kennedy airport, the Atlantic City and Colts Neck radio beacons, and the Sates intersection.

of just one small sachet of sugar increases fuel consumption by one gallon per year.

The problem for airline captains, on the other hand, is that one of the most useless things in aviation is fuel left in the refuelling bowser. Fuel on the ground may be expensive, but fuel in the air is priceless. Although, once airborne, aircraft are able to dump fuel if required — on a 747 at the rate of two tons a minute from nozzles in the wingtips — mid-air refuelling of civilian aircraft is not possible and it is essential that sufficient fuel is carried. Captains may be under pressure to carry the lowest amount of fuel commensurate with safety and the law but, with unpredictable bad weather in certain areas and frequent unexpected delays due to traffic increases in others, the dividing line between carrying sufficient fuel and running out in flight can be very thin indeed. Not surprisingly, crews still tend to err on the side of safety and, of course, if poor weather or landing delays are likely the captain has no choice but to carry excess fuel. On occasions, however, even the most conscientious of commanders can be caught out.

On 20 October 1979, a Pan Am 747 approached New York's John F. Kennedy Airport with the weather reported as poor. Low cloud and bad visibility were causing landing difficulties. The flight had departed about three hours earlier from Houston Intercontinental Airport, Texas, for the 1,200 nm journey, and now faced landing delays at its destination because of worsening conditions. The 747 had pushed back from the gate at Houston with 42.3 tons of fuel in the tanks but owing to congestion at the airport had used 1.9 tons of fuel in taxying. The flight had eventually taken-off at the weight of 225.7 tons, with 40.4 tons of fuel remaining: 28.9 tons for the trip, 8.8 tons in case of diversion and 2.7 tons in reserve. The 747 had passed over the VOR radio beacon at Gordonsville, Virginia, cruising at 37,000 ft (11,280 m) and had been cleared to proceed direct to Waterloo VOR, situated in Delaware on Delaware Bay, 128 nm south-west of Kennedy. The captain was now further cleared to descend to 21,000 ft (6,400 m) and was instructed to join the stack at Waterloo with turns to the left. Because of the poor visibility causing landing delays at New York he would have to hold at that point before proceeding. The stacks or holds are flown in a precise racetrack pattern, normally over a radio beacon, with aircraft being stacked one above the other at 1,000 ft (300 m) intervals. Normally the holding procedures are conducted near airports at lower levels, so the instruction to Pan Am to hold at such a height so far out clearly indicated the backlog of flights. It looked as though it was going to be a long delay.

The captain spoke to the passengers on the public address system and told them the bad news. He had enough fuel to hold for about forty-five minutes before commencing an approach to New York, so there was no undue worry. In the meantime they would just have to go round and round until their turn came. On the descent to 21,000 ft, the crew established contact with Pan Am ground personnel on the company radio frequency and a series of messages passed between the two in an attempt to establish a landing time. It was also agreed that if Kennedy closed they would proceed to Newark, New Jersey, where the weather was known to be better. The 747 joined the holding pattern over the Waterloo beacon, still descending, and after one or two left circuits the Captain was instructed to change to right-hand turns. The Pan Am aircraft changed its turns to the right and levelled at 21,000 ft.

While established in the hold awaiting onward clearance, the crew began to work out the exact fuel required for a diversion to Newark. There was every intention of landing at New York, of course, but it was as well to be prepared. At the beginning of the hold the tanks still contained fifteen tons of fuel and using a 'flight conduct summary' table for fuel management, a diversion fuel figure of 6.5 tons was computed. The calculations were based on an estimated landing weight at Newark of 195 tons, and using a stated distance of 25 nm between the two airports. This distance, however, was as the crow flies and, since aircraft don't normally fly in straight lines, the use of the summary tables resulted in a somewhat pared diversion fuel figure. It would be unusual, of course, for a flight to be right down to this fuel figure before commencing a diversion, so there would normally be something in hand.

After holding for fourteen minutes, the Pan Am aircraft was cleared to Sates intersection, thirty nm south of New York, via a 'Kennedy Two' arrival route, which proceeded over the radio beacon at Atlantic City. There would be a further delay at Sates after which the flight would be radar vectored to runway 22L for landing. At Sates the 747 joined the other holding aircraft. As flights were cleared from the bottom of the stack to commence their approach, Pan Am was instructed to descend lower in 1,000 ft steps. Eventually, after thirty-three minutes of holding at Sates, the 747 departed the stack on a radar heading, level at 7,000 ft (2,130 m). 8.2 tons of fuel remained in the tanks and, with aircraft ahead landing safely, the captain was satisfied with their progress. The crew kept a close ear on the weather information which indicated the visibility along the runway, or runway visual range (RVR), to be varying from 550-850 m (1,800-2,790 ft) at the landing end, to as low as 200 m (650 ft) at the rollout end. With both autopilots engaged the 747 could land automatically with an RVR as low as 400 m (1,300 ft), so there was some room to spare.

In case a go-around was required with the low fuel state, however, the flight engineer suggested preparing the aircraft for the 'minimum fuel go-around' procedures. There was a danger, if a missed approach procedure was initiated, of the fuel pumps being uncovered in the tanks by the low fuel levels. An engine could be starved of fuel and could run down. All boost pump switches were turned on and all cross feed valves were opened. It was also recommended on the go-around not to accelerate rapidly and to reduce the nose-up angle to eight degrees.

The Pan Am flight was instructed to call Approach Control, and the first officer established contact.

'Descend to 3,000 feet and reduce to 180 knots,' radioed Kennedy Approach.

The captain commenced descent and called for 5° flap to be set as he slowed the aircraft. Shortly they would be turned on to the final approach course, but before the controller could issue a heading the weather took a sudden sharp turn for the worse. The landing runway visual range dropped to 600 m (1,970 ft) and then to 300 m (985 ft). The visibility was now below the aircraft's landing limit and there was no way they could land. Nor could anyone else, for that matter, and they could hear on the radio the aircraft ahead requesting a diversion to Newark.

'Remain in line,' called back Approach, 'and continue to fly the runway course for traffic sequencing.'

Kennedy Approach then advised all aircraft that flights on the approach to land would have to be vectored along the 22L runway centre line for spacing before proceeding. The Pan Am 747 flew down the runway direction at 3,000 ft (910 m) and, with the weather still below limits, the first officer informed the controller that they would also like to go to Newark. Only 6.7 tons of fuel remained according to the total fuel weight indicator, or fuel totaliser gauge, with a calculated minimum fuel figure requirement of 6.5 tons. It was going to be close.

'Turn on to a heading of 240°,' called back Approach, 'vectors for Colts Neck, and contact Departure.'

Colts Neck VOR radio beacon lay to the south west, about twenty-five miles (forty kilometres) in front of them, and was situated at about the same distance to the south of Newark. They appeared to be going the long way round. The first officer changed frequencies and called the next controller.

'Proceed direct to Colts Neck,' replied Departure Control, 'maintain 3,000 feet and increase to 250 knots. Leave Colts Neck heading 335° for radar vectors to runway 22L at Newark.'

Over the Colts Neck radio beacon the captain turned the aircraft to the right on to the assigned heading, but as he did so he was instructed to roll out on 320°. The aircraft proceeded on the north-westerly heading maintaining 3,000 feet and 250 knots. The 747 still had to route all the way round to the north of the airport before turning back onto a south-westerly direction for landing. The total distance covered would be nearer eighty-five nm than twenty-five nm. Passing several miles to the west of Newark the flight engineer scanned the indicators once more. The totaliser gauge now showed 2.7 tons of fuel remaining, about fifteen to twenty minutes' flying time to dry tanks, which would be just enough to get there with a fraction to spare. The fuel quantity gauges confirmed the amount remaining in the tanks but the fuel left seemed uncomfortably low. Again he checked the calculations. The figures tallied but the amount, even if they had gone on a direct route, hardly seemed enough. What the flight engineer did not know at the time, nor the captain or anyone else for that matter, was that the 'flight conduct memory' table on board the 747 which had been used for the fuel management computations, was in error. The correct calculated fuel figure for diversion was 7.9 tons, 1.4 tons more than assumed. The Pan Am aircraft was seriously short of fuel.

Suddenly, to the flight engineer's horror, he saw the low pressure lights of the forward and aft boost pumps illuminate for number one tank. The fuel was so low the pumps were being starved of supply. The number one tank fuel gauge indicated 800 lb (360 kg), just over one third of a ton, but not much more fuel could be pumped from the bottom. The other tanks held only a little more, and he surmised that their pumps would also run dry when the fuel dropped to that level. By a quick reckoning he estimated that only 1.3 tons of the 2.7 tons indicated remaining was usable. The other 1.4 tons couldn't be taken into account because it had to be assumed it wasn't there. The pilots, already under pressure to land quickly, were shocked by the news. There was little more than five minutes' flying time remaining and a potential disaster was only moments away. The captain thought of turning quickly to the right and landing in an easterly direction on runway 11, but there were no instrument approach charts available for that runway and the aircraft was still in cloud. By now the first officer was in contact with Newark Approach and he requested their time to touchdown.

'Five minutes,' replied the controller.

There was barely enough time and the captain declared an emergency. The strain on the crew was now enormous and they were under tremendous pressure. Newark Approach radar vectored the 747 directly on to the 22L runway course and within minutes they were established on the instrument landing system. Just before the outer marker the aircraft broke cloud and the runway could be seen ahead. About two minutes remained to touchdown. Newark Tower was contacted and the controller requested the nature of the emergency.

'Fuel,' replied the co-pilot briefly, his heart in his mouth.

The captain maintained the flap set at 20° and waited till he was certain of getting in before selecting the full 30° landing flap setting. After passing the outer marker the landing gear was lowered but the captain flew the aircraft high on the approach path and kept the speed about thirty knots fast. If the engines suddenly stopped through fuel starvation he hoped to be able to glide to a landing.

'What fuel do you have remaining?' asked the Tower controller. With virtually nothing left there wasn't much that could be said.

'The gauges are unreliable so we don't know,' replied the first officer. 'One tank is feeding all engines.'

Approaching 200 ft (sixty m) the flight engineer informed the captain that all the fuel low pressure lights on all the boost pumps were illuminated. The 747 was moments from running out of fuel. Passing 200 ft the captain felt that a landing was certain and he called for the selection of full flap. The engines were now running on thin air. If they cut out at this moment he felt he could reach the threshold, but it would be a close run event. The three cockpit crew held their breaths in the tense atmosphere. Fifteen seconds later the wheels gently touched the runway surface and a mightily relieved crew felt the aircraft settle on terra firma. All four thrust levers were pulled into reverse and the engines responded with a roar, but it was a noise that did not last long. The aircraft slowed and the captain cancelled reverse thrust, but as he did so engine numbers one and four ran down from fuel starvation. The 747 taxied from the runway and proceeded along a parallel taxiway where, after about a mile, number two engine also ran down from lack of fuel. The captain shut down number three engine and waited for a tow truck to pull them to the terminal. In the meantime, the flight engineer checked his fuel panel and noted that the fuel totaliser indicated 1.4 tons remaining. According to the fuel quantity gauges about 1.5 tons of fuel remained in the tanks so the figures cross-checked. The four main fuel tank gauges read, from left to right: 800 lb (360 kg), 400 lb (180 kg), 1,100 lb (500 kg) and 1,100 lb again. The small amount of fuel which was indicated remaining should have been usable but was obviously not available. This discrepancy in the gauges and the error in the fuel management chart had placed the 747 great jeopardy. If the engines had stopped only a few minutes earlier while the aircraft was still in cloud the 747 would have landed short of the runway and a disaster would have been inevitable. By good fortune and a quick thinking crew a catastrophe was only narrowly averted.

The instances of airliners running out of fuel in flight are extremely rare, which is just as well, for a big jet trying to land without engine power, especially with flaps and landing gear set, has the flying properties of something close to a brick. The light aircraft pilot may be used to practising forced landings from height, usually simulating an engine failure, but such a prospect for the airline pilot is a different matter. If the incident occurs at night or in cloud the chances of success are about nil.

A big jet can, in fact, glide reasonably well and, indeed, when descent is initiated from cruise level the thrust levers are closed to flight idle and the aircraft literally becomes a giant glider. The descent rate is normally about 2,500 ft (760 m) per minute for a 747, so the rate of descent without idling engine power would be something greater. If all engines suddenly failed on a 747 at cruise height, therefore, the flight could probably remain airborne in the glide for about twenty minutes or so — as seen in Chapter 9.

At the lower levels, however, it would be necessary to select the landing gear down for an emergency powerless landing and that would be another story. The big jet would drop like a stone. A touchdown without power is referred to as a deadstick landing and such a procedure on a big jet aircraft can be considered extremely hazardous. Great skill would be required to judge height and rate of descent and to execute a safe deadstick landing. There would only be one chance and more than a little luck would be needed as well. It would be hard to find quickly somewhere suitable to land for, unlike the light aircraft pilot, a grass field would not suffice. If a big jet suddenly lost all power in flight, attempting a forced landing and accomplishing the task safely would be very difficult indeed. Not, perhaps, entirely impossible.

On a warm afternoon of 23 July 1983, Captain Robert Pearson and his co-pilot, Maurice Quintal, boarded Air Canada's Boeing 767 wide-body jet in Montreal, Quebec. The aircraft, registered C-GUAN, had only just arrived from Edmonton and Ottawa and, with a fresh crew, was about to turn round and fly the same journey back.

The Boeing 767 is an ultra-modern, two-crew, twin-engined machine with advanced electronics, and the aircraft was brand new to Air Canada. The flight deck has an uncluttered appearance with most details being presented on cathode ray tube type displays. The 767 is a pleasure to fly and is liked by pilots. On arrival in the cockpit on the afternoon of 23 July, however, Captain Pearson found they had a problem. The fuel indicating system on C-GUAN was faulty and there was no display of fuel load on the flight deck. The 767 fuel gauges are situated in the middle of the pilot's overhead panel and display fuel quantities in the two main wing tanks and the central auxiliary tank, as well as total fuel load. The minimum equipment list carried on board each aircraft stated that departure with this defect was not permitted. Only one main wing tank fuel gauge was allowed to be inoperative, and then the refueller had to dip the tank with a stick to confirm the level. The procedure, of course, was designed to safeguard against insufficient fuel being loaded.

In spite of the total fuel gauge failure, however, the 767 had received special dispensation to operate in that condition from Maintenance Control. Aircraft are often dispatched with systems unserviceable which are considered more of an inconvenience than a safety factor, but the minimum equipment list was designed to prevent departure in an unsafe condition. There are occasions, however, when dispensations are granted as long as proper precautions are taken.

The problem with the fuel quantity indicating system on

Air Canada's 767, *C-GUAN*, had begun at the start of the month when a fault on the equipment was found to be intermittent. In fact, inconsistencies had been discovered months earlier on 767s operated by other airlines and Boeing had issued instructions for the systems to be checked regularly. A United Airlines 767 on a delivery flight had shown that discrepancies could exist between the quantity of fuel displayed on the gauges and the actual amount in the tanks. A situation could arise where the pilots thought they had more fuel than was actually available.

On 5 July, in Edmonton, an Air Canada certified aircraft technician, Conrad Yaremko, conducted a routine check on *C-GUAN*'s fuel gauge system. The aircraft had arrived from Toronto with a fuel processor channel unserviceable and he found that during the check all fuel quantity gauges went blank. Two fuel quantity processors channels on the aircraft compute fuel quantities which are then displayed on the gauges. Each processor computer channel sums the quantities independently and the two systems then cross-check each other. If one fails the other can operate on its own.

Yaremko discovered, however, that there was a fault in the number two processor channel and that this was

An Air Canada Boeing 767. (Air Canada)

affecting the entire system and causing all fuel indicators to go blank. He found that if he isolated the number two processor channel computer by pulling its electrical circuit breaker he could get the system to work. All indicators would display as normal, but since there was only one processor channel operating there would be no computer cross-check of the calculated amount. It was necessary, therefore, as in the case of a main wing tank gauge failure, for a mechanic to dipstick the tanks to confirm the displayed quantity. The aircraft duly returned to Toronto and the number two processor channel was checked. Surprisingly, it was shown to be within tolerance. The circuit breaker was reset and the processor appeared to be working normally.

On 14 July, en route from Toronto to San Francisco, the number two fuel processor channel computer failed again and all fuel gauges went blank. In San Francisco the equipment in the electronics bay was re-racked and the system operated normally. On 22 July, again in Edmonton, in the evening before the day in question, *C-GUAN* arrived on another flight from Toronto. The system was operating normally but, during the routine check, the fuel gauges blanked once more. Yaremko checked the equipment and found the same number two processor channel failed again. He was unable to clear the fault but no spare fuel processor unit was available. He ordered one from the stores to be available the following evening when the flight returned once more to Edmonton. Having encountered the trouble before he simply isolated the number two processor channel and the fuel indications returned. In this condition the flight could depart in the morning.

Early the next day, 23 July, the 767 was satisfactorily dispatched but, before the flight left, Yaremko spoke to the departing commander, Captain John Weir. The two men agreed that the condition satisfied the minimum equipment list but that a fuel tank dipstick check would also be required. During the conversation Yaremko mentioned that on 5 July the aircraft had arrived from Toronto with the same problem and he had cleared the fault in a similar manner. In a misunderstanding, however, Weir thought he referred to the previous evening when the same aircraft had also arrived from Toronto, and the captain was left with the impression that the fault had been running from the day before.

The 767 left Edmonton on time and the flight operated via Ottawa to Montreal, arriving in the afternoon. On going off duty in Montreal, Captain Weir met Captain Pearson and First Officer Quintal on their way to work and passed on the news of the problem. He mentioned that it would be necessary to dip the tanks and added, incorrectly, that the fault had been like that from the previous afternoon. He suggested that they fuelled in Montreal for both return sectors because by doing so they would save themselves some bother during the transit in Ottawa. The conversation touched on previous problems with the fuel indicating system in general and Captain Pearson, in a further misunderstanding, mistakenly believed that the fuel indicating equipment was completely unserviceable. What's more he believed he was being told that it had been like that for the last day and a half.

When Captain Pearson and his co-pilot entered C-GUAN's flight deck, they saw before them what they expected to see; the fuel quantity indicators were blank. But the flight had arrived with the system working and only the number two fuel processor channel computer unserviceable. This was the failure that Captain Weir had been referring to in his brief conversation with Pearson and that, of course, was why the tanks had to be dipped. In Edmonton the previous evening, Yaremko had tripped the number two processor channel electrical circuit breaker and after doing so had attached to it the relevant inoperative label. Why had the fuel indicators now gone blank? Unknown to Captain Pearson, an unfortunate sequence of events was beginning to unfold.

Before the new crew arrived at the 767, a Mr Ouellet had been sent to the aircraft by his foreman to dipstick the tanks after fuelling was completed. While waiting to perform his task he sat on the flight deck and noticed the inoperative label on the number two fuel processor channel circuit breaker. Although Ouellet was not qualified to check the system he thought he might be able to help and he reset the breaker. Immediately the fuel indicators went blank. On checking the equipment he found it deficient but, like

Yaremko, he was unable to obtain a spare. He was told that one was being positioned to Edmonton for the flight's return. At about this time he was called to dipstick the tanks, and, unfortunately he forgot to re-trip the number two fuel processor channel circuit breaker. The breaker remained pushed in and its position was masked by the inoperative tag which was still attached. To the eye it appeared that the breaker was tripped and all the screens remained blank.

Captain Pearson checked the minimum equipment list (MEL) which confirmed that he was not permitted to depart with the fuel indicating system inoperative. At that time, however, the MEL on the newly introduced 767 was incomplete with many items blank and alterations taking place to it constantly. In the few months since the 767's introduction, over fifty changes had been made. The list was not considered reliable and it was Maintenance Control's practice then to authorise flights contrary to the MEL.

Captain Bob Pearson.

Pearson checked the paper work and the fuel flight plan simply stated: FUEL QTY PROC # 2 INOP. DIP REQD. The maintenance log was also inspected and two entries were apparent. One by Yaremko in Edmonton read: SERVICE CHK — FOUND FUEL QTY IND BLANK — FUEL QTY # 2 C/B PULLED & TAGGED — FUEL DIP REQD PRIOR TO DEP. SEE MEL. Yaremko, of course, referred to the indicators going blank during the check but that was not clear from the text. The other entry by Ouellet stated: FUEL QTY IND U/S. SUSPECT PROCESSOR UNIT AT FAULT. NIL STOCK. The maintenance log had then been signed out as satisfactory.

The captain also discussed the situation with the mechanics in Montreal and he was informed by them that a special dispensation had been received to operate in this manner. The case was supported by the chat with Captain Weir, the blank fuel gauges, the maintenance log and the belief that the machine had flown in this fashion from the day before. If others had flown it this way then he would have to do so as well and Captain Pearson accepted the aircraft. A fuel processor was to be ready in Edmonton for the flight's return and that provided the justification for the dispensation. The idea that the blank fuel indicating system was acceptable, however, was *not* correct and the aircraft, in spite of Maintenance Control's approval, was not permitted to depart in that condition.

Captain Pearson and F/O Quintal both believed they would be operating in accordance with the applicable rules and regulations or they would not have considered proceeding with the flight. By an unfortunate sequence of events the captain had been deceived into accepting an aircraft which was unsatisfactory. There was still the fuel dip check to be performed and that would cross-check the fuel quantity on board against the volume pumped into the tanks from the bowser plus the load remaining on arrival. If the calculations were performed carefully, what could possibly go wrong? What, indeed!

Captain Pearson made the decision to carry sufficient fuel out of Montreal for the two sector flight via Ottawa to Edmonton. The required fuel load amounted to 22.3 tons, or more correctly 22.3 tonnes — one tonne being equivalent to one metric ton or 1,000 kilogrammes — for the calculations were being conducted in kilogrammes. The system of units used in aviation throughout the world is not standardised and the present situation can only be described as messy.

The International Civil Aviation Organisation (ICAO) units are mostly metric, exceptions being distance which is stated in nautical miles and speed which is given in knots. Very few nations comply completely with the ICAO basic standard and most signatories abide by what is known as the Blue Table, with height, for example, being measured in feet. The Republic of China and the Soviet Union use metric units throughout with height expressed in metres and speed in kilometres per hour. Wind speeds are given in metres per second. Flying in a metric country with aircraft which comply with the Blue Table is not easy.

The USA uses its own modified 'Imperial' system where many of the same problems apply. Almost all foreign aircraft have to convert just about everything for calculations: degrees Fahrenheit to degrees Celsius, pounds to kilogrammes, inches of mercury to millibars and US gallons to litres. The modern world trend, however, is towards metrication in spite of America steadfastly adhering to its own version of 'avoir dupois'. The names of units are also moving to a standardised form and are now being referred to mostly by the names of people prominent in their particular field: centigrade has become Celsius, after its Swedish inventor, a cycle per second has become Hertz, after the famous German physicist; and more recently, a millibar has become a hectoPascal, after the French scientist Blaise Pascal.

In the 1970s, nations as far apart as the UK and Australia began the painful task of converting to the metric system, and in the early 1980s Canada also commenced the transition. For most countries the changeover was smooth and gradual, if not always without problems. The aviation industry welcomes any move towards a standard, if not least because the profusion of units within its own ranks was, and is, still confusing. Fuel, for example, is pumped aboard an aircraft by unit volume, and at a busy international airport like London's Heathrow, airlines ask for their fuel in litres, US gallons or Imperial gallons. The fuel quantity is then converted to pounds or kilogrammes for trim purposes and if a dipstick check is required the tank depth is measured in centimetres or inches. The general attitude is that it is a wonder that more mistakes are not made.

Air Canada's aircraft had been refuelled for some time using litres which, in a mixture of units, were than converted into pounds. In line with the nation's transition to metric, however, the airline was in the process of changing, and the 767 fleet was the first Air Canada type to have its gauges calibrated in kilogrammes. On Captain Pearson's 767, *C-GUAN*, the refuellers discussing the fuel load with him were aware the amount he required was a kilogramme measurement, but when the maintenance personnel calculated the quantity in litres to be pumped aboard they used the incorrect conversion factor. The conversion employed was for changing litres into pounds (1.77 instead of 0.8 for kilogrammes), and only sufficient fuel was loaded to give a combined litre volume in the tanks equivalent to 22,300 lb (10,115 kg). The tank quantities were checked using a dipstick which measured the depth of fuel in centimetres which the ground personnel, using a table for conversion, then changed into litres. This volume compared with that

Flight 143's routeing and the position of Gimli airfield.

loaded by the refueller, plus the amount in the tanks on arrival. When the captain conducted a cross-check, however, he was also given the incorrect conversion factor, and when he checked the calculations he confirmed the mathematics were correct. The refueller had also used the same figure before converting to litres and both were in agreement. Having both used the wrong factor, however, the volume of litres in the tanks was only equivalent to 22,300 lb instead of 22,300 kilogrammes. One pound is less than half a kilogramme so the fuel load on board was less than half required. With no fuel quantity indicators on the flight deck, the crew had no warning of the situation.

Before departure, the flight management computer (FMC) was loaded with the fuel quantity. A page in the Boeing operating manual at the time gave instructions which showed how fuel quantity from dipsticking the tanks could be entered in the computer. After engine start, fuel consumption would be recorded, permitting a total fuel readout to be constantly displayed throughout the flight, and *en route* fuel checks could be conducted normally. The FMC, however, was calibrated in kilogrammes and when the fuel load of 22,300 was entered, it was accepted by the computer as kilogrammes.

A radio call was received from the maintenance section before push back clearing the flight for the trip.

Captain Pearson took off from Montreal on the afternoon of Saturday 23 July operating Flight 143's first short hop to Ottawa. The aircraft arrived safely at the transit station and the turn-round was conducted expeditiously. No extra fuel was added but, as a precaution, the fuel tanks were dipped again to check the quantity before departure and to update the FMC. By an amazing stroke of misfortune, the same incorrect conversion factor was used by the ground personnel and the error was not discovered. Maintenance staff there also approved dispatch of the aircraft in the unsatisfactory condition. Flight 143 departed from Ottawa in the evening for the longer westbound sector to Edmonton. Only sixty-one passengers were on board, being looked after by six flight attendants led by Robert Desjardins, which gave a total, including the two cockpit crew, of sixty-nine. The lightly-laden 767 climbed rapidly to 41,000 ft (12,500 m) and the aircraft quickly settled in the cruise. It was a fine evening, the visibility was good, and the pleasant circumstances offered a feeling of well-being to the passengers and crew. In the tanks, however, was less than half the fuel needed for the journey and Flight 143 had no chance of reaching its destination.

The first sector had been flown by Captain Pearson and now F/O Quintal handled the aircraft on the way to Edmonton. As Flight 143 approached the border of Ontario with Manitoba, the 767 was about halfway on its journey. At 20:00 Central Daylight Time (CDT), Quintal spoke to the passengers.

'Good evening ladies and gentlemen, this is your first officer. We're presently coming up over Red Lake and are cruising at 41,000 feet. In Edmonton it's a beautiful day.'

Below, the countryside stretched before the cockpit and Red Lake could be clearly seen.

'I'm going to sit here and watch the trout swimming in the lake,' joked Pearson.

Ten minutes later, as the 767 crossed the border into Manitoba, the jesting stopped. If the fuel monitoring system had been operating properly, the first sign of trouble would have been a visual and aural low fuel state warning as the fuel quantity dropped below two tons. This would have been just sufficient fuel for an immediate descent and landing. With the equipment unserviceable, however, the first indication of a problem was when the instruments indicated a low fuel pressure in the left forward pump. Beep, beep, beep, sounded the warning.

'Holy . . .!' shouted Captain Pearson.

The first officer checked out the systems.

'Something's wrong with the fuel pump.'

'Left-forward fuel pump', confirmed Pearson. 'OK, what have we got here? I hope it's just the . . . pump failing, I'll tell you that.'

Moments later a second warning light illuminated indicating low fuel pressure in another pump. The captain's first reaction was that he had a computer problem but it would be safer to have it checked before going any further. It was too

much of a coincidence that two fuel pumps should fail on a
brand new aircraft, so Pearson decided to divert.

'Let's go to Winnipeg.'

Winnipeg was the nearest major airport and lay 120 nm
away to the south-west. Clearance was received for the
aircraft to proceed direct and to commence descent. Captain
Pearson resumed control, closed the thrust levers and began
the descent from 41,000 ft towards Winnipeg. Seconds later,
warning lights indicating loss of fuel pressure in both right-
hand pumps also illuminated. At that point the crew realised
that so many pumps failing simultaneously on a brand new
aircraft was highly unlikely and that they must have a fuel
problem. The chief flight attendant, Desjardins, was called
to the flight deck and told to prepare the passengers for an
emergency landing. A few minutes later the number one
engine was starved of fuel and ran down.

'We've just lost an engine,' radioed Quintal to Winnipeg
Control. 'Request the fire trucks standing by for our arrival.'

Three minutes later the number two engine ran out of fuel
and flamed out. The aircraft was now totally without engine
power and with no fuel left in the tanks it was not possible to
restart the engines. The 767 could only glide to a landing. At
the moment of total engine failure the 767 was descending
through 25,000 ft (7,620m) and was sixty-five nm from
Winnipeg. A small air turbine dropped from the belly of the
aircraft to supply power to operate the flying controls while
emergency instruments in the cockpit were fed from the
batteries. The cathode ray tube screens went blank and all
that was left was a standby magnetic compass, an artificial
horizon, an airspeed indicator and an altimeter. The captain
expected to see the compass display of the radio magnetic
indicator still functioning, but it did not work. Although it
was mid-evening it was still bright daylight outside and the
visibility was excellent. In the cockpit, however, 'it became
the blackest place in the world,' Captain Pearson was to
comment later. A Mayday call was transmitted.

'Centre, 143, this is a Mayday, and we require a vector on
to the closest available runway. We are 22,000 feet on . . .
with both engines failed due to, looks like fuel starvation,

and we are on emergency instruments . . . now please give us a vector to the nearest runway.'

In the cabin the attendants secured galley equipment and briefed the passengers on the emergency landing and evacuation procedures. The cabin occupants were informed only that the aircraft had fuel trouble, but with both engines stopped it was obvious there was a major problem. It was very quiet. Two points were in the passengers' favour, however: Captain Pearson was a very experienced glider pilot and F/O Quintal knew the area well. He had been stationed near Winnipeg while serving in the Canadian Air Force. Their knowledge and skills would be greatly needed this day. The captain slowed the aircraft to about 220 knots which he guessed would be the best speed for a long glide. Steering the aircraft according to the controller's instructions proved to be another matter. The standby compass was situated in the centre of the flight deck at the top of the glare shield and was difficult to read. It was swinging wildly and became impossible to use for flying headings.

'So I steered by the clouds underneath us,' explained the captain after the event. 'I would ask Winnipeg Centre for a heading, they would say "left twenty degrees" and I would turn left about that much, judging by the clouds, and then I'd ask Winnipeg how my heading was. Using the clouds, I kept eyeballing it.'

Judging the rate of descent and planning a descent profile proved to be the most difficult task of all. No vertical speed indicator was functioning. In an attempt to calculate a descent path, F/O Quintal repeatedly asked the controller for distances to go to Winnipeg and compared those with the altitudes indicated. At the same time he also had to complete the emergency check lists, so he was kept very busy. As the 767 descended through 14,500 ft (4,420 m) its distance to Winnipeg was forty-five nm and the aircraft was dropping much faster than either of the pilots expected. By 9,500 ft (2,900 m) the Winnipeg radar controller informed them that they still had thirty-five nm to go. Flight 143 had dropped 5,000 ft (1,520 m) in ten miles and at the most they could only glide for about another twenty nm.

'We'll never make it,' said Quintal.

A hasty replanning of the situation was required.

'What about Gimli?' suggested the co-pilot.

Gimli Air Force base was about forty nm north of Winnipeg, situated on the west coast of Lake Winnipeg, and Quintal had spent some time there during his military service. The 767 was only just near the south of the lake and they could see its waters on the right hand side. Gimli couldn't be far away but some cloud obscured the view.

'Gimli's about twelve miles away from your position,' reported the radar controller.

F/O Quintal informed his captain that the base had two parallel runways and both were long enough to use. Pearson made an immediate decision to aim for Gimli, which at that time was in their four o'clock position, and they were instructed by radar to turn right 120 degrees. Descending below the cloud, with the sun about ten degrees above the western horizon, they proceeded almost northbound under radar assistance for several miles. Suddenly Quintal spotted Gimli Airfield. The time was 20:32 CDT and in the cabin all preparations were complete. Now it was up to the captain. He had only one chance at a landing. He would also be unable to select flap without power so the landing would be fast, but before touchdown they would have to lower the landing gear. It could be dropped by the force of gravity but since it would increase their rate of descent enormously it would have to be left to the last moment. Captain Pearson then asked the controller for more details of Gimli. The Air Force base was disbanded, he was told, but the right runway was still used by light aircraft and was 6,800 ft (2,070 m) long. It would be best to go for that one.

'There will be nobody on the runway when we get there, eh . . . nothing?' questioned Pearson.

'I don't know,' replied the controller, 'I can't tell you for sure.'

Quintal could see the runway clearly ahead now and he called out to his captain.

'We're going to make Gimli OK,' radioed Pearson to Winnipeg.

'Great! We show you about six miles to touchdown.'

The only problem now was that the 767 was too high

and fast. Pearson could make a quick orbit but if he did so he would lose sight of the runway and he might lose too much height. There was only one thing to do and that was to side-slip. The technique is used effectively by light aircraft pilots to lose height quickly but it is not recommended on a big jet. The captain pushed on right rudder and at the same time banked the wings in the opposite direction to the left. The crossed controls had the desired effect, and as the aircraft crabbed sideways through the air the drag plummetted the machine earthwards. In the cabin, the passengers felt the 767 plunge close to the ground and most people assumed the captain had lost control. On the contrary, however, the speed and height were both dropping rapidly and their situation was improving.

'Five miles to touchdown,' called the controller.

'Roger,' acknowledged Quintal, 'we have the field in sight.'

With the speed back to 180 knots and sufficient height lost, the captain straightened the aircraft on the final approach. He was satisfied now that he could commit himself to a landing and he called for the landing gear to be lowered. Quintal selected the landing gear lever down but nothing happened. His heart sank. Quickly he checked the handbook but he could find no reference to free-falling the wheels. The secondary procedure for landing gear extension was, in fact, located at the back of the section on hydraulics, but by an oversight the detail had been omitted from the index. He was unable to find the relevant information so, of his own volition, he selected the alternate gear extension switch to the down position. At last he heard the gear fall down into place but when he checked the indicators he was shocked to see the nose wheel had not locked down. Frantically he searched the pages of the handbook once more in a desperate attempt to find the required drill, but before doing so the time ran out.

The captain had judged the descent beautifully and he crossed the threshold at 180 knots, about fifty knots faster than normal, at just the right height. It was then that the mistake was noticed. The right runway which had been recommended for landing was darker in texture than the other and had remained unseen as it blended with the countryside. The runway on which the 767 was about to land was the lighter, left runway. Its colour had been easier to pick out from the air but, although it was longer at 7,200 ft (2,195 m), it was disused. The problem with landing on the left side was that the abandoned runway was employed over weekends as a racing car circuit and the last race of that Saturday evening had only just finished.

Captain Pearson touched down perfectly within 800 ft (245 m) of the threshold at about 175 knots but as he did so the two pilots saw to their horror that people and vehicles milled about at the far end of the runway. Children were playing and cycling in the area. Beyond the activity there were tents and caravans in which the racing drivers and their families were staying for the weekend. The 767 sped towards the gathering with no reverse power or ground spoilers available to help slow the machine. In one camper vehicle parked near the runway a racer's wife, Jo Ann Barry, was washing dishes after their evening meal. Suddenly she heard a boy shout that a jet was landing.

'I opened the camper door and there was this huge plane coming at us.'

Pearson hit the brakes hard and the aircraft reduced speed, but as it did so the unlocked nose wheel collapsed. The nose dropped to the ground and the nose wheel was forced back into the housing. Showers of sparks were thrown into the air as the nose section scraped along the ground. As it turned out, the fallen nose gear was a blessing in disguise for the friction slowed the aircraft rapidly and the 767 shuddered to a halt well short of the race meeting.

As the aircraft stopped, the forward section filled with smoke and the captain ordered an emergency evacuation. The flight attendants operated the escape slides: six in total with two at the front, two at the overwing emergency exits and two at the rear. With the nose tilted down the forward chutes sloped to the ground at a gentle angle but the rear slides were very steep. In the event, however, there was no problem with so few passengers and all aboard evacuated quickly with only minor injuries being sustained. No flames could be seen but thick, oily smoke continued to billow from

The 767 at rest at Gimli. Apart from the damage in the nosewheel area, no other damage was sustained. (Captain Bob Pearson)

the front of the aircraft and about ten large fire extinguishers, borrowed from the Winnipeg Sports Car Club, were required to dampen the emission. The fuel tanks, when checked later, were found to be completely dry.

The incident proved a lucky escape for all concerned and but for the skill of the pilots the result could have been much worse. Captain Pearson had displayed his abilities to the full and had executed a brilliant forced landing.

At the summing up of the subsequent Federal Government Public Inquiry Mr Justice Lockwood said of the crew, 'Thanks to the professionalism and skill of the flight crew and of the flight attendants, the corporate and equipment deficiencies were overcome and a major disaster averted.'

# Chapter 6
# The Blackest Day

The day did not start too well. To begin with, Pan Am's Flight 93 was late leaving Brussels and was behind schedule on its arrival into Amsterdam. The journey had been routine but there had been no chance to make up time on the short hop. The ground staff would try their best to speed the transit in Amsterdam but the Boeing 747 was a new aircraft type for the airline and had not been in service for long. Preparing the 747 would take time. The next stop was New York, and at least 100 tons of fuel would be needed for the Atlantic crossing; just pumping the fuel quantity into the tanks would take over thirty minutes. The passenger load was light, with only 152 travelling on the Amsterdam-New York sector, so time could be saved on boarding, but the number was disappointingly low for the airline. Pan Am's brand new 747, named *Fortune,* could hold 360 people, double that of the Boeing 707, and less than half the available seating capacity would be filled. The profit margin on this flight would be thin.

The day was a cool, cloudy Sunday in northern Europe, 6 September 1970, and 49-year-old Captain John Priddy, Flight 93's commander, would be pleased to be on the way. His co-pilot was First Officer Pat Levix and his flight engineer was Julius Dzuiba, known to his colleagues as Zuby. In the cabin he had fourteen flight attendants, led by Flight Service Director John Ferruggio, bringing the total on board to 169. Among the passengers was France's new deputy delegate to the United Nations, M. Francois de la Gorce, a deadheading crew returning to New York as passengers and Captain Priddy's wife, Valerie.

At about 13:30 GMT, 15:30 local time at Amsterdam's Schiphol Airport, Flight 93 was finally ready for departure.

The big jet pushed back from the gate and taxied out to the runway. The air traffic control flight clearance was given and confirmed the routeing as across the North Sea to overhead London, then westbound over the UK to begin the Atlantic crossing. Approaching the threshold Captain Priddy was instructed to hold position to await landing traffic and was told take-off clearance would be given shortly. As the crew waited for the arriving aircraft to land, a radio message was received from the control tower with the controller using Pan Am's call sign, 'Clipper'.

'Clipper 93, change to Ground Control for a minute, they have a message for you.'

The first officer re-selected the ground frequency and established contact.

'We have just been informed,' radioed ground, 'that there are two passengers on your flight that were refused passage by El Al.'

'For what reason?' asked Priddy.

'We have no idea.'

It seemed just another little problem to add to those of the day for the information was too vague to be conclusive.

'If you can give us the names of the passengers we'll check them out,' suggested the captain.

'The names are Diop and Gueye.'

Captain Priddy called his flight service director to the cockpit and they discussed the situation. Ferruggio did not recognise the names and he knew nothing about them. The captain felt it advisable to have a talk with the two suspects so he and his service director left the flight deck to seek them out. Meanwhile F/O Levix contacted the Pan Am operations office, known as Panops, in Amsterdam and spoke to a representative on their company frequency. Any additional information they could be given would be appreciated.

Priddy and Ferruggio descended the stairs from the upper deck to the first class cabin and the service director paged the two men on the public address (PA) system. The captain and his chief flight attendant walked through first class, right down one aisle to the back of the aircraft, then crossed over to the opposite side and walked all the way back. No one came forward. A second PA announcement was made and, this time, as Captain Priddy returned to the first class cabin, the two men revealed themselves.

'Hey, that's us,' they shouted.

They were sitting in the middle of the last row of seats. Immediately it could be seen that they were young men of Middle East or Arab origin and that they were very well dressed. They seemed pleasant people, and the captain felt uncomfortable as he approached them. He didn't know what he was looking for and he felt he had no right of search. And, after all, they had paid first class fares. As tactfully as possible he explained that an alert had been received and that their names had been mentioned. The two suspects spoke very good English and they talked with the captain for a few minutes. They were polite, well mannered and helpful. Captain Priddy could see no cause for alarm.

'Well, there's been some sort of misunderstanding,' he assured them, 'but I'll either have to take you back or give you the option of being searched.'

'If you want to search us, go ahead,' the men replied obligingly.

The captain searched their persons and belongings but nothing was found. They each had only a small Samsonite briefcase containing a few papers and it was obvious they were clean. Captain Priddy was satisfied they did not pose a threat.

'I'm sorry,' apologised the captain, 'apparently there has been some mistake.'

On returning to the flight deck, Priddy found that no further information on the suspects was available and, since the warning seemed a false alarm, he decided to depart.

Flight 93 took-off from Schiphol Airport at just before 14:00 GMT (now used throughout) and climbed south-west across the North Sea, reaching level cruise approximately 25 minutes later. At about 14:30, the Pan Am aircraft flew overhead London and, with the aircraft settled comfortably in the cruise, the decision to continue seemed justified. Captain Priddy contacted Panops at Heathrow and discussed the situation with them. He explained that he had searched the two suspects but had found nothing. Suddenly the flight deck door burst open and the captain stopped mid-sentence.

Pan Am Boeing 747. (John Stroud)

Standing behind the flight crew at the back of the cockpit were Diop and Gueye, each brandishing a pistol in one hand and a grenade with the pin pulled out in the other. The nearer of the two men held the first class purser before him as a shield, with an arm around her neck. Pan Am Flight 93 had been hijacked!

The day for Captain Priddy and his colleagues could now not get much worse, but just how black it had become for aviation at large was not known to Pan Am's crew. The first blow of the day was struck at 11:15 when a TWA Boeing 707 was hijacked on departure from Frankfurt, West Germany. The flight had originated in Tel Aviv and was bound for New York. The aircraft was commanded by Captain C. D. Woods who was forced by a group of armed guerrillas to fly to an unknown destination in the Middle East. Only fifteen minutes later, at 11:30, the hijacking of another Boeing 707 began, this time of airline El Al, by two passengers, a man and a woman. Their names were Patrick Arguello and Leila Khaled. Like TWA's aircraft, El Al's Flight 219 had also originated in Tel Aviv and was bound for New York, but it had, instead, transitted Amsterdam.

About thirty minutes after departure from Schiphol Airport, Arguello had let out an 'animal type bellow' and, with a small .22 pistol in his hand, he had rushed towards the front of the aircraft. He was quickly followed by Khaled who pulled a couple of grenades from her bra and charged down the aisle with one in each hand. As Arguello approached the flight deck door he was intercepted by Steward Shlomo Vider and a scuffle ensued. Armed sky marshals raced into action but before they could do anything Vider was shot in the chest. In the first class cabin a guard lunged at Khaled but she managed to pull a pin from one of the grenades. He grabbed her elbows from behind but as he pushed her down the grenade tumbled to the floor. Miraculously it failed to explode.

Another security guard rushed forward from the rear, his pistol firing, and Arguello dropped, fatally wounded. Khaled was securely bound with string and a necktie and Flight 219's commander, Captain Uri Bar-Leb, informed London he required an emergency landing at Heathrow. The captain also radioed Tel Aviv with news of the attempted hijacking and received a request for an immediate return to Israel. The authorities there would have liked very much to get their hands on the hijacketer, but Captain Bar-Leb insisted on landing in London. The wounded steward was seriously ill and urgent medical attention was needed.

On Flight 219's arrival at Heathrow a brave crew member ran from the aircraft with the unexploded grenade and placed it some distance away on the tarmac. Vider was rushed to hospital, the body of Arguello was removed and Khaled was placed in custody. The 707 was thoroughly searched and after a short delay was permitted to proceed on its way. Steward Vider later made a full recovery from his injuries.

In the afternoon, three hours after the incident, Pan Am's Flight 93 had followed El Al's route out of Amsterdam and had suffered a similar hijack attempt. The 747, however, did not carry armed sky marshals and the Pan Am big jet had been commandeered without resistance. Captain Priddy, at this stage, had no knowledge of the previous events and it was only later that the authorities were to realise how closely connected were the El Al and Pan Am hijack incidents.

As if the morning's attempts at air piracy were not enough — with one successful and one failed — another hijack occurred in the early afternoon before Pan Am became involved. At 12:15, a Swissair DC-8 en route from Zurich to New York was also overcome by a group of armed guerrillas. The hijacking had taken place near Paris and the commander, Captain Fritz Schreiber, was also forced to fly to an unknown destination in the Middle East.

Captain Priddy's 747 was the fourth aircraft that Sunday to be boarded in as many hours by armed hijackers and 6 September 1970 was a black day indeed. It was the worst for piracy in the history of civil aviation. Had the Pan Am captain been made more fully aware of the earlier events and had the warning of the Schiphol Airport police regarding the two suspects been more specific, he would never have left the ground. The police certainly knew of the attack on El Al before the 747 departed. The polite and helpful young gentlemen Captain Priddy had interviewed earlier now stood on his flight deck, armed and nervous guerrillas, determined to carry out their task. With the pins removed from the grenades each held, any attempt at opposition would have been suicidal and there was no choice but to obey the hijackers' demands.

Soon after the 747's take over the guerrillas ordered Flight 93 to turn back to Amsterdam. 3100 was selected on the transponder, at that time the hijack squawk code, and London Airways requested the 747 to descend to 27,000 ft because of traffic. A few minutes later the hijackers changed their minds and decided on Beirut, the capital of the Lebanon, as their destination. Priddy received clearance to climb back to a more suitable level and continued the flight eastwards to Beirut.

'Are we going to land there?' asked Captain Priddy.

'I don't know,' said Gueye, 'I'll tell you when we get there. I have to talk to my people on the ground.'

The reply was an indication that perhaps not all had gone according to plan and further instructions were required. The 747 had plenty of fuel for the expected Atlantic crossing so the four-hour flight to Beirut in the opposite direction did not give the captain cause for concern on that account. He hoped, once on the ground in Lebanon, to be able to persuade the guerrillas to release the passengers. Unaware of the facts, he was not to realise the outcome of the events.

As the 747 flew towards Beirut the hijackers began to relax a little, but one or other of them remained on the flight deck for the entire journey. At all times the grenades were grasped with the pins removed. On one occasion one of the guerrillas played with the spare pin in his fingers and accidentally dropped it. For a while it couldn't be found and a shiver ran down F/E Dzuiba's spine at the thought of being unable to secure the grenade. The flight engineer rummaged on the floor with his flashlight and the commotion attracted Priddy's attention.

'What the hell's going on?' asked the captain.

'Never mind, keep flying,' called back Dzuiba. 'I'll find it.'

Eventually a relieved flight engineer recovered the pin and returned it to its owner.

Meanwhile in Amsterdam, the authorities had not been inactive and details of the hijackings began to be pieced together. Diop was identified as Mazn Abu Mehana, a Palestinian from Haifa, and Gueye as Samir Abdel Meguid, a Palestinian from Jerusalem. Both men, like their colleagues who had hijacked the other aircraft, were members of the Popular Front for the Liberation of Palestine (PFLP), an organisation dedicated to furthering the Palestinian cause by whatever means available. Aircraft of the enemy, Israel, or of their supporters, American or European, were considered legitimate targets.

Diop and Gueye, it transpired, had originally been booked on El Al's Flight 219 which had departed Amsterdam with Arguello and Khaled aboard a few hours ahead of the Pan Am 747. A team of four was considered the minimum required to tackle an El Al aircraft with armed sky marshals but, with the two men denied access to Flight 219 and no time to find replacements, the attempt had failed. El Al's suspicions regarding Diop and Gueye had arisen ten days earlier when they had tried to make a booking on the Amsterdam-New York flight. Security officers checked the men out and found the facts didn't tally. Both men carried

Senegalese passports and claimed to be students travelling
to South America. The journey they had chosen via New
York to Santiago in Chile, however, was not the cheapest
route to fly and, what's more, they had bought one-way first
class tickets paid for in cash. Students from Senegal did not
normally travel in this fashion! Diop and Gueye were
eventually told that the El Al flight out of Amsterdam to
New York was full and they were unable to carry them. The
airline simply marked the paid-for El Al tickets with an 'open
endorsement' which allowed them to fly with any other
airline.

Three days before Sunday the 6th, the two men booked on
Pan Am's Flight 93. At check-in, the counter clerk noted the
El Al 'open endorsement' tickets but received the two men
for the flight. Pan Am representatives, however, became
concerned that they might have unwittingly accepted rejects
from another airline and they checked the names with El Al.
At about the same time, news of the attempted hijacking of
Flight 219 reached Amsterdam and El Al security agents
became aware of the potential danger to the 747. Pan Am's
Flight 93 was already taxying out for take-off at this stage so
the Schiphol Airport police were contacted immediately.
Unfortunately the police did not take the threat as seriously
as the airline, and the information, when passed via
the ground controller to Captain Priddy, was vague and
incomplete.

When the Pan Am captain descended the stairs to
interview the suspects, unknown to him at the time the two
men had been sitting in the third row on the right side of first
class. After the PA announcement calling for them the
guerrillas had slipped back to the last row of seats in the
middle. Captain Priddy had searched the right men in the
wrong place.

The original intention of the PFLP was to hijack three
aircraft that September Sunday: the TWA 707, the El Al 707
and the Swissair DC-8. When Diop and Gueye were found to
be spare they had been switched to Pan Am to cover any
possible failure of the attack on Flight 219. The plan had been
carefully organised and executed and success in three out of
four attempts was quite remarkable. All four aircraft had

been hijacked at the beginning of transatlantic flights and carried plenty of fuel. The one problem facing Pan Am's hijackers, however, was that they expected the aircraft to be a 707. The Boeing 747 had been only newly introduced into service and it had caught them by surprise.

As Flight 93 flew towards Beirut, Diop and Gueye re-arranged the seating of the passengers. With one on the flight deck at all times, the other, pistol in hand, herded all the cabin occupants into the rear of the economy section. Passports were collected and were thoroughly checked. Any potential trouble makers — military personnel, diplomatic staff, crew members — were then isolated from the main group and seated in first class. A special watch would be kept on them. All passengers were firmly ordered to stay in their seats and to remain still. If any rescue was attempted the perpetrators would face grave consequences.

After several hours the captain was finally permitted to talk to the passengers and he informed them on the PA that the aircraft was no longer under his command. He explained, in as calm and reassuring a manner as possible, that the flight was now not going to New York, but to Beirut Airport, 2,000 miles (3,707 km) to the east of their departure point.

As the Pan Am 747 approached Beirut Airport, Captain Priddy was instructed to remain at height and to circle overhead. He obtained permission to descend to 27,000 ft (8,230 m), below the airway structure, and at the speed of 250 knots he prepared to begin orbiting. Meanwhile, in Jordan, 100 miles (160 km) to the south, another drama was unfolding. The two aircraft which had been hijacked earlier — the TWA 707 and the Swissair DC-8 — had been forced to land at a disused desert airbase in northern Jordan, known as Dawson's Field, situated near the town of Zarqa, fifteen miles (twenty-four kilometres) to the north of Amman. The landings on the rough and uneven desert strip had been hazardous and the passengers had been badly shaken. One woman aboard the TWA aircraft had sustained a broken wrist. The parked aircraft were immediately surrounded by armed commandos of the PFLP.

Detachments of Israeli airborne helicopter troops crossed the border and landed near the towns of Irbid and Jerash in preparation for an attempt to release the two airliners, but their efforts were too late. Armed factions of the PFLP also feared that the Jordan Army, with which they had been in recent conflict, would attempt a rescue, but they too were helpless. King Hussein opposed the PFLP action in hijacking the aircraft and Jordan in fact, heavily infiltrated by Palestinian guerrillas, was on the brink of civil war. About 300 passengers, 155 aboard the DC-8 and 145 aboard the 707, were held hostage in the desert against their will.

Unaware of the circumstances, Captain Priddy began circling the 747 overhead Beirut Airport at 27,000 ft. The time was now about 18:30 GMT, 20:30 local Lebanese time, and darkness had fallen, but the lights of the town could be seen five miles (eight kilometres) below. Priddy established contact with Panops Beirut and was instructed by the hijackers to order an Arabic speaker to be brought to the mike. The guerrillas wanted to converse in their own language to conceal their discussions from the crew. An Arabic speaker was quickly acquired and he was told by one of the hijackers to summon a PFLP official to the airport to discuss the situation. A few minutes later the hijacker called back again.

'Brother, have you made contact with any of the responsible officials?'

'We are now in contact with a responsible official,' replied the Arabic speaker, 'and he shall communicate with you on this frequency when he comes to the office.'

As the arrival of the PFLP official was awaited a conflict of interest arose between Captain Priddy in the circling 747 and the Lebanese authorities at the airport. Priddy, unaware of the hostages held in the desert, was convinced the best course of action was to land in Beirut. He was confident that once on the ground he could persuade the hijackers to release the passengers, or at least the women and children. He had learned that Diop and Gueye were fairly knowledgeable about aircraft operations but their one area of weakness seemed to be in fuel management of the 747. He became aware that they had no idea of how long they could continue flying with the remaining fuel and he sensed he could force them into landing at Beirut by declaring a fuel shortage. On

the ground, a Mr A. Bedran, the deputy manager of Beirut
Airport, and a Colonel Salloum of the Lebanese Army, had
other ideas. To them the 747 was trouble and they wanted
nothing to do with it. They had their own plans for
dissuading the aircraft from landing.

'For your information,' radioed Mr Bedran, 'the main
runway at Beirut Airport is closed at the present time due to
work in progress. The other runway cannot tolerate the
weight of the Boeing 747. We suggest that the aircraft be
directed to Damascus Airport, which airport is presently
ready to receive this type of aircraft.'

'We will not land at Damascus Airport, but will land at
Beirut Airport. Did you hear? Answer, answer! We will land
at Beirut Airport and will not land at any other airport unless
contact is established with a responsible official from the
Popular Front. I want an answer.'

'We are in contact — attempting to contact — the Popular

The routeings of the four aircraft hijacked on 6 September.

Front to send a representative to the airport,' reaffirmed the deputy airport manager. 'Therefore please fly overhead Beirut until contact is established and agreement reached to head to another airport as Beirut Airport is not technically ready to receive this aircraft.'

News was then received that representatives of the PFLP would arrive imminently and that they would be in the control tower within ten minutes. If the 747 crew also selected the tower frequency of 118.9 MHz on another radio box the hijackers could communicate with them shortly. It then transpired that the Palestinian officials were arriving from Bhamdoun, a mountain town some distance away, and it would take at least thirty minutes just to drive into Beirut.

An hour passed and still there was no sign of the representatives. The Pan Am 747 continued to fly in circles above the airport and by now it was obvious to all concerned that the big jet's arrival overhead Beirut was unexpected.

'It's taking a long time to get these people,' commented Priddy.

'Well, you know the traffic in Beirut on a Sunday night,' Gueye replied casually as if in everyday conversation.

Meanwhile Bedran, the deputy airport manager, tried again to stress that Beirut was not technically suitable to receive the 747. The main runway had been closed for over a month, the hijackers were informed, and the first 2,300 ft (700 m) of the second runway were unusable. It would be extremely difficult for the 747 to land. He did not reveal, however, that it *was* possible for the big jet to use the shortened runway for landing. Whether Bedran's remarks were bluff or fact was not known to anyone aboard the Pan Am aircraft but when the deputy airport manager offered the information that Damascus had been contacted and the airport could receive the big jet the hijackers became hysterical. Bedran had no authority to speak to Damascus, one of the guerrillas shouted over the radio, and on no account was the 747 going anywhere until a responsible Palestinian official was contacted. Captain Priddy, however, was concerned that there might be some truth in the statements and he, in conversation with Panops Beirut on the other radio box, enquired if Baghdad would be a suitable alternative. Unfortunately, neither the airport there nor Iraqi Airways were able to handle the big jet.

On the tower frequency, the hijacker, still in conversation with Bedran, asked about one of the other events of that Sunday.

'An El Al aircraft was hijacked today en route to London. Where did it land?'

'It looks like it has landed at London,' replied the deputy airport manager.

'Who is responsible for its hijacking?'

'Oh, by God, we don't know, excepting that it has landed at London at the present time.'

'Thanks.'

Diop and Gueye had, of course, more than a passing interest in the event and it appeared from what had been said that the attempt had failed. Unaware of the other successes they, too, felt that their day had not gone according to plan.

About one-and-a-half hours after the initial request for a PFLP representative, two responsible officials, Abou-Khaled and Abou-Ahmad, finally arrived in the control tower. Abou-Khaled spoke over the radio to Gueye, now identified in Amsterdam as Samir Maguid, but neither of the men knew each other personally and both were very cautious.

'Hello, hello.'

'Yes, go ahead,' said Gueye.

'Hello, hello, this is Abou-Khaled speaking, do you hear me?'

'Who?'

'Walid Kaddoura speaking, do you hear me? Hello, who is talking to me, brother? Who is talking?'

'Samir.'

'Samir?'

'Yes.'

'We have news from Amman that you could not land at the airport there,' said Abou-Khaled.

'Of course we cannot land there.'

'Who is talking, brother? What squad?'

'Well . . . do you want to disclose names?'

'No, the name of the squad, the name of the squad! You

originated from Amsterdam, is that right?'

'Yes, from Amsterdam.'

'What happened?' asked Abou-Khaled.

'What happened when we entered the Amsterdam Airport is that those responsible on the aircraft were suspicious and started to search us but could not find the weapons. When the aircraft took off, its destination was diverted in accordance with instructions we received.'

'Can you go to any other place? Can you go to any other place?'

'Where do you want us to take it?'

'Is there enough fuel?' questioned Abou-Khaled.

'Is there enough fuel? I will ask the captain . . . Hello, hello, he informed us that he has fuel enough for forty minutes.'

'Can you go to Amman? Is the fuel sufficient to reach the destined place?'

'Yes, it is, but landing is impossible. We can reach the destined place, but landing there is impossible.'

'Brother, if anything happens to the aircraft there, it does not matter. Is this possible?'

'It doesn't matter if anything happens to the aircraft there?' asked Gueye, surprised.

'It does not matter if anything happens to the aircraft. It did happen to the TWA's Amman landing to a certain extent, but it did not matter.'

'Does this mean that we can land there at the destined place? What I want you to understand is that this is a 747 aircraft and it weighs many times the weight of a 707 aircraft. It is impossible to land at the destined place under any circumstance whatsoever. The destined airport definitely cannot stand it, and if it lands there it will be a wreck.'

The radio conversations were in Arabic and were, of course, not understood by the Pan Am crew, but the language difference could not disguise the hijackers' concern. Not only did Captain Priddy not want to be hijacked, but the guerrillas had not wanted to commandeer a Boeing 747! If the aircraft had been a 707 it would by now be sitting at the 'destined place' — Dawson's Field — with the other two machines, but it was impossible to land such a big jet on the rough desert strip. The PFLP, therefore, were left with a rather large embarrassment circling five miles overhead Beirut: they didn't want the 747 nor did they know what to do with it.

Captain Priddy's estimate of forty minutes' fuel was on the low side and he had in fact much more than he was telling. Since Beirut Airport appeared unable to accept the 747, the hijackers suggested to the PFLP officials that they land at either Baghdad or Cairo for refuelling. With what they assumed was little fuel remaining, however, they required an answer quickly. Priddy had already established that Baghdad Airport could not handle a 747 but he did not understand the discussion in Arabic. When questioned he simply said he could remain overhead for about a further twenty minutes after which he would have to land at Beirut. If they wanted to go elsewhere they would have to decide soon.

'So I beg of you,' pleaded Gueye with Abou-Khaled, 'to give an answer in less than fifteen minutes.'

'Within five minutes we will give you an answer, brother.'

By now the Beirut Airport manager had joined those in the tower and Abou-Khaled confronted him face to face. He called his bluff and demanded to know the true situation at the airport otherwise he would order the destruction of the 747 in the air. A Colonel Hamdan of the Lebanese Army telephoned the Transport Minister, Pierre Gemayal, and relayed the threat. Could permission be given for the 747 to land? With little choice the Minister relented and allowed Beirut Airport to accept the Pan Am aircraft.

Meanwhile, in Flight 93's cockpit, the hijackers were becoming impatient.

'Hello, Abou-Ahmad, what shall we do? Have you received an answer, or not yet?'

'Abou-Ahmad talking to you. I will give you an answer in three minutes.'

'Okay, I am listening to you. Didn't you expect us here, or what? Is that why you cannot give us a quick answer? Four minutes are over, and we are still waiting.'

'They will allow you to land at the airport to refuel,' a relieved Abou-Ahmad at last reported.

'Land at what airport?'

'Instructions will be given to land at Beirut Airport to refuel, which will take forty-five minutes, after which we will give you instructions as to where to go.'

'Does this mean that the Lebanese authorities agreed to our landing at Beirut? They said technically the airport was not fit for landing.'

'Technically you can land, you can land,' affirmed Abou-Ahmad. 'The authorities have approved landing at the airport for refuelling.'

'Please inform them of the following message: If any attempt is made to approach the aircraft, we will destroy the aircraft completely.'

It was agreed that, on landing, the two PFLP representatives in the tower could board the aircraft for discussion, and descriptions of the men were radioed to the hijackers for identification. In the darkness it would be difficult to see who was approaching the 747. Gueye, however, was still unhappy about the fact that he was not known to those in the tower and he expressed his concern.

'I am astounded that you do not know who is talking to you as long as you know that I originated in Amsterdam.'

'Brother, it was not planned for you to land at Beirut, remonstrated Abou-Ahmad. Ashraf* and Abou-Hani* did not tell you to land at Beirut. This is an emergency. I am not supposed to know.'

'I know it is an emergency. We also did not expect it to be a 747.'

'Therefore, it *is* an emergency, and we do not know.'

Captain Priddy now prepared the aircraft for landing and the tower controller butted in to the radio conversation to pass on the relevant details.

'Okay, Clipper 93 — calling for landing — you have to be very smooth on landing and you have to choose either 03 which is landing from over the sea or runway 21 from over the sea. The full length will be available, I mean runway 03. On runway 21 the first 600 metres are to be avoided, and anyhow on runway 03 and 21 there will be a VASI* which will guide you in for landing.'

* Amman PFLP leaders.

'What is the field elevation?'

'The field elevation is eighty-seven feet, sir.'

'Eighty-seven feet, okay,' repeated Priddy. 'What is the wind direction and velocity?'

'Easterly at five knots, runway length available 3,180 metres.'

The Pan Am 747 had no airport charts on board for the arrival at Beirut and all relevant details had to be passed by radio, but Priddy was not over-concerned about the landing. He had already been in touch with a Pan Am unit in Frankfurt on HF long range radio and had received much information. He was suspicious the poor conditions at Beirut had been exaggerated by the authorities to prevent a landing and he did not expect any problems.

Suddenly the PFLP officials in the tower spotted Lebanese Army vehicles and troops massing on the manoeuvring areas and they became extremely agitated. Word had also spread amongst the Palestinian community in Beirut of the excitement at the airport and a number of heavily-armed PFLP commandos had positioned themselves in front of the terminal building. An ugly scene was brewing and there was a great deal of tension.

'Do not land pending further instructions!' ordered Abou-Ahmad from the tower. 'There are army vehicles at the airport. Do not land now!'

'Delay the aircraft landing? Why?' demanded Gueye, confused.

'In case an attempt is made to approach the aircraft, they are not going to be happy at all.'

'Who is attempting to approach the aircraft? Answer! Who is attempting to approach the aircraft? Answer!'

'Can you postpone landing for the time being, brother?'

'Why? Give me convincing reasons.'

'Brother, brother. Abou-Ahmad is talking to you. We now see on the ramp army vehicles moving here and there, therefore any attempt to approach the aircraft from the army will not be tolerated by us at all. So please postpone the landing a few minutes to enable us to agree with them to pull out all army vehicles.'

* Visual Approach Slope Indicator.

'Okay, will inform the captain of this. I want to tell you something which you must accept and understand quickly, in that, if any obstacles develop and we could not land at Beirut, in about ten or fifteen minutes we will not be able to go to any other airport as the fuel would not suffice.'

'Okay, I heard you, you will definitely land at Beirut Airport for refuelling, but we beg you to postpone landing for a few minutes in order for us to come to an agreement with the army to withdraw all his vehicles.'

'Fifteen minutes enough?'

'Fifteen minutes in order.'

'Okay, will postpone landing for fifteen minutes.'

'Clipper 93 calling Tower,' radioed Priddy.

'Go ahead.'

'Okay, this is the captain speaking. How about clearing that runway so that we can get down, huh? Do not cause us any more trouble. These folks are serious and are willing to destroy the airplane.'

'Okay, sir. We are going to give the military here orders to clear all the military around the runway so as to give way for landing safely.'

'Okay, as fast as you can, huh?'

'Okay, as fast as we can.'

'We just want to land at Beirut,' restated the captain.

'Do you prefer to land on runway 03 or runway 21?'

'We'd rather land on 03.'

'Roger. Stand by, please.'

Unknown to any of the communicators, other ears were listening to the conversation. The border with Israel lies less than sixty miles (ninety-six kilometres) to the south of Beirut and Israeli controllers were monitoring the Lebanese airport's frequencies. Suddenly a new voice was heard on the air.

'Hey, Clipper 93, this is Tel Aviv Control. Come on down! We've got two beautiful, long, lighted runways — we got emergency equipment standing by — we'll give you fighter escort. You just make a dash for it.'

The two hijackers went through the roof and Gueye became hysterical. He waved the grenade around and threatened to detonate it immediately. The Israeli controller kept trying to persuade the 747 to turn south for Tel Aviv, in spite of Captain Priddy's protestations, and Gueye was going to blow them all up on the spot. Eventually the captain managed to persuade the Israeli controller to keep quiet and he was able to pacify the hijackers. Alarmed now at how easily the situation could get out of hand Priddy stressed his concern once again.

'From Clipper 93. They say they know the airport and if there are any tricks they will blow up the airplane. So cut out the horsing around down there and get the runway cleared and get us down, huh?'

'Okay, that is what we are doing now.'

The tower controller repeatedly asked the captain for his endurance — how long he could stay in the air — but Priddy, not wanting to reveal that he still had plenty of fuel, simply kept saying that an immediate landing was required. He also radioed Panops Beirut on the other box, asking them to impress upon those concerned that the hijackers were serious in their intentions to blow up the aircraft.

'Understand,' replied Panops. 'For your information, I personally saw some groups of forces, policemen and army groups, pulling out of the airport in order to avoid a clash with the men on board. I would say that it is about to be cleared.'

Ten minutes later, after almost two hours of circling, descent clearance for landing at Beirut Airport was finally received. F/O Levix changed frequency to radar control and the Pan Am aircraft was vectored on to the approach for runway 03. After a short while the 747 at last lined up on the final approach to land and a large crowd, including many armed PFLP commandos, gathered to watch its arrival.

'Clipper 93, eight miles from touchdown,' informed the radar controller.

'Okay, we will stay with you for the moment . . . now we have the runway in sight.'

'Understand you have the runway in sight. Take over visually to runway 03 and call Tower, frequency 118.9.'

'Okay.'

Levix changed frequency but before he could establish contact the tower controller transmitted.

'Clipper 93, Beirut Tower, your range please.'

'Okay, we are about eight miles out and we have the runway in sight.'

'Roger, we have the VASI on now. Cleared to land on runway 03, wind east at five knots.'

'Okay, understand the wind is east at five knots and cleared to land, runway 03.'

'Okay, and I suggest you try to stop as soon as possible, please. We will take you to the parking.'

'Okay, I will try to run short if we can. I will stay on your frequency for taxy and instructions. Do you understand?'

'It is correct,' replied tower, 'remain on this frequency.'

'Okay.'

'East section cleared to parking. Use the first left intersection and pick up the follow-me jeep.'

'Okay, we understand that.'

'Clipper 93, this is Beirut Tower.'

'Okay, go ahead.'

'After you stop, call the frequency 121.9, please, and let somebody of the people who are with you talk to us.'

'Okay.'

At 20:40 GMT, 22:40 local time, the Pan Am 747 touched down safely, if a little roughly, on the uneven surface and observers watching from the terminal clapped as it landed. A follow-me truck led the aircraft from the runway to the east parking area and as the big jet approached the terminal it turned to face away from the building. Captain Priddy set the parking brake and called for the engines to be shut down.

Abou-Khaled and Abou-Ahmad descended from the tower and mounted a jeep while another PFLP party member, Salah, maintained contact from the control tower on the ground frequency of 121.9 MHz. The hijackers could also communicate by radio with the officials in the jeep and as the vehicle approached they were ordered to stop and disembark. Anxiously the hijackers, on edge and suspicious of every move, watched from the flight deck. The jeep sped rapidly back towards the terminal and the two PFLP men approached the big jet on foot. Neither group could see clearly what was happening in the darkness but the men on the ground were accepted and the left forward door was opened. After conferring with the officials, instructions were given to the captain to order maintenance steps which were eventually placed by the door and the PFLP men boarded the aircraft. The door was closed and the steps were removed.

As the four men on the aircraft discussed the situation, Salah, in the tower, awaited instructions from the party members in Amman. A reply was expected in approximately half an hour regarding the fate of the Pan Am aircraft and its occupants. In due course orders were received and Salah transmitted the details to Abou-Khaled in the 747 cockpit.

'Take the following instructions,' commanded Salah. 'News received from Amman to the effect that you first refuel. This means that the first thing you do is refuel, and if they refuse refuelling here, we will blow up the aircraft at Beirut Airport, of course after you disembark. Also, of course, we have notified the airport manager of this, and he is making the necessary arrangements for you to refuel. After you refuel, the same guys who are commanding the aircraft now will head on it to Cairo. In Cairo they will precisely act in like manner as Abou-Doummar and Leila Khaled have acted. Clearly, they will act the way Abou-Doummar and Leila Khaled have acted, but they have to avoid all the mistakes that occurred in the operation of Leila Khaled and Abou-Doummar at Damascus Airport. You remember what happened at Damascus Airport? — the way Abou-Doummar and Leila Khaled acted — but they have to avoid the mistakes that occurred. This means that the operation must be accomplished in perfect manner, the front and the rear, that is, the nose and the tail.'

In August of the year before, Abou-Doummar and Khaled had hijacked a TWA 707 en route from Rome to Tel Aviv via Athens. The jet had been forced to land at Damascus where a bomb had been detonated only moments after the passengers and crew had been evacuated. Fortunately for the airline the damage was not irreparable and about one-and-a-half months later the aircraft had been returned to service. There was to be no mistake this time. The 747 was to be effectively wired with explosives at both the front and the rear of the fuselage and to be completely destroyed.

The destination, Cairo, had not been chosen without reason. The Egyptian president, Nasser, had permitted peace negotiations to be conducted with the Israelis in New York and the parties were moving towards agreement. The Palestinians, however, had been excluded from the talks and the blowing up of a 747 at the Egyptian capital's airport, would effectively demonstrate their displeasure.

Discussions between the PFLP men in the control tower and the 747 now centred on the refuelling of the aircraft. The hijackers were extremely nervous that the process might be used to launch a rescue attempt and instructions were given that only the minimum number of refuellers necessary would be permitted to approach the aircraft. They were also to be closely monitored. The Lebanese Army, although withdrawn, could be quickly recalled, and the large number of armed PFLP men in the airport area created a very tense atmosphere. The situation was very delicate and in the darkness any wrong move could turn the parking apron into a battle ground. The hijackers also had a problem in explaining to Salah that they had no explosives on board and these items — code named 'sandwiches' — would have to be loaded. Eventually the message was understood and arrangements were made to secure the explosives from downtown.

'During this period,' radioed Abou-Khalad from the 747, 'kindly secure the items required by the guys here for travel to Cairo. There is possibility that one of us would travel with the guys to Cairo. Did you hear me, Salah?'

'I heard you, Abou-Khaled,' replied Salah, 'and have arranged everything. All the items will be available quickly. Samir El-Saheb and Captain Ali are going to supervise five other elements to refuel the aircraft. And "sandwiches" will be sent to you so that the comrades may have dinner.'

The Lebanese authorities, only wanting to see the back of the Pan Am flight, offered Captain Priddy as much fuel as he wanted. Full tanks would have been ideal, of course, but the aircraft was restricted in the fuel load it could carry because of the short distance to Cairo. The flight from Beirut to Cairo was less than a hour and the 747 would have to land at its destination at or below the maximum landing weight. A figure was agreed and refuelling began. Meanwhile, Salah passed over the radio further instructions from Amman to one of the hijackers on the 747 flight deck.

'You will execute the plan you will now work out at your end. That is to say that you, Abou-Khaled, the comrade you have, and Abou-Ahmad will work out a plan as to how you should act there. With regards to the passengers, deplane them quietly and smoothly. After the passengers deplane, determine the distribution of your responsibilities as to who goes in the front and who in the rear. The quantity of the sandwiches which we will give to you — you will amuse yourselves with them on the way — arrange them properly in order for your plan to be a complete success. This means that you will work out all the details with Abou-Ahmad and Abou-Khaled. Tell them this for me. You have received the instructions. Make out the arrangements, work out a detailed plan. That is your mission. Consider all plans previously made as cancelled. All of you aboard the aircraft work out a complete plan as to how you should act there. Secure the passengers deplaning. Of course, it is important for us that the passengers deplane safely.'

As the preparations for departure progressed the tension on the aircraft eased and the passengers were able to relax a little. Drinks were served and they were even permitted to stretch their legs on board. A political statement was read over the PA by one of the guerrillas. While waiting, the hijackers then took it in turns to walk through the cabin to talk to the passengers. Where did they come from? Had they any questions? The Palestinians' manner was friendly and polite, but the pistol in one hand and grenade in the other were readily evident. Few cabin occupants wanted to converse with them.

The explosives arrived about halfway through the refuelling process and arrangements were made to bring them to the 747. The 'sandwiches' were packed in a large seaman's bag which weighed about eighty lb (thirty-six kilogrammes) and two men were needed to carry it. The maintenance steps were drawn up again to the left forward door and nine guerrillas, including one woman, brought the heavy explosives bag and a quantity of small-arms on to the aircraft. The Palestinians aboard welcomed their comrades warmly and they embraced each other by the door. When all were gathered in the 747 the door was closed and the steps were removed once more. A conference was held in first class and one of the joining group who had accompanied the refuellers to the aircraft, a Captain Ali, discussed the distribution of the 'sandwiches' on the aircraft. He was the explosives expert who was going to travel with the two hijackers on the trip to Cairo. Captain Priddy and his colleagues were waiting in first class when the group of guerrillas boarded and the meeting was held, but with all conversation in Arabic they understood nothing. Priddy asked if he could go back to talk to the passengers and he had a few words with each and every one. The captain was later followed into the cabin by several members of the guerrilla group who, like the hijackers, were friendly towards their hostages and encouraged questions. They also tried to justify their behaviour and to advertise the Palestinian cause.

By now the refuelling was nearing completion and Captain Priddy returned to the flight deck to supervise the details. He sat in the cockpit with the hijacker, Gueye, and tried to persuade him to release the passengers. Couldn't he fly to Cairo with just the crew as hostages?

'No, you don't understand,' admonished Gueye.

'What will happen when we get to Cairo?'

'Everyone will get out of the airplane, I promise you,' assured Gueye.

The fact that the aircraft was going to be blown up was left unmentioned, as were a number of other details, but Gueye had never lied to the crew and the captain felt encouraged. As Priddy checked the calculations, Salah in the tower spoke some last words to the hijacker, urging him to be extremely cautious and offering him encouragement.

'Now I am going to go down,' replied Gueye, ' and I will leave the captain for a little while in the cockpit, in order to make the arrangements for the Cairo trip. This means that I will be away from the cockpit for fifteen minutes in order for him to get ready and also to send the crew to him.'

By now Diop had returned to the flight deck and he was

left in charge as Gueye descended the stairs to supervise the final preparations. The two other flight crew were sent back to their posts and Captain Priddy and his team began to get the 747 ready for the flight. Departure was expected in forty-five minutes. About half an hour later, at 22:52 GMT, just before 01:00 local time on Monday morning, the refuelling was completed and the fuel bowser and ground personnel were withdrawn from the aircraft. The forward left cabin door was opened once more and a group of PFLP represent-atives on the ground spoke to those on the aircraft. All of the joining group were instructed to leave, except Captain Ali, the 21-year-old explosives expert, and the maintenance ladder was repositioned at the door for them to disembark.

All preparations were now completed and as the door was closed and the area around the aircraft cleared, the engines were started. A few minutes later all engines were running and at 23:30 the 747 taxied out to the runway. F/O Levix radioed for air traffic control instructions from the tower and the controller read back a flight clearance to Amman.

'We want clearance to Cairo,' corrected Levix. One of the hijackers also butted in saying that they were not going to Amman.

'Well, you're cleared for take-off,' sighed the tower controller, 'for wherever you want to go.'

Approaching the runway a clearance to Cairo was finally received and one of the PFLP representatives in the tower informed the hijackers that radio communications were to cease. The 747 was to take-off and proceed en route in radio silence. On no account were other stations to be informed of the aircraft's destination.

Captain Priddy started the take-off roll at 23:36 and one minute later, almost three hours after touch-down, the Pan Am aircraft lifted off for Cairo. The flight soon settled down to routine and all was as usual except for the lack of radio communications and the one hijacker who remained constantly on the flight deck. The passengers were served a meal and the children were permitted to run free. A pretence of normality returned to the situation and all on board remained calm. Only one young man, Captain Ali, busied himself on the aircraft, swiftly planting the explosives in closets, toilets and other parts of the structure. Between the charges he cut and laid the explosive fuze, a simple burning type which would have to be ignited by a naked flame to start the sequence. At the beginning he cut just sufficient for an eight-minute delay. He knew his business well and he was cool and efficient. His quiet manner masked his actions and many passengers were unaware of what he was doing. Ali concentrated on the front section of the 747 and as he worked in the first class cabin he was observed by those people segregated in that section. Amongst them was the Service Director, John Ferruggio, who later asked one of the hijackers what was going to happen.

'We will give you eight minutes,' he answered.

'Eight minutes for what?' questioned Ferruggio.

The hijacker refused to reply.

'What about this?' asked the service director, pointing to the explosives.

'What do you care about this imperialistic piece of equipment?' sneered the guerrilla as he looked about the 747.

'I think it's a beautiful piece of equipment and, imperialistic or not, I do care.'

The hijacker paused for a moment then added matter of factly.

'It's going to be blown up. You will have eight minutes to get out.'

At this stage the 747 was passing to the south of Cyprus, in the Nicosia flight information region, and about forty-five minutes flight time remained to Cairo. Ferruggio was concerned about the short period allowed for evacuation and he asked if he could brief the crew and passengers on procedures. He summoned all the available crew, including the four flight crew travelling passenger, to first class and told them what he knew. He suggested that the passengers be broken into groups and each section be instructed by flight attendants on evacuation procedures. The four off-duty flight crew were each asked to position by a door carrying a baby. When the chutes were deployed they were to jump first with the infant and the mother was to follow immediately. The parent was to take the child on the ground and the crew member could then help the evacuees at the bottom of the slide.

The task of dividing the passengers into groups and instructing them in evacuation procedures was carefully undertaken. An impression of urgency had to be imparted without telling everyone that from the moment the wheels touched the runway they would have only eight minutes to get out before being blown to pieces. Remarkably, much to the credit of the crew, the passengers remained calm and prepared themselves mentally for the immediate evacuation. All knew exactly what to do. They could take with them only the valuables they could wear and the ladies could carry nothing larger than a small, soft shoulder bag. All shoes were to be removed and thrown into blankets in piles for later return. When they got on the ground they were to run as fast as they could away from the aircraft.

As the 747 entered Cairo flight information region, the aircraft began descent in the darkness maintaining radio silence. The night was clear and approaching the city at 00:50 GMT, 02:50 local Egyptian time, Cairo Airport could be seen below. The tower controller tried many times to establish contact but the flight crew was forbidden to respond. By now Captain Ali had effectively completed his grim task and he had joined Gueye on the flight deck. Diop remained on guard in the cabin.

'Circle over the city,' ordered Gueye.

Ali and the hijacker spoke excitedly to each other in Arabic, pointing to sights they could see on the ground. The guerrillas were taking no chances and were checking carefully that Priddy had led them to their desired destination. As they flew over the Nile in the centre of the city Gueye confirmed their position.

'OK, it's Cairo, go ahead and land.'

Captain Priddy flew the 747 onto final approach at 01:20 and Gueye broke radio silence, telling the controller in Arabic that they were about to land and confirming that the aircraft would be blown up on the ground. Cairo had already been informed from intercepted radio communications that the aircraft would probably be destroyed and they were anxious not to have their entire runway blocked. The controller asked that the 747 be stopped at the far end of the runway, and the hijacker obligingly agreed. The captain, however, had a different thought. Priddy and his colleagues had been isolated in the cockpit when the plan to blow up the aircraft had first been revealed to Ferruggio, and they had no idea of the hijacker's intentions. Captain Priddy knew, however, that the handling facilities at Cairo for a 747 would be non-existent. He felt that the best course of action would be to halt at a suitable turning point on the runway, manoeuvre without the aid of the towing truck, and taxy back to the terminal building.

On the final approach to land Captain Ali left the flight deck and returned to the forward cabin. He spoke to First Class Purser Augusta Schneider and casually asked her for a match. There was little she could do except hand him a box. Ali simply struck a light and ignited the fuze. The aircraft at this stage was still airborne and the lit fuze began to burn away time. The evacuation would have to be very quick indeed.

Captain Priddy landed safely in the darkness at 01:24, and as the aircraft rolled down the runway he began braking to stop at a suitable point.

'Go all the way to the end of the runway,' instructed the tower controller. Gueye also shouted at him to go all the way but Priddy butted in on the radio.

'I want to stop short enough that I have room to turn round.'

Priddy kept braking and stopped the aircraft. Gueye screamed at him to keep moving and the controller shouted over the radio to continue to the end. In the cabin, Service Director Ferruggio felt the aircraft come to a halt and, using a megaphone, he immediately ordered the evacuation. All doors flew open and the chutes deployed satisfactorily. Instantly the dead-heading flight crew, each holding a baby, slid to the ground, followed closely by the mothers and the other cabin occupants. The flight attendants were cool and efficient and the evacuation was orderly. It was just as well, for half the fuze time had already gone and only four minutes remained to detonation.

In the cockpit, Captain Priddy was still being shouted at

by both Gueye and the controller to continue further down the runway and, unaware of the circumstances, he opened up the thrust levers. Service Director Ferruggio was horrified to hear the noise of the engines and to feel the 747 begin to move while people rushed down the slides. He mounted the stairs to the upper deck two at a time and from half way up bellowed through the megaphone.

'For God's sake, stop. We're evacuating.'

Priddy jammed on the brakes and called for the emergency evacuation check list. Quickly the flight crew completed the checks, shutting down the engines and systems. Ferruggio rushed back below, the trip up and down the stairs taking only about thirty seconds, to find all the cabin occupants, including Ali and Diop, had gone. They had been evacuated in less than a minute and a half. The service director grabbed two blankets laden with shoes and threw them down the slide, then followed the bundles himself. When he hit the ground he joined the passengers running clear. By now the security forces were closing in on Ali and Diop who were mingling with the passengers and the two men opened fire. Ferruggio could hear the crackle of shots behind him as he ran and he feared that Gueye had shot the flight crew still sitting in the cockpit. Less than two minutes' fuze time remained.

On the flight deck, Captain Priddy and his colleagues, still very much alive, had completed their tasks and were ready for departure. Gueye still stood behind them, one eye on his watch, and he told the flight engineer, Dzuiba, to go. The two pilots rose at the same time but Gueye shouted at them.

'No, you two guys stay.'

Dzuiba left, and Priddy and Levix had no choice but to remain seated. The seconds ticked by on Gueye's watch. Were they going to be made to die with the hijacker?

'OK, go,' Gueye cried at last, 'and good luck.'

The two men rushed down the stairs leaving Gueye on his own. They quickly ran along the entire length of the 747 and back, Priddy down the right aisle and Levix down the left, to check that all the passengers had gone, but when they completed their search they found Purser Schneider still picking up shoes. Priddy shouted at her to get out and she jumped down the nearest chute while the two men slid from the left forward door. By now Gueye was in hot pursuit and he followed the two pilots to the ground. The security forces at the airport were returning the guerrillas' fire and a lot of shooting could be heard. Tracer bullets arced through the night, striking the side of the big jet. In the darkness the situation was very confusing. Priddy and Levix took to their heels and ran for their lives. Any second now the 747 would go up and they would need to be well clear to avoid injury. As the men were only twenty-two yds (twenty m) from the fuselage, still inside the wingspan of the aircraft and fleeing past the outboard engine, the bombs planted at the front of the big jet exploded. The entire cockpit area was blown to pieces and the pilots could feel the blast in their backs, but fortunately they escaped injury. The night sky was lit up with the eruption. Moments later an enormous blast occurred at the rear, and soon after the entire top section lifted off. In seconds the 747 was a burning inferno.

Somehow everyone managed to scramble clear and only minor injuries were sustained. When the captain reached an airport bus nearby he found passengers lying on the floor,

The charred remains of the brand new 747 on the runway at Cairo the following morning. (Captain Pat Levix)

staying low to avoid the gunfire. The Egyptian driver was frozen with terror. From too close a range the occupants caught glimpses of the 747 disintegrating, but the driver refused to move. Priddy quickly took over the driver's seat and drove the bus to safety. Captain Priddy's action was typical of his conduct throughout the hijack, for his behaviour had been outstanding. His calm voice over the PA and his reassuring manner in the cabin, much of the time with a pistol at his head, had sustained the passengers throughout the event and his coolness had brought them through safely. It took over an hour to round up all the passengers and crew but eventually each and every one was accounted for. The brand new aircraft, unfortunately, was totally destroyed and only part of the tail was left standing. The three guerrillas were arrested by the security forces and seven passengers were hospitalised, while the remainder were accommodated in the airport hotel. Later that day the runway was cleared and a Pan Am 707 was dispatched to Cairo from London to collect those people fit to travel and to speed them on their way. The hijack had been a harrowing ordeal for the passengers and crew of the 747 but at least they were now free from danger. The entire crew had behaved in an exemplary fashion and their efforts had undoubtedly saved many lives.

At Dawson's Field in northern Jordan, the hostages aboard the hijacked TWA 707 and Swissair DC-8 aircraft were still being held and faced the first of many a hot and uncomfortable day in the baking desert. That afternoon, about 100 women, children and elderly passengers were freed. In return for the safe release of the approximately 200 remaining detainees and the two airliners, the PFLP demanded the release of seven Palestinian captives: three guerrillas serving twelve-year sentences in Switzerland for a machine-gun and grenade attack in February of the previous year on an El Al aircraft at Zurich Airport, three terrorists from a rival group, the Action Organisation for the Liberation of Palestine, being detained in Bavarian jails in West Germany for a bomb attack in the same month on a bus load of El Al passengers at Munich Airport, and the lovely Leila Khaled, being held by the police in the UK.

A few days later, on 9 September, in order to press the British for the release of Khaled, a BOAC VC-10 was hijacked. The aircraft was flying en route from Bombay to London, via Bahrain and Beirut, and was commandeered as it departed Bahrain with 105 passengers and ten crew on board. The captain, Cyril Goulbourn, was forced to refuel at Beirut and was made to fly at gunpoint to the desert strip. The PFLP then held three aircraft at Dawson's Field and over 300 hostages. The airliners were surrounded by heavily armed PFLP commandos with anti-tank and anti-aircraft guns. Beyond the Palestinian positions, the Jordanian Army, helpless to interfere, ringed the defensive circle at a discreet distance with tanks and other armoured vehicles.

Representatives of the five nations involved, Britain, Israel, Switzerland, the United States and West Germany, met to discuss joint action and, with little bargaining power, moved to succumb to the PFLP demands. Hostages continued to be released in batches to join the women and children freed earlier until by 13 September only 56 people, mostly Israeli or dual American-Israeli nationals, were still held. On that day, amid negotiations for their release and return of the aircraft, the three airliners were blown up and totally destroyed. In retaliation the Israelis arrested 450 prominent Arabs as an assurance against the safety of their nationals. Two weeks later, by 29 September, negotiations were finalised and only six hostages remained. In Amman, battles flared between Palestinian commandos and the Jordanian Army and open war erupted. The next day, President Nasser died of a heart attack. By the end of the month all the hostages had returned home safely and on 1 October the seven terrorists held by Britain, Switzerland and West Germany were freed. Hundreds of detainees and prisoners were released by the Israelis. So ended the blackest period in the history of civil aviation.

# Chapter 7
# Ice Cool

Alaska lies to the north-west of Canada and is America's most northern state. Its vast area stretches from 130° west at the border with British Columbia to 173° east at the far end of the Aleutian Island chain. At the Bering Strait, lying between the USSR and the USA, only fifty-six miles (ninety kilometres) of ice separates the two antagonists. Alaska, in fact, was purchased from the Soviet Union in 1867 for $7.2 m, and to this day its sale must upset the Kremlin. The land is rich in minerals, and oil is a major industry. Fishing is prominent too, and there is also a strong military presence. The Distant Early Warning (DEW) radar line stretches from Alaska to north-eastern Canada and defends the North American continent from attack by Soviet missiles.

Alaska is a cold and mountainous land and the early pioneers who first trekked north in search of gold, and then of oil, were as rugged as the landscape they conquered. Alaska, however, is also a land of beauty, and the State boasts America's highest mountain, Mount McKinley, standing at 20,650 ft (6,194 m). The scenery, as well as the ice cold air, takes your breath away.

Anchorage, the State capital, lies on the shores of Cook Inlet, so named after Captain Cook, who anchored in its sheltered waters on his third voyage in 1778. Hence, also, the name of the town. In the pioneering days Anchorage was a tough and wild place, but today it is a modern and sophisticated city of 200,000 inhabitants. Situated at 61°N, just south of the Arctic Circle at 66½°N, which marks the extent of perpetual daylight in the northern summer and perpetual darkness in the northern winter, the days are long in the brief summer and short in the many months of winter. The weather is harsh, being cold and snowy for most of the year, with only a three-month respite from June to August.

Travel in the rough and extensive territory is mostly by air, with many of the excellent cross-State highways being impassable for months during the winter. Light aircraft in Alaska are used as much as automobiles elsewhere. Alaska Airlines connects the north-western State with 'outside' America while many small carriers ably operate within the region. One such local airline is Reeve Aleutian Airways (RAA) which, from its base in Anchorage, serves the 10,000 inhabitants of the Aleutian Island chain. The communities are remote and stretch from the southern shore of Alaska to Shemya Island, 1,500 nm away. RAA was started in 1932 by Bob Reeve at 'about the time that the aircraft was replacing the dog team'. Today the company is run by his son, Dick, who is owner and president of the airline. Reeve Aleutian operates nine aircraft, two Boeing 727-100s, four Electra L-188s and three Nihon YS-11s, and employs 240 staff. The 727 operations are limited to Cold Bay, which has a 10,500 ft (3,200 m) runway, constructed during World War Two, Adak, a US Navy base, and Shemya Island, a US Air Force Station at the end of the chain. The Electra and YS-11 turboprops fly the entire route network from King Salmon, near the mainland, through such places as Port Heiden and Dutch Harbor, to Shemya at the tip of the Aleutians.

Along the line of the islands, cold air from the frozen

A Reeve Aleutian Airways YS-11. (Reeve Aleutian)

Bering Sea to the north meets warm air from the Pacific currents to the south, and intense frontal activity results. Weather conditions are difficult and changeable with fog in the summer and storms in the winter, and operations are rarely planned for night: the environment in the daytime is enough to cope with. The Aleutian Island chain, however, hooks down as far south as 53°N and the temperature variation is not as bad as might be imagined. Winter temperature lows in the islands are of the order of −7°C and summer highs are around 13°C. In the moist atmosphere, however, the temperature range is ideal for icing and it is a major hazard to aircraft.

Most freight to the Aleutians is shipped by sea, but RAA carries a lot of mail and all the airline's aircraft are in a combined cargo/passenger arrangement with the cargo compartment at the front. At short notice the configuration can be changed, if required, to carry extra passengers. Load factors tend to be low but, surprisingly, Reeve Aleutian carries 50,000 passengers annually, with half that total being carried in the three months of summer. The Electra is the workhorse of the airline and seems to be ideally suited to the conditions and terrain, with the YS-11 giving useful support. Both can fly in weather and to airports unacceptable to the 727. The YS-11s are costly to run and maintain, and in the combi role have only 2.2 tons cargo capacity and eighteen seats available, but the airline owns them outright and can make a useful profit from their operation.

Weather conditions, especially in winter, are a major problem, and the long experience of the airline in flying in such harsh surroundings is of paramount importance. Stormy, violent and changeable weather, bad visibility, poor landing aids, gale force winds and icing in sub-zero temperatures all combine to form a working environment for Reeve Aleutian crews which is a tough one indeed. Fortunately the pilots are as robust as the machines they fly and as cool as the ice with which, in the long winter, they have to contend daily.

Early on the morning of 16 February 1982, a Nihon YS-11A, registered *N169RV*, was prepared to operate Reeve Aleutian Airways Flight 69 from Anchorage to Cold Bay, via

Map showing the Anchorage-King Salmon routeing.

King Salmon and Dutch Harbor. The aircraft had been in the hangar all the previous day and while there fuel had been drained from the fuel sumps to check for water. No contamination was found. At 06:00 local Alaskan time (now used throughout) on the day of departure the YS-11 was removed from the hangar and towed in the darkness to Gate 18 at the terminal. The sky was overcast at 1,200 ft (366 m) with five miles (eight kilometres) visibility in light snow, but fortunately the wind was light. The temperature indicated − 21°C. The wing fuel tanks were topped up with 900 gallons (4,090 litres) of Jet A fuel to give a total fuel load of 1,350 gallons (6,137 litres). Once again, following standard practice, the fuel sumps were drained for a further contamination check, but no water was detected. The examination was conducted with great care for any water remaining would quickly freeze in the very cold conditions and would block filters and disrupt the fuel flow.

*N169RV* was a sturdy, twin-engined turboprop powered by Rolls-Royce Dart 542 engines. The aircraft was the Japanese equivalent of the HS748 and had been manufactured in 1971. At just over ten years of age it had completed only 4,385 flying hours. The machine had been acquired by RAA two years previously and had given good and reliable service. Flight 69 was carrying little cargo and the seating area had been expanded to accommodate thirty-six passengers who were travelling on the route. By 07:45 all the cabin occupants were on board and the commander, Captain Thomas Hart, prepared for departure. Captain Hart was forty-five and had 13,500 flying hours to his credit, 4,200 of which were on the YS-11. He was a check captain with the company and was also qualified to fly the Electra, DC-3 and C-46 aircraft. His co-pilot was 34-year-old Roger Showers. First Officer (F/O) Showers had only just converted on to the YS-11 but he had flown 6,500 hours on other types. He was a qualified flight instructor, a certified mechanic, and was also rated to fly helicopters. In the cabin one flight attendant, Cecilia Allen, looked after the passengers. She was known to the crews as Ceecee and she had kept secret that she was pregnant and was about to leave the company.

As the door was closed the co-pilot copied the clearance. The take-off runway in use was 32 and Flight 69 was cleared for an Anchorage 4 departure: after take-off the YS-11 was to climb on runway heading till 400 ft (122 m) and then to turn left on to a track of 300° magnetic. On that course the aircraft would be issued headings on to the assigned low-level airway, Victor 456, which routed via Kenai, then southwest down the Aleutian Peninsula abeam Mount Iliamna and on to King Salmon on the Naknek River. The planned cruise altitude was 12,000 ft (3,660 m).

At 07:55, in the darkness with light snow failing, Flight 69 lifted off from runway 32 at an all-up-weight of 54,220 lb (24,594 kg); 8,800 lb (3,992 kg) of fuel was contained in the wings. About ten minutes after departure the YS-11 established on airway Victor 456, climbing to 12,000 ft towards Kenai. The outside air temperature began to drop rapidly and the crew had to keep an eye on the conditions. The potential problem in the cruise was not so much with airframe and propeller icing, for the air in the frozen north in winter is mainly free of moisture, but with the freezing of water droplets suspended in the fuel.

Checks of the fuel for free visible water had, of course, been conducted in the hangar, and after refuelling, but it was impossible, using such a method, to detect in the fuel dissolved water or water suspended as submicroscopic particles. Such dissolved or suspended water is usually present in jet fuel but its extremely small quantity does not affect normal combustion. When the fuel in the tanks is subjected to very cold temperatures at cruise altitude, however, it is a potential source of ice in the fuel system. Tiny ice crystals can form which can block fuel filters and the engines can stop with the disrupted fuel flow. To prevent fuel icing, therefore, fuel heating systems are installed on most aircraft.

On the YS-11 each engine is supplied with fuel from its respective wing tank. An engine-driven fuel pump first draws fuel from the tank via a fuel heater which is a fuel-air heat exchanger using hot compressed air bled straight from the engine compressor. The heated fuel is then fed through a filter and into a pump from where it is delivered at high pressure to the fuel control unit. The metered fuel is then directed to fuel nozzles in the combustion chambers. The

Captain Tom Hart.

fuel heater is controlled by a three-position switch on the flight deck, marked manual, off and auto. The normal setting for the switch is auto.

Any icing of the fuel filter results in a blockage which causes a difference in pressure between the inlet to the fuel heater and the outlet of the fuel filter. When the pressure differential reaches a certain limit a detector illuminates a warning light which is positioned by the fuel heat switch. With the switch selected to auto, compressor air is automatically bled from the engine and fed to the fuel heater. The fuel heat switch 'auto' position, therefore, is a safety setting designed to operate with inadvertent icing. With the switch in the manual position, compressor air is fed continuously to the fuel heater.

As the YS-11 climbed towards its cruising altitude a request was made to climb to 14,000 ft (4,270 m) and Anchorage control approved. Approaching 10,000 ft (3,050 m), however, passing over the Kenai VOR, the crew noted that the OAT was −25°C, lower than expected, and F/O Showers moved the fuel heater selector switches from auto to manual. Immediately a rise in the fuel temperatues was checked on the gauges as the fuel heaters began to operate. A few minutes later Flight 69 levelled in the cruise at 14,000 ft and, with the temperature now indicating −37°C, the fuel heaters remained on. A serious risk of fuel icing existed without their use. Some thin stratus cloud was encountered en route but no airframe icing was evident.

Flight 69's cruise towards King Salmon was routine, except for the very low temperatures, and by over halfway along the journey, abeam Mount Iliamna and the Iliamna Lakes, the OAT had dropped to −40°C. Later the temperature rose slightly to −38°C, but it was still well below normal for that altitude. F/O Showers established contact with King Salmon Approach at fifty miles (eighty kilometres) out and descent clearance was requested.

'Roger, Reeve 69,' radioed back approach, 'descend and maintain 7,000.'

After forty-five minutes in the cruise, at 08:50 and forty nm north-east of King Salmon, Captain Hart eased back the throttles to a reduced setting. The descent from 14,000 ft was commenced at a speed of 240 knots with constant engine power.

King Salmon Airport is used by both civilian and military traffic and the responsibilities are shared; the Federal Aviation Administration provides air traffic control personnel and the US Air Force supplies the fire and rescue services. There are two paved runways: 11/29 being the main runway at 8,500 ft (2,590 m) long and 18/36 the shorter at 5,000 ft (1,525 m). The airport lies almost at sea level and is bounded to the south and west by the meandering Naknek River which in winter freezes in parts to a depth of three feet (0.9 m). The weather in King Salmon was good and on the descent the crew copied the details from the automatic terminal information service (ATIS). The wind was 320° at ten knots and runway 29 was in use. Flight 69 was heading south-west and the aircraft would simply be able to position on a right base leg before turning right through 90° on to finals to land toward the north-west. The cloud cover was scattered at 5,000 ft and the visibility was a good fifty miles. The altimeter setting was 29.32 inches of mercury.

The crew set and checked their altimeters and approaching 7,000 ft (2,134 m) the captain advanced the throttles and held the aircraft level with the speed still steady at 240 knots. After one minute, Reeve Flight 69 was instructed to descend to 5,000 ft. Again Captain Hart eased back on the power and at the same speed slowly descended the YS-11 to 5,000 ft. The captain called for the descent and approach check lists and the drills were completed. Flight Attendant Allen reported that all the passengers were strapped in and that the cabin was ready for landing. Captain Hart set the power to 12,500 rpm and 850 lb (385 kg) per hour fuel flow, and began to decrease speed to 210 knots. The controller was slow in clearing the aircraft for further descent and the YS-11 was becoming a little high on the approach. The time was now just before 09:00 and the half-light of the northern winter day had dawned, but the visibility was very clear in the unpolluted atmosphere. As Flight 69 neared 5,000 ft the aircraft was positioned ten to fifteen miles (sixteen to twenty-four kilometres) to the north-east of King Salmon and the airport could be seen clearly ahead and to the right.

'Approach,' radioed Showers. We're just levelling 5,000 feet and we have the airport in sight.'

'Roger, Flight 69, you're cleared for right base for a visual approach to runway 29.'

The approach controller's instruction automatically cancelled the YS-11's flight plan and Captain Hart was now free to control his own progress. He could judge his own heights and speeds and could position the aircraft as he desired for approach and landing by visually sighting the airport. The YS-11 continued descent at 210 knots and at just after 09:00, as the aircraft passed 2,600 ft (792 m), five miles (eight kilometres) from touchdown, instructions were given to contact the tower.

'King Salmon Tower, Reeve 69,' called Showers, 'five miles right base for 29, been cleared for a visual.'

'69, King Salmon Tower, roger. Report turning final, runway 29.'

'69.'

'Three zero at one zero,' called back the tower, giving the wind velocity, but making a slip.

'Three zero at one zero?' questioned Captain Hart.

'Say again the last part of transmission,' radioed Showers.

'Roger, the wind at this time is three two zero at one zero, you are in sight and cleared to land runway 29.'

'Three two zero at one zero,' said F/O Showers to his captain, 'that was in the ATIS.'

'Thought he was giving us a squawk,' admitted Hart, referring to the four-figure code normally issued by radar controllers for setting on the transponder. 'He's not very clear today,' he continued, 'sounds like he's talking through a wet sock.'

'No, it's not very clear,' confirmed Showers.

The YS-11 was now two to three minutes from landing and, with the aircraft a bit high and fast for the short distance remaining, Captain Hart levelled off at 1,800 ft (549 m) and let the speed drop. The power setting was left constant but the speed fell to below 200 knots and continued to decrease. Height and speed would also be lost on the 90° right turn onto finals, so the situation did not pose a problem. Meanwhile, the co-pilot began to perform the before-landing check. The list would not be completed till the landing gear was down and locked but some items could be initiated by the co-pilot of his own volition. Once the gear was set he would read the check list in a challenge and response manner whereby he would call the items and both pilots would confirm the tasks accomplished. The sequence of the before-landing check list was as follows and, for visual approaches, was to be performed upon entering the traffic pattern and completed before turning onto final approach, except for the final flap settings.

| Item | Response |
| --- | --- |
| Landing gear | Down and three greens |
| High pressure (HP) fuel cocks | High stop withdrawal lock (HSWL) |
| Landing lights | On below 165 knots |
| Fuel trim | Set |
| Prop lights | 3 on and 3 off |
| Fuel heaters | Off |
| Flaps | Off |
| Water/methanol | On |
| Spill valves | Manual |

Most of the items such as the landing gear, landing lights and flaps, etc, would be set in the normal flow of events but at this stage the first officer could set the HP cock to HSWL and could switch off the fuel heaters. The 'high stop' referred to in the second item above is a mechanical propeller pitch stop which is a safety device engaged during take-off and cruise. The propellers are variable pitch and if, for example, an engine fails at take-off, the stop prevents the windmilling propeller blades from decreasing to a flat pitch, i.e. from turning flat to the airflow, and so creating enormous drag. If such an incident happened during take-off or in the cruise, control of the aircraft could be lost, and the stop is designed to prevent its occurrence. The stop is removed during the before-landing check to permit finer pitch angles for landing and is accomplished by moving the HP cock to the high stop withdrawal lock. Two blue lights then illuminate to confirm the high stops have been removed.

Another selection for the HP cock is the 'feather' position and is used with an engine failure to reduce the windmilling propeller drag to a minimum. The HP cock is first selected to 'feather' to cut off the fuel to the engine and this is followed by the pressing of a 'feather' button. The propeller blades are then hydraulically driven in line with the fore and aft axis of the aircraft to allow the blades to cut through the air like a knife, reducing drag to a minimum.

The selection of fuel heat to off as part of the before-landing check is also a precautionary measure. As mentioned previously, hot air is bled directly from the engine com-pressors to feed the fuel heaters, and extracting air in this manner causes a reduction in engine power. At the full power setting, for example, power is reduced by four per cent when compressor air is bled for fuel heat. For maximum power availability in the event of a go-around, therefore, the fuel heaters are turned off during the approach to land.

With the HP cock selected to the high stop withdrawal lock and the fuel heaters switched off, Showers routinely scanned the engine instruments. The aircraft was now two minutes from landing; the first officer had performed the drills properly and the two pilots had complied correctly with procedures. Unknown to the crew, however, the fuel in the tanks, in spite of stringent checks, had been contaminated with more than the usual minute quantities of water. The amount would probably have remained unnoticed in normal circumstances but, operating the YS-11 in such extreme temperatures, fuel freezing problems were likely, even though the water content was very small and the fuel heaters were switched off at a very late stage. During the flight, with temperatures down to −40°C, the fuel in the wing tanks would have been very cold because of the long exposure to such icy air. As long as fuel heat was supplied any ice crystals in the system were melted and easily passed through to the engine as liquid. The fuel heater on this occasion, however, only raised the temperature of the fuel entering the system to slightly above freezing. As soon as the fuel heaters were turned off, the microscopic water droplets suspended in the cold fuel began to freeze. Ice crystals began to form in the small orifices and screens in the fuel control units and pumps, and began to impregnate the fuel filters and to restrict the fuel flow.

'Barrier one,' called the tower controller to another aircraft, 'what's your position now . . . ah, I've got you in sight. Remain clear of runway one one and two nine, landing traffic a YS-11 on right base.'

After a few seconds 'tower' informed both flights that men were working near the runway.

'Barrier one and Reeve 69, there will be men and equipment on the departure end of the runway on the left side. They are clear and outside the lights.'

First Officer Showers ignored the radio call for, as the controller spoke, he could see that there was a problem with the right-hand, number two, engine. The torque pressure indicator was dropping, as was the fuel flow. Approaching 09:02, with the height just under 1,800 ft (550 m) and the speed dropping below 190 knots, Captain Hart felt the aircraft yaw as power dropped on number two engine and the nose swung to the right. He pushed on the left rudder to hold the machine straight.

'We've lost one!' shouted Showers.

The number two fuel flow was well below 500 lb (227 kg) per hour when it should have been 850 lb (385 kg) per hour.

'Fuel flow . . . ' he called, pointing to the gauge.

The number two torque pressure was also down, indicating forty lb per square inch (psi) (2.8 kg/cm²) instead of the 100 psi (7 kg/cm²) it should have read with the throttle position at 12,500 rpm.

'Torque's very down.'

The captain advanced the number two throttle but there was no response. It was obvious the engine had failed. He turned on both relight switches and pushed the throttle forward once more, but to no avail. With the little extra height and speed in hand the YS-11 was, fortunately, in a good position for a single-engine approach and landing. The captain felt it was better to eliminate the drag from the right engine, thereby easing the control difficulties, rather than continue attempts to restart it, and he decided to shut the engine down.

'Okay, feather the . . . ' called Hart.

Showers selected the number two HP cock to 'feather' and pressed the 'feather' button. Fuel was cut to the engine and as it ran to a stop the propeller blades moved to the feather position.

'Feathered?' questioned the captain.

'It's feathered.'

Neither of the fuel filter differential pressure warning lights, which would have indicated a filter blockage, illuminated, nor did the low fuel pressure warning lights. Since the crew had complied properly with procedures the two pilots did not at first associate the engine failure with icing.

Feathering of the number two engine was completed as the speed dropped below 170 knots and under the circumstances the YS-11 seemed safe. The aircraft was still on base leg at just below 1,800 ft and as the speed dropped to 165 knots the captain continued the descent.

'Tell 'em we've got one shut down,' said Hart, 'and would like the fire trucks out.'

'And, ah, Anchorage King Salmon, Reeve 69,' radioed Showers, 'ah, get the fire trucks out. We've lost one engine on . . . we're turning final at this time.'

At this stage the flaps were selected to the approach flap setting and, with the YS-11 still a little high, Hart called for the landing gear to be lowered. As the wheels dropped he advanced the number one throttle to increase power on the left engine to stabilise the approach. Suddenly popping sounds could be heard from the number one engine and a smell of smoke could be detected on the flight deck.

' . . . . it!' exclaimed the captain, 'we're losing the other one.'

Fuel icing was also affecting the left engine but in a different manner. As the throttle was moved forward, ice crystals in the fuel control servo system caused large fluctuation in the fuel flow. Blocked orifices or screens in the system were preventing the fuel pump output from matching the throttle position and too much fuel was flowing into the engine. Excessive fuel was being admitted to the combustion chambers and an intense rise in heat was occurring without a corresponding increase in the propeller rpm to drive air through the engine for cooling. The insufficient cooling airflow was causing a severe over-temperature condition in the turbine and the engine was literally burning itself out.

The number one engine power began to drop as the popping sounds continued and the smell of smoke on the flight deck increased. The engine fire was close to the air conditioning duct for the cabin and fumes were being drawn into the aircraft. No engine fire warning was given. Immediately Captain Hart began the right turn to line up on the runway. At 1,200 ft (366 m) his height and position seemed good for a safe landing but the rate of descent increased rapidly and as a precaution the captain brought the flaps up.

'Say your fuel aboard and persons,' requested tower.

The controller was obviously trying to obtain the information for the emergency services but Showers was too busy to respond. As the wheels fell into place and were checked locked the co-pilot confirmed their condition.

'Gear down and three greens,' he called to his captain.

The number one engine now began to surge and the power dropped and then increased at random. With the number two engine shut down and the landing gear lowered the rate of descent increased dramatically.

'Okay,' said the captain, 'tell the girl in the back we've got a problem.'

Showers pressed the call button to the intercom in the cabin.

'Hello,' replied Flight Attendant Allen.

'Yeah,' said Showers, 'we've got a little problem here. We've shut down one engine and we're losing the other one. Prepare the passengers for an emergency landing and evacuation.'

Cecilia Allen went about her duties and as she did so the tower controller radioed with permission to land.

'Reeve 69, cleared to land runway two niner. The ah, emergency equipment has been advised.'

'69, roger.'

'Get the other one going,' said the captain to his co-pilot.

The number one engine continued to pop and surge and the YS-11 was losing height rapidly. Large fluctuations were noticed in the left engine fuel flow, approximately centered around 1,000 lb (454 kg) per hour, and at drops in the power the captain could feel the aircraft yaw to the left. The number one engine power now began to fade and there was a danger they might not reach the runway.

'Get the other engine going,' urged the captain. 'Get it going.'

The first officer had already moved the number two engine HP cock lever forward to the start position and he was in the process of pushing the 'feather' button to unfeather the engine. They were quickly running out of time but the number two engine resolutely refused to start. With both props now unfeathered and the landing gear lowered the drag on the aircraft was enormous. Rapidly the YS-11 dropped towards the ground.

'We'e not going to make it,' stated the captain simply, 'we're not going to make it.'

Keeping a cool head and thinking quickly, Captain Hart turned the aircraft 90° to the left and headed south-west towards the Naknek River. There was no time now to do anything except land on the frozen surface. That, however, was going to be easier said than done, for not all the river was frozen. At the sharp bend in the river to the south of the airport the stream slowed sufficiently for the river to freeze to a depth of about three ft (0.9 m) in the extreme temperatures. About one mile (1.6 kilometres) up and down stream from this point, however, the water was still unfrozen and only one week earlier, in warmer conditions, a water channel had been open along the length of the river. Captain Hart aimed for the two-mile (3.2 kilometres) stretch of ice.

'69 has lost both engines,' radioed F/O Showers, 'on final here to the river.'

'69, roger,' replied the controller, as he watched the stricken aircraft dive to the south of the airport. Immediately he alerted the fire and rescue services and directed them toward the Naknek River.

Captain Hart aligned the YS-11 with the banks of the ice-covered river and, with the speed about 120 knots, prepared for a rough landing.

'You want the gear up?' asked the co-pilot.

If a wheel caught in a rut on the ice it could tear off the undercarriage, but the smooth belly of the aircraft would glide easily over the frozen surface. There was also another consideration: the ice in the centre of the river was clear and appeared green in texture as the water could be seen flowing below the surface. It did not look to either pilot as if the ice would hold but there was nowhere else to go. If the surface gave way it would be better to land with the gear retracted rather than have an undercarriage leg smash through the ice.

'Yeah, put it up,' said Hart.

The first officer selected the landing gear lever to the up position but the retraction was slow because the hydraulic pumps were not operating fully with the engines windmilling. At the same time the captain selected both HP cocks to 'feather.' The right prop feathered immediately but the left side was slow to respond and Hart had a great deal of difficulty in controlling the machine. Both hands were needed to fly the aircraft. As the YS-11 rapidly approached the icy surface, the ground proximity warning system sounded its alarm.

'Pull up, pull up, pull up . . .'

Captain Hart wrestled to level the wings but he was unable to raise the left wingtip. With great skill he managed to pull the powerless machine out of the dive but just before landing the left aileron struck the ice. Fortunately little damage was caused. A moment later, with the gear still retracting, Hart touched down on the frozen river as gently as possible. The belly of the aircraft gradually settled onto the surface as the wheels retracted completely and the aircraft began to slide across the ice. Both props were now in the feathered position but with the right side stopped and the left one still turning. Immediately the prop blades on both sides dug into the ice and slashed the surface. The aircraft bumped across the ice, which was remarkably smooth, and banging and scraping sounds could be heard in the cabin. The nose gear doors were crushed, the fuselage belly skin was buckled in a number of places, but fortunately did not rip from the airframe, and the rotating safety beacon and several antennas were broken and bent. The YS-11 continued to slide and rumble over the ice. Captain Hart, still concerned that the ice might give away, applied right rudder and steered the aircraft towards a sand bank on the north side. Slowly the machine curved in an arc to the right. Suddenly, a red warning light illuminated and a bell rang indicating a fire in number one engine.

'We got a fire,' called the captain.

The required drill was to place the HP cock to the 'feather' position to cut off fuel at the control unit and to pull the fuel shut-off 'T' handle to cut off fuel at the engine, as well as to isolate the services. The fuel cocks were already in the 'feather' position so it was simply a matter of pulling the 'T' handle and pressing the button.

'Pull 'em both?' asked Showers.

The captain nodded and the first officer pulled the fuel shut off handles.

'Gang bar, fire bottles,' said Hart.

Showers pushed up the electrical gang bar and shut off the aircraft electrics.

'Fire bottles,' repeated the captain as the aircraft continued to bump over the ice.

The first officer pressed both fire buttons and discharged the extinguishant from the bottles into the engines.

As the YS-11 skidded over the frozen river it continued in a gentle curve to the right. After sliding for about half a mile (800 metres) it eventually came to an abrupt stop facing towards the west with the left wingtip resting on the surface. The aircraft still weighed in excess of twenty tons and, in spite of the three feet of frozen water covering the river, the ice began to crack as it settled. Immediately, Captain Hart ordered an emergency evacuation. The number one engine was still burning in spite of their efforts and, with the possibility of ruptured fuel tanks, there was a serious risk of fire. Showers quickly left his seat while the captain remained to secure the flight deck. The co-pilot ran to the back of the cabin and assisted Flight Attendant Allen in evacuating passengers via the aft cabin door on the right side.

In the cockpit Captain Hart completed his tasks then quickly radioed King Salmon tower with news of their predicament.

'Hey, this is Reeve 69,' called Hart. 'We're down on the ice, nobody's hurt, we're still on fire over here, though. And, ah, we had a fire in the air and lost power on the engines and couldn't get to the end of the runway. We had to make a quick left turn here but we're still on fire.'

Unknown to Captain Hart, help was already on the way and the fire trucks were speeding to the scene. Hart rapidly left the flight deck and went back to the cabin where he found some passengers struggling to open the right over-wing exit. Flames could be seen on the left side through the passenger windows and smoke was entering the cabin. It was imperative to get the people out quickly. The captain swiftly released the catch of the over-wing exit, pulled the handle, and threw the door out of the opening. He then assisted the passengers in evacuating by that escape route. In a matter of moments all thirty-six passengers and three crew were out of the aircraft and standing safely on the ice. Only one passenger received a minor knee injury while fleeing from the aircraft. Almost immediately the fire trucks also appeared on the scene and the fire in the number one engine was quickly extinguished. Fortunately the frozen surface, in spite of the cracking, held the additional weight. In due course transport arrived to take the passengers and crew to the terminal building, but not before some people suffered frostbite in the severe temperature.

A rescue operation was mounted to save the YS-11 and stakes were driven into the frozen river to secure the aircraft to prevent its movement on the shifting ice. Air bags were

The YS-11 back on its feet. Note the smooth surface of the ice.
(Reeve Aleutian)

The YS-11 being towed up the river bank on the specially constructed ice ramp. (Reeve Aleutian)

then placed below the wings and nose and inflated in turn to raise the machine to a sufficient height for the lowering of the landing gear. The YS-11 was then towed three miles (4.8 km) across the ice and was hauled from the frozen surface up a specially constructed ice ramp on to the river bank. From there it was moved to the airport for repair. The entire rescue operation took five days and was only just completed in time, for the next day the ice river melted. Two weeks later, YS-11 *N169RV* flew out of King Salmon Airport; an engineering feat almost as remarkable as the landing on the ice. The cause of the water contamination in the fuel was never discovered.

The incident had developed very quickly and a normal approach had swiftly developed into a potentially disastrous situation. Keeping cool heads, Captain Hart and First Officer Showers had reacted calmly and efficiently to the emergency and the captain's quick thinking and great skill had saved his passengers and aircraft from an almost certain catastrophe. Both pilots received Superior Airmanship Awards from the American Airline Pilots' Association.

# Chapter 8
# Roll Out the Barrel

Aircraft manufacture is a highly refined engineering art and modern jets are built to be extremely robust. The strength of contemporary airframes lies in their monocoque structure, whereby the skin takes much of the load although supported by a reinforcing frame. The central section of the aircraft is the strongest part with the form of the machine being more or less built around it; at this location the wings are attached and the landing gear fitted so the region is subjected to all flight and ground loads.

During normal operational flying aircraft are exposed to a variety of stresses: extremes of weather, large temperature changes — from +40°C on the ground to −70°C in the air — cabin pressurisation, wing flexing, landing and take-off loads and engine vibration. The aluminium-copper alloys mostly used in aircraft construction are light and flexible yet strong enough to cope with such conditions. Heavy landings, violent weather or severe turbulence can also be handled by modern jets with safety, although airframe checks may subsequently be required. Normal maximum manoeuvring loads in flight for modern jets are +2.5g to −1.0G, where 'g' is the force of gravity and negative 'g' the impression of weightlessness.

On completion of a new aircraft design, a full test programme is implemented, with an airframe being tested to destruction in a test rig. The wings are bent upwards by large jacks to test strength, and to witness the wingtips almost touching before failure occurs would dispel any fear of flying. On occasions, admittedly inadvertently, aircraft are put to the test in earnest during flight. Fortunately, in the few incidents recorded, the airliners involved have survived and the events have borne witness to the impressive

strength of modern machines. One such incident occurred to
a Boeing 747 SP (special performance) on 18 February 1985.

China Airlines Flight 006 was en route from Taipei, the
capital of Taiwan, to Los Angeles, California, with the
aircraft under the command of Captain Ming Yuan Ho. The
B747 SP was shorter than the standard 747 model and was
specifically constructed for such long-range flights, being
designed to fly at high altitudes to conserve fuel. At just after
10:00 local time, Flight 006 was cruising at 41,000 ft (12,500 m)
over the Pacific, with the aircraft lying 300 nm north-west of
San Francisco. One and a half hours flying time remained to
Los Angeles. The journey so far had been routine and the
254 passengers had just finished breakfast. Extra crew
members were carried for the long duty day, and the five
flight deck members and fifteen flight attendants brought
the total on board to 274.

In the rarefied atmosphere at 41,000 ft and at a weight of
245 tons, the 747 SP's margin between the maximum and
minimum flying speeds was narrow, and could have been as
small as thirty knots. At too fast speeds, high speed
buffeting caused by shock waves on the wings occurs and
the aircraft can be damaged. At too slow speeds, low speed
buffeting caused by turbulent airflow over the wings occurs
and lift is lost from the wings. If the speed is allowed to

China Airlines 747. (John Stroud)

decay further the wings can stall and the aircraft can drop from the sky.

The China Airlines 747's autopilot was engaged and the autothrottle of the Performance Management System (PMS) was selected to control the speed at Mach 0.85 (i.e. 85 per cent of the speed of sound at that level). Flying conditions in the daylight were clear, with cloud 10,000 ft (3,050 m) below covering the ocean, but the changeable wind was causing turbulence and was upsetting the delicate balance of the flight. The speed fluctuated from Mach 0.84 to Mach 0.88 and the autothrottle moved in response in an attempt to stabilise the speed. Suddenly, as the thrust levers retarded automatically to flight idle to reduce excessive speed, number four engine suffered a problem. On achievement of the desired speed numbers one, two and three engines increased to the required setting, but number four engine

Flight 006's spiral dive.

failed to respond. It remained in what is known as a 'hung condition'.

Before flight, Captain Ming had noted from the technical log that number four engine had a history of ceasing combustion, or flaming out, when decelerating. In the turbulent conditions, with the autothrottle advancing and retarding the thrust levers in an attempt to hold speed, the number four engine had required special attention. If engine flame-out occurred, there would be insufficient power from the remaining engines to maintain speed in the rarefied atmosphere and the delicate balance of the flight would be impaired. Captain Ming would have no choice but to descend into the more dense air at a lower level.

The flight engineer attempted to restore power to number four engine but his efforts failed and ninety seconds later the engine flamed out. The speed began to decay and the aircraft yawed and rolled to the right. With no automatic rudder, the autopilot applied full left aileron to compensate for asymmetric thrust. Captain Ming disengaged the PMS and the height lock and eased the nose down in descent using the autopilot control wheel. The actions of the captain, however, were insufficient to contain the situation and when Ming disengaged the autopilot to revert to manual control he, and the other 273 occupants aboard Flight 006, received the shock of their lives. Instantly the control wheel snapped to the central position and the aircraft bank increased abruptly 63° to the right, with the speed dropping to Mach 0.75. The big jet began a steep dive towards the ground. Flight 006's nose pitched down to 67° and the aircraft rolled on its back to a bank angle of 160°. The 747 plummetted earthwards at 15,000 ft (4,570 m) per minute and entered the cloud layer which lay below. The crew were caught completely by surprise and in seconds were totally disorientated.

In the cabin all hell broke loose. 'Dishes crashed against the walls and floors,' recounted William Peacock, a Vietnam veteran and colonel in the Marine Corps Reserve. 'Baggage compartments opened up and window shades were forced down by vibration.' 'You could feel bits popping off,' commented another passenger. Those people not in their seats were thrown about the cabin and fifty passengers received minor injuries. Two flight attendants suffered serious back damage. The aircraft continued its spiralling plunge, screaming almost vertically towards the earth as it dropped at three miles per minute. As the 747 spun through the cloud the airframe and wings were subjected to five g, five times the force of gravity and twice the structure's design limit. The aircraft shook violently and the vibrations caused large portions of the horizontal stabiliser to break off. Both outboard elevator sections detached, the auxiliary power unit broke free and the right wingtip high frequency radio antenna separated. By rights the aircraft should have broken apart completely, but somehow the machine held together.

Captain Ming tried desperately to regain control but, with no visual reference and pinned to his seat with the 'g' forces, he faced a difficult task. There seemed little chance of recovery as the aircraft shuddered in a steep diving turn when, to complicate matters, the landing gear suddenly deployed. The powerful uplatches locking the undercarriage in the bays had released under the excessive 'g' forces and the landing gear had fallen down into place. The two body landing gear doors were ripped from their hinges and flew off into space. The lowered undercarriage, however, had an unexpectedly beneficial effect as the wheels biting into the airflow seemed to stabilise the aircraft. This gave Captain Ming the chance he needed and by an extraordinary effort he righted the falling machine. Passing 11,000 ft (3,350 m), with only forty seconds to go before the 747 plunged into the sea, he managed to pull the aircraft out of the dive. The three good engines were still functioning and the captain applied power. As Ming regained control, Flight 006 broke from the cloud and the aircraft was levelled off at 9,500 ft (2,895 m). Flying in the clear conditions, the crew were able to regain their composure and to take stock of the situation. Quickly Captain Ming spoke to the passengers and in a 'pretty shaky' voice instructed the cabin occupants to fasten their seat belts.

The captain made the decision to land as soon as possible to inspect the damage and Flight 006 was cleared to divert to San Francisco, the nearest suitable airport. Ming climbed the aircraft back to 27,000 ft (8,230 m) and one hour later, without further incident, the 747 commenced its final approach. Fortunately the crew were able to lock the landing gear down and to obtain a safe display on the indicators. Flight 006 landed safely and on touchdown Captain Ming and his crew received a spontaneous round of applause.

Mystery surrounded the incident for some months until a subsequent inquiry verified the facts. It was concluded that

Computer-animated sequence of the 747's spiral dive. (NTSB)

the actions of the captain when dealing with the engine failure in the delicate circumstances of the high altitude cruise had been on the tardy side. As a result the autopilot inputs required to maintain control had been excessive. When Ming disconnected the autopilot he was caught completely off guard by the out-of-balance forces, and the machine had spun from his grasp. In defence of the captain, the International Federation of Airline Pilots (IFALPA) stated that too often on long distance flights aircraft commanders are compelled to fly at very high altitudes to lower fuel consumption in order to complete their journeys. Captain Ming had also done a fine job in regaining control of the stricken aircraft, albeit with some luck from the falling landing gear, and he deserved his applause on landing. The passengers, perhaps, should also have clapped the Boeing Aircraft Company, for the 747 was the real hero of the event. The aircraft was subjected to probably the greatest 'g' forces sustained by any wide-bodied civilian airliner, and survived. No clearer demonstration of the strength of modern aircraft could have been presented and the successful outcome was a fine testament to the skill of the aircraft designers.

Unfortunately the gross jet upset suffered by the China Airlines Boeing 747 was not the only such event recorded in aviation history in the last decade. In 1979, another Boeing machine, in this case a 727, was involved in a similar upset. The mystery surrounding that incident was never properly resolved and to this day the repercussions of the episode still affect those involved.

On 4 April 1979, TWA Flight 841, a Boeing 727-100, registered *N840TW*, prepared for departure from John F. Kennedy (JFK), New York, for a scheduled service to Minneapolis/St Paul International Airport in Minnesota. In command of the aircraft was Captain Harvey 'Hoot' Gibson. His co-pilot was First Officer Jess Kennedy and at the flight engineers' station was Second Officer Gary Banks. The crew was a very experienced trio with Captain Gibson having amassed a grand total of 15,710 flying hours at the relatively young age of forty-four. He had learned to fly at only thirteen years of age and after a period serving as an air traffic controller in Chicago had joined TWA in 1963. Gibson was not only qualified to fly the 727 but also had his licence endorsed to fly the DC-9, L1011 Tristar and the Boeing 747. He was one of aviation's 'all-rounders' and he flew helicopters and piloted balloons as well. Captain Gibson had not flown the B727 regularly for some time, however, for he had been operating as co-pilot on the B747 for just over one year. In December 1978 he had broken his ankle and the injury had kept him off work for three months. He had only just returned to his duties as captain on the B727 three weeks earlier and had completed ground school refresher, simulator and aircraft handling details. On 28 March he successfully completed a route flight check of over five hours' duration.

First Officer Kennedy was forty years of age and had joined TWA in 1967. He had operated as a flight engineer for eight years and in 1978 had transferred to the right-hand seat as co-pilot. He had a total of 10,336 flying hours, of which an impressive 8,348 hours had been acquired on the B727. Second Officer Banks was thirty-seven and had operated as a flight engineer for nine years. He was also a qualified commercial pilot. In the cabin were four flight attendants providing for the eighty-two passengers, bringing the total on board to eighty-nine.

The trip for the flight crew began in Los Angeles, California, the day before, on 3 April, and it was Captain Gibson's first time in command without supervision after his spell as first officer on the 747 and his sick leave. Duty had commenced at about 08:30 local time (11:30 Eastern Standard Time, now used throughout) and after a series of short sectors had terminated in Colombus, Ohio, at 22:00. After a night's rest the crew had recommenced duty the following day, Wednesday 4 April, at 13:45, and in the afternoon had operated Flight 841 via Philadelphia, Pennsylvania to JFK, New York. The B727 had arrived at Kennedy in the evening at 17:20. With only eighty-two passengers scheduled for the next sector to Minneapolis/St Paul, a comfortable turn-round should have been accomplished, but it was not to be. New York in the 1970s suffered from a surfeit of aircraft movements, and the mid-week traffic congestion was causing extensive delays.

Night fell as Flight 841 prepared for departure, and while

waiting for take-off a score of anti-collision lights could be seen twinkling ahead in the darkness. After forty-five minutes of taxying, three quarters of a ton of fuel had been consumed from the sixteen-ton load on board, even with one engine shut down to conserve fuel. Finally the B727 was given clearance for take-off, and at 20:25 Flight 841, weighing sixty-five tons, lifted off from JFK. The aircraft climbed steadily in the blackness to its planned cruising height of 35,000 ft (10,670 m) and twenty-nine minutes later, at 20:54, levelled in the cruise. The cockpit crew settled down to their usual routine and all was normal except for an exceptionally strong headwind.

The scheduled flight time for the 900 nm journey was just over two hours, but the very high winds being encountered slowed their progress. The ground speed was down to about 380 knots and at this rate the flight time would be nearer two-and-a-half hours. The B727 would be further delayed and additional fuel would be consumed from the load already eroded by the waiting time at Kennedy. Captain Gibson hoped the winds might slacken later in the flight and in the meantime the crew ate their evening meal.

Flight 841's routeing crossed the border into Canada over the northern end of Lake Erie, then passed over London, Ontario, before re-entering the States over Michigan. About one hour after departure the 727 entered Canadian airspace and First Officer Kennedy established contact with Toronto Control. Captain Gibson was still concerned about the very strong headwind which blew in excess of 100 knots and, with the aircraft now light enough to climb, he felt it might be prudent to change altitude. The decision, however, was not taken lightly. The 727-100 was not considered by pilots to be a comfortable aircraft to fly at such a high altitude, but it was felt the slacker winds expected at the upper level would make the climb worthwhile.

'Toronto Centre,' radioed Kennedy, 'have you any reports of winds from flights at other levels?'

'Negative,' replied Toronto, 'no reports.'

'We're encountering headwinds in excess of 100 knots and we'd like to climb to 390.'

'Roger, TWA 841, climb and maintain level 390.'

Captain Gibson disengaged the autopilot and initiated a manual cruise climb, gradually ascending the aircraft to the upper level. At 21:38, 39,000 ft (11,890 m) was achieved, and the autopilot and altitude hold were reselected. Second Officer Banks adjusted the thrust levers to maintain Mach 0.81. The winds at the new level were down to 85 knots, which helped improve the ground speed, and the fuel consumption was better. The outside air temperature indicated −57°C. The flight engineer estimated that about six-and-a-half tons of fuel had been used and at 21:40 he noted the aircraft weight of fifty-eight-and-a-half tons in the flight data log. The night was clear with cloud cover far below and a half moon shone about 50° above the horizon. The ride was smooth and the climb to 39,000 ft seemed justified. First Officer Kennedy set about recalculating the aircraft's ground speed and adjusting the leg times in the flight log while the captain monitored progress.

Flight 841 crossed the Canadian/US border into Michigan state and continued north-west between the city of Detroit to the south and Lake Huron to the north. The city of Saginaw, situated just south of Saginaw Bay, lay ahead. The sky was clear and bright, almost like daylight with the brilliant, near-full moon, and a thin but solid overcast lay directly below at 35,000 ft (10,670 m). Captain Gibson began sorting his charts for the onward route and he turned briefly to his left to extract fresh maps from his flight bag which lay by his left side on the cockpit floor. The time was 21:47. As his attention was momentarily distracted he suddenly felt a strange buzzing sensation. Within seconds the buzzing increased to a light buffet and he could feel the effect through the airframe.

Quickly Gibson looked at the instruments and checked his visual reference in the clear night. The aircraft wings were level but the autopilot had turned the control wheel 20°-30° to the left. The situation seemed very strange indeed. The other two on the flight deck were still busy with their calculations and at first had not noticed the development. Captain Gibson disconnected the autopilot and maintained the wings level by holding the control wheel to the left. Suddenly, the aircraft yawed sharply to the right, followed

TWA Boeing 727. (John Stroud)

by another severe right yaw. All on the flight deck were surprised by the manoeuvre. The second yaw continued with the aircraft rolling and skidding in a turn to the right. The nose dropped swiftly and a rapid roll to the right developed. The captain gradually pulled back on the control column to the limit with a slight backwards pressure and applied full left aileron. Neither input was sufficient to halt the manoeuvre. As the aircraft banked through 30°-45° to the right, Gibson applied full left rudder. For a moment the roll rate slowed, then the rapid right roll continued. The sky was crystal clear in the bright moonlight and, with the situation deteriorating so swiftly, all control inputs and decisions were made with reference to the visual horizon. Gibson managed a last glimpse of the artificial horizon as the machine banked through 45°-60° to the right and felt the aircraft was about to turn over. In a desperate effort to save the situation he took his right hand from the control column and quickly retarded the thrust levers to flight idle. His efforts, unfortunately, were to no avail. The aircraft continued to roll rapidly in a right diving turn, with the nose dropping sharply, and there seemed nothing the captain could do.

'We're going over,' he shouted.

The 727 flipped over on its back and, with the nose below the horizon, plunged earthwards close to the city of Saginaw. The engines hiccuped with the disturbed airflow and two quick, loud bangs of the compressors stalling could be heard in the cabin. For less than a second a feeling of absolute terror gripped Captain Gibson and then, strangely, a near calm returned almost as quickly. It was as if he knew that in spite of any recovery attempt his efforts would not be sufficient and that it was all over. Suddenly he felt relatively cool and his mind was clear. The rapid roll rate continued and by the end of the first roll, as the wings passed through level again for the first time, the nose had dropped 30°-40° below the horizon.

'Get them up,' shouted Gibson, referring to the speed brakes.

Kennedy did not understand the command so the captain pulled the speed brake lever himself. The operation seemed to have no effect so he recycled the speed brakes to check the function. The fast roll rate continued unabated and by only one-and-a-half rolls the nose was pointing near vertically downwards towards the cloud layer below. What had begun as a barrel roll had quickly developed into a vertical, scream-ing dive. The aircraft was now pulling 3.5g or more (727s are stressed to +2.5g or −1.0g) so the machine was already being strained beyond design limit. The 727 continued to race earthwards almost vertically with the wings rotating at about 50° per second. Gibson fought desperately to regain control. As the aircraft broke through the cloud layer at 35,000 ft (10,670 m) the captain could see, framed in his windscreen, the ground spinning directly below. It was not a panoramic sweep of the horizon as experienced in a flat spin in a light aircraft, but a vertical, rotating dive. Gibson could see a large dark patch, possibly a forest or lake, and one large city and three small cities spinning before his eyes.

The 727 plunged towards the ground at an average descent speed of 46,000 ft (14,020 m) per minute, with the rate of descent at moments reaching 76,000 ft (23,165 m) per minute. At such speed the aircraft broke the sound barrier and sonic booms could be heard clearly on the ground. On board, the noise level was painful to the ears. Still the 727 raced downwards in the darkness, rolling continuously, and the aircraft buffeted and shook with the fast speed. The artificial horizon which, in level flight, normally showed the top half sky blue and the bottom half earth black, displayed only a solid black. By 30,000 ft (9,145 m), the airspeed indicated about 450 knots on the instruments and the altimeters ran down so quickly the numbers were blurred and were difficult to read. The situation appeared hopeless and all Captain Gibson's efforts seemed of no effect. Still the machine dived and rolled inexorably towards its destruction. The spinning 727 still subjected the airframe to an increasing gravity force and in the cabin passengers were pinned to their seats. Those people standing at the beginning of the manoeuvre were forced to the floor. No one could move and fortunately only minor injuries were sustained. Many passengers found difficulty in breathing and some passed out for a few seconds under the strain.

On the flight deck Gibson watched the airspeed race past the limit and reach 470 knots in the dive. The captain estimated the aircraft to be descending through 20,000 ft (6,095 m), still out of control after about five to six rolls, and drastic action was needed. Quickly he called for extension of the landing gear. It was not permitted to raise or lower the undercarriage above 270 knots because of risk of damage to the gear doors, but in this situation that was hardly a consideration. Kennedy immediately selected the lever to the down position and the crew heard what sounded like an explosion as the landing gear dropped into the excessive airflow. The noise was unbelievable and for a moment Gibson thought the wings had separated. Both main landing gear doors and operating mechanisms were severely damaged and hydraulic line 'A' was ruptured. The right landing gear nearly came off, being blown past the over-centre position. It twisted rearwards into the trailing edge flap track and canoe fairings, jamming the flaps. The lowering of the undercarriage, however, appeared to have the desired effect and the speed at last began to reduce. The 'g' force decreased and the captain noticed some response return to the control column. At the completion of the last spin he managed to stop the aircraft rolling in just over one second, but as he fought to gain recovery the wings continued to rock about 20° to either side with little control. The nose, however, still pointed downwards almost vertically and with the height passing through 11,000 ft (3,350 m) and the aircraft still dropping rapidly, swift action was required.

Maintaining the wings level, he heaved steadily back on the controls and desperately tried to pull the aircraft from its dive. The 'g' forces quickly increased as the 727 began to respond and at about 8,000 ft (2,440 m) the captain appeared to have regained control. N840TW, however, was still descending and it was another 3,000 ft (914 m) before it bottomed out of the dive. At 5,000 ft (1,525 m) Gibson continued to pull back on the control column and he could feel his stomach drop to his knees as the aircraft was subjected to six g. The wings were tearing at their roots as they withstood six times the aircraft's normal weight. Miraculously they held. The Boeing jet had dropped 34,000 ft (10,360 m) in forty-four seconds, an average descent rate of 46,000 ft (14,020 m) per minute, or over one mile about every eight seconds.

Gibson had pulled the nose from near vertical to arrest the descent, but before the captain could react it passed through the level position and the aircraft shot skywards again. The nose pitched up to about 50° above the horizon and the speed dropped rapidly. Captain Gibson was so intent on not hitting the ground he nearly looped the plane. He had to work hard to prevent the machine from stalling out of the sky and plummeting earthwards once more. Climbing through 8,500 ft (2,590 m) the airspeed decreased to 280 knots and by 11,000 ft (3,350 m) it was down to as low as 160 knots. Using the moon as reference and with Kennedy and Banks both calling out pitch attitudes from the artificial horizon, Captain Gibson managed to regain his bearings and gradually he eased the nose forward. The 727 descended below 10,000 ft (3,050 m) again but, with the speed increasing to 180 knots, he was able to ease the stricken machine back into the climb. By 13,000 ft (3,960 m) he managed to level the aircraft with guidance from the other two and he was able, finally, to make a full recovery. It was an amazing feat of airmanship.

Under the circumstances there was no choice but to land as soon as possible and the captain informed the passengers that everything was now under control and that they would be making an emergency landing at Detroit. By now the flight engineer had taken action over the warning light indicating failure of hydraulic system 'A' and the flap extension drills were commenced. The trailing edge flaps were jammed by the twisted right landing gear and would not move and the leading edge flaps could only be extended by the alternate system.

On completion of the leading edge slats extension, Gibson once more experienced control difficulties. At speeds below 200 knots and above 220 knots the aircraft rolled uncontrollably, this time rapidly to the left, and it was necessary to fly at about 210 knots to maintain control. Attempts to retract the leading edge slats failed. Only inboard ailerons were available, compounding the problem, for the outboard ailerons, which normally come into play with the selection of trailing edge flaps, were still locked in with the flaps being jammed. Part of the rudder was also inoperative with 'A' system hydraulic failure.

The aircraft buffeted severely, making it impossible to read some of the instruments, and Gibson was unable to verify his height. In the distance the crew could see the lights of Chicago, where the captain had once been an air traffic controller, but it was feared too far for a landing. The aircraft might not hold together till then, so the nearer Detroit Airport had been chosen, although the weather there was much worse with a low cloud base. The damaged landing gear also displayed an unsafe condition with three red warning lights indicating all three gears unlocked. Nothing could be done for the two main landing gears, but a manual wind down facility was available on the flight deck for extending and locking the nose gear. Second Officer Banks began to crank the mechanism. As the three cockpit crew performed their emergency checklist procedures, the flight attendants in the cabin prepared the 82 passengers for an emergency landing.

After about thirty minutes, approaching Detroit, Banks succeeded in locking down the nose gear and stowing the doors. The nose gear light now glowed green and the stowed nose gear doors reduced the buffeting by about forty per cent, which at last enabled the captain to read all the flight instruments.

The aircraft was proving very difficult to handle and

Captain 'Hoot' Gibson at the controls of a Ford Trimotor.

Captain Gibson gingerly commenced an approach to Detroit's 03L runway, fighting the aircraft down through the cloud. He did not intend to land from this first approach but planned to execute a low level pass over the airport to allow an examination of the landing gear. Over 90° of aileron control wheel input were required, with the rudder held fully to the right, to maintain control. Even with maximum right trim selected, the strain on Gibson's right leg was enormous and he could feel his leg pulsating to the beat of his heart. The weather did not help either with freezing drizzle falling from a cloud base only a few hundred feet above the ground. The 727 broke from the cloud at about 400 feet and Gibson flew down the runway on a low altitude pass at about 50-57 ft (15-23 m) while crash rescue personnel shone searchlights on the landing gear. The gears were checked in place by the tower controllers but much damage could be observed and the right gear appeared misplaced.

On being so close to the runway, Captain Gibson had the greatest urge to jump from the aircraft and place his feet firmly on solid ground rather than go back up into the weather. The captain commenced a left circuit of the airport, staying low and trying to keep in visual contact with the runway. Turning to the left at the start of the downwind leg he concentrated hard on maintaining sight of the lights as he executed the uncomfortable manoeuvre. The aileron control was still held almost fully to the right, with hard right rudder, and his right leg still pulsated with the strain. Suddenly the captain lost control and he was unable to level the wings. The left turn continued and the 727 headed back towards the airport. The co-pilot also grabbed the control wheel, holding on full right aileron, but was unable to stop the turn. Gibson pushed the number one thrust lever to high power and retarded the centre and right engines to idle. Gradually the asymmetric power took effect and, just before crossing the runway, he managed to gain control and to bring the wings level.

The next approach, this time for a landing, was flown at about 205 knots and the 03L threshold was crossed at the same fast speed. Gibson flared the aircraft with full right rudder and aileron applied and at 22:31 executed a beautifully smooth landing. The 727 landed with the left gear touching down first at a speed of 197 knots. Fortunately it held. On closing the throttles, however, the machine rolled uncontrollably to the left. Reverse thrust was selected as normal and the nose wheel was lowered to the ground. As yet the right gear had not touched and the crew feared it had gone. As the 727 edged towards the left side of the runway the captain slowly lowered the right wing and at a considerable angle the right main landing gear finally touched. By good chance it also held and the aircraft continued its rollout down the runway with a pronounced right wing low attitude. Sparks showered from the dragging right landing gear and the tower controller radioed advising of a possible fire. Nose wheel steering was not available with the loss of hydraulic system 'A' and Gibson had to steer the aircraft off the runway along a high speed turn off using differential braking and asymmetric reverse power. On the taxyway, the 727 was met head-on by fire trucks racing towards the stricken aircraft and Gibson finally brought the machine to a halt. It was a fine demonstration of flying skills in very trying circumstances.

Foam was sprayed on the damaged areas and one of the firemen on the ground called the captain on intercom to advise that 'fuel was running all over' and that an emergency evacuation using escape slides might be prudent. Captain Gibson felt that his passengers had been through enough and that with fuel and fire trucks all over the place in the darkness it would be safer to walk the passengers off the aft exit. He replied accordingly. The plane was only about half full anyway and it would not take long to disembark the passengers from the rear. Quickly all on board evacuated by the aft steps and a relieved group of passengers and crew were finally taken to the terminal. They had faced death and survived.

An attempt was made later to tow the 727 from the high speed turn off but when the aircraft had been moved less than ten feet the right landing gear started to separate. The machine was jacked up to examine the damage but as the wing was raised the right landing gear broke from the wheel well and fell in three separate pieces.

A further inspection of the aircraft the next day revealed extensive damage. Wing skin panels were buckled, bolts had been sheared and large pieces of the machine had virtually been torn off. Wrinkling of fuselage panels was evident at the wing roots and clearly indicated the strain to which the wings had been subjected. Fuel leaked from around several structural fasteners in the left wing. A speed brake section had been wrenched from its hinges, an aileron bolt had been severed, a trailing edge flap carriage had been damaged and a flap transmission mechanism had been broken. All landing gear doors were extensively damaged and hydraulic system line 'A' was fractured. A flap track fairing was missing, as were some engine panels, and a leading edge lift device had sustained damage. To be precise, the number seven leading edge slat mechanism had suffered sheared bolts and twisted tracks and more significantly the slat itself was missing. Could this be the cause of the spiral dive of the 727? A search of the Saginaw area was conducted for the missing aircraft parts and the number seven slat, broken in two, the flap track fairing, and most of the speed brake section were found about six to seven miles (ten kilometres) north of the city. The stricken 727 lay at the side of the runway while the landing gear was made safe and was eventually towed to the hangar for repairs. Several days after the incident the aircraft was sufficiently repaired to permit a ferry flight to the TWA maintenance base at Kansas City, where major repair work was conducted.

Captain Gibson and his crew received just praise for their skills in saving the stricken 727 and the captain received a letter of commendation from the Federal Aviation Administration (FAA) via TWA's vice-president of operations. The cause of the incident was unknown but both the FAA and TWA exonerated the crew from any blame.

Immediately the National Transport Safety Board (NTSB) began an investigation of the accident, including the part played by the crew in the upset. As a formality, Captain Gibson was required by the FAA to be re-rated in the 727 simulator, as well as on the aircraft, and to attend a high altitude awareness course. He passed with flying colours and TWA received a further letter from the FAA complimenting the captain on his abilities. Ten days after the incident Gibson was promoted to Lockheed L-1011 captain.

The investigation of the upset proved to be a lengthy affair and it was to be more than two years before the NSTB reached a conclusion. Fortunately the B727 involved in the incident was not compromised by the delay and, although damaged extensively, N840TW was repaired within a matter of weeks. It was duly returned to service, none the worse for its ordeal, in late May 1979. Sadly, the same could not be said for the flight crew. As the inquiry continued, the three men found the situation changing for the worse. Adverse rumours began to circulate that more was involved than met the eye and Gibson and his colleagues were placed unfairly under suspicion, as much by the piloting fraternity as anyone else. The trio faced a harrowing ordeal and the mental anguish suffered made their return to duties and a normal life substantially more difficult.

The initial suspicion that the number seven slat was responsible for the gross upset prevailed, but how and why the slat had extended whilst cruising at 39,000 ft (11,890 m) remained a mystery. Lift devices on the leading and trailing edges of the wings of modern jet aircraft are essential for take-off and landing but are not designed for use at such high altitudes. On modern jets the wings are swept back at a large angle (on the B727, 34°) to allow the aircraft to fly high and fast by delaying the onset of shock waves as airflow over the wings approaches the speed of sound. At slow aircraft speeds, however, the lift producing qualities of the wings are poor. To improve lift, high lift producing devices in the form of slats (see diagram) are required at the wing leading edges*, and flaps are required at the wing trailing edges. When extended these devices increase the wing surface area and the camber of the wing shape. With slats and flaps fully extended the wing area is increased by twenty per cent and the lift by over eighty per cent. To improve lift at take-off, some flap and all slats are extended, any increase in drag being more than compensated for by increase in lift, and take-off without slats and flap is not possible at normal operating weights. On landing, slats and full flap are always selected in normal circumstances. Leading edge slats and trailing edge flaps are set together by the operation of a single lever on the flight deck. With selection of 2° of trailing edge flap the numbers 2, 3, 6 and 7 slats automatically

Boeing 727 flight control system surfaces.
(NTSB)

* The Boeing 727 also has a type of leading edge flap, but these are not relevant to the story.

extend, and with selection of 5° of trailing edge flap the remaining slats, numbers 1, 4, 5 and 8 also automatically extend. With 5° of trailing edge flap set, all the leading edge devices are extended, and further operation of the flap lever selects only additional trailing edge flap extensions until full landing flap is set.

At cruise speeds and levels there is no requirement to select slats or flaps, and operation of these lift devices on the B727 is expressly forbidden above an indicated airspeed of 230 knots and an altitude of 25,000 ft (7,620 m). Rumour later had it, however, that flaps on the B727 were being extended by crews at higher altitudes than permitted to improve performance, and that the habit was not just confined to a few people but was fairly widespread. Since the use of leading edge devices was dangerous at the higher flight levels and speeds, 727 crews, it was alleged, were pulling the electrical circuit breaker which shuts off the hydraulic valve feeding the leading edge slats, thereby isolating the mechanisms in the retracted position, and then extending the trailing edge flap to 2° by use of the flap lever. The hydraulic valve cut-off circuit breaker was situated beside the crew wardrobe, on the right of the cockpit in a recess aft of the flight engineer's panel.

The effect of the small amount of trailing edge flap in the cruise, it was rumoured, tucked the nose down and improved speed and fuel consumption. The implications were, therefore, that the pilot of Flight 841 had deliberately selected the trailing edge flaps and that by some error the number seven slat had extended and become isolated in that position. In a landing configuration, an extended number seven slat would provide extra lift and would raise the right wing, rolling the aircraft to the left. In a fast, high altitude cruise with a low nose attitude, however, the device would create the opposite effect. When extended the number seven slat would produce negative lift on the right wing and the aircraft would roll sharply to the right.

Flight and simulator tests subsequently appeared to demonstrate that extension of the number seven slat had caused the incident and that it had detached near the end of the last vertical roll, at about the time of lowering the landing gear, and had allowed Captain Gibson to regain control and save the aircraft. Whether the extension was an unscheduled movement or, as whispered, an irresponsible crew action, however, remained unresolved. No proof of any crew involvement was forthcoming although the stigma remained. Rumours implicating the pilots in the event continued unabated and it appeared, on hearsay alone, that a crew who should have been treated as heroes were being seriously maligned. The crew protested that they had never even heard of such a malpractice, but it was to no avail. At the time of Gibson's incident few, if any, knew of the action of selecting flaps in the cruise, but afterwards rumour had it that the practice was widespread. Suddenly everyone seemed to know someone who had tried it although no one who had actually used the procedure emerged. In answer to the accusations of tampering with the flap controls, Captain Gibson, in a deposition to the inquiry in Los Angeles, California on 12 April 1979, one week after the incident, issued a sworn affidavit.

'At no time prior to the incident did I take any action within the cockpit either intentionally or inadvertently, that would have caused the extension of the leading edge slats or trailing edge flaps. Nor did I observe any other crew member take any action within the cockpit, either intentional or inadvertent, which would have caused the extension.'

The first and second officers also both issued sworn statements at the same place and time denying tampering with the flaps. The deposition was conducted in the full glare of publicity with TV cameras and a battery of twenty-six microphones.

These testimonies seemed sufficiently clear but they did not satisfy the NTSB. A statement, allegedly made by one of the investigators a few months later, clearly laid blame on the crew's shoulders. 'I think those guys were fooling around up there and I don't think we really know what they were doing yet,' a 'spokesman' revealed to Aviation Consumer magazine on 15 October, 1979. Such a statement, if accurately reported, was a disgraceful breach of ethics, for the investigation was still at a premature stage. Soon the national press echoed the comment and a countrywide accusation of guilt resulted. The crew seemed convicted before any hearing had begun. Meanwhile, Captain Gibson and his colleagues, desperately trying to pick up the pieces of their careers, were restrained from issuing public statements in their own defence.

A number of points surrounding the incident were also found questionable by members of the inquiry. To begin with, the cockpit voice recorder (CVR) tape on the 727 had been erased after Flight 841's emergency landing at Detroit. Cockpit voice recorders are installed on aircraft to record flight deck conversations which might be useful to investigators following an accident. CVRs are not permitted to be used by the FAA in any disciplinary action. The recorder tape operates on a continuous, thirty minute loop and would not have recorded details of the dive, but the NTSB were suspicious that conversations on the flight deck after the incident could have revealed details of the crews' actions and were deliberately erased. In 1979 the CVR had been only recently introduced and crews distrusted the equipment. Most pilots feared misuse of its information and regularly erased the tape after a trip. Under questioning by counsel, Captain Gibson admitted that he, too, normally erased the tape after a flight but that in this instance he could not remember doing so.

'Did you erase the recorder?'

Captain Gibson: 'Not to my knowledge.'

'Did anyone erase it?'

Gibson: 'Not to my knowledge. I didn't see anyone erase it.'

'Do you usually erase the recorder?'

Gibson: 'I usually do, yes. I don't recall erasing it.'

'Can you erase it in the air?'

Gibson: 'No.'

'What is required to erase the CVR?'

Gibson: 'The parking brakes have to be set.'

'How many minutes of recording are there on the CVR before previous contents are erased?'

Gibson: 'Thirty minutes. It was forty-five minutes to an hour [after the incident] before the aircraft was shut down and we got off.'

'So if the tape had not been bulk-erased at the time of shut-down would there have been anything meaningful on the tape?'

Gibson: 'No, the tape could only have made my other two crew members look good. They did a real good job. All that would have been on the tape would have been the other crew members complying with the check list.'

'Can you explain why it is your habit and routine to erase cockpit voice recorder data on landing?'

Gibson: 'It is an accepted practice, and as far as I am concerned at the time it was done by everyone. It is done by an awful lot of people. When they put the cockpit voice recorder on the airplane I would say 100 per cent of people always erase it on landing after they park their brakes.'

'Why do you do it?'

Gibson: 'Because I might say something unkind about some of the people in management, and they might take that tape out and send it someplace.'

Both Kennedy and Banks also swore that they had not erased the tape. It seemed reasonable that, in the highly charged atmosphere after such an event, crew members might by force of habit, take actions which they might later forget, but the investigators were not to be convinced.

'We believe the captain's erasure of the CVR is a factor we cannot ignore and cannot sanction. Although we recognise that habits can cause actions not desired or intended by the actor, we have difficulty accepting the fact that the captain's putative habit of routinely erasing the CVR after each flight was not restrainable after a flight in which disaster was only narrowly averted. Our scepticism persists, even though the CVR would not have contained any contemporaneous information about the events that immediately preceded the loss of control, because we believe it probable that the twenty-five minutes or more of recording which preceded the landing at Detroit could have provided clues about causal factors and might have served to refresh the flight crew's memories about the whole matter.'

The investigating team clearly felt that the erasure of the CVR was deliberate. If the inadvertent operation of the number seven leading edge slat was also to be proved part of a deliberate act by the crew, then any mechanical failure of components would have to be discounted. The NTSB instigated a thorough investigation of the possibilities of an unscheduled extension of the slat. If some kind of mechanical fault had resulted in accidental operation of the number seven slat, the Safety Board would do their utmost to find the cause. A total of 118 trials were conducted in a Boeing flight simulator to try to identify the condition that precipitated the aircraft's upset and to duplicate and evaluate its manoeuvre.

'The flight simulator traces showed that the simulated aircraft could be returned to wings-level flight with relatively little loss of altitude provided corrective action was begun before the roll and airspeed were allowed to increase excessively. In the simulations, the pilot could delay reaction for about sixteen seconds and regain control with an altitude loss of about 6,000 ft (1,830 m). However, when the pilot delayed corrective action for seventeen seconds or more, a manoeuvre was entered that approximated Flight 841's airspeed, altitude, and g-traces. In this manoeuvre, the aircraft continued throughout the descent to roll to the right, in spite of full left aileron and rudder, until the slat was retracted to simulate its loss from the aircraft.'

During none of these tests, however, was yaw induced at the beginning of the upset.

A thorough inspection of the damaged aircraft and the retrieved debris was conducted but no evidence of a malfunction which might have caused an inadvertent slat extension was discovered. An examination of the slat locking devices also proved fruitless. The slats are locked in the retracted position by hydraulic pressure from system 'A' and by a mechanical locking mechanism. Both systems would have had to fail before the slat could have extended and there was no evidence to suggest that this had occurred. Loss of hydraulic system 'A' and/or failure of a mechanical lock would have illuminated warning lights in the cockpit, and neither were reported by the flight crew.

A repair of the hydraulic system line 'A', which ruptured on extension of the landing gear, was implemented, and the slat and flap systems were found to function satisfactorily. Number seven leading edge slat, the offending device, could not be tested since it had separated from the wing, and its extending and retracting hydraulic mechanism, or actuating system (see diagram), could not be checked since it was broken. The investigating Board acknowledged, however, that failure of the actuating system, namely, fracture of the actuating piston or separation of the piston from the actuating rod, could have resulted in inadvertent extension, but Boeing convinced the NTSB that the safety margins, particularly regarding an actuator piston fracture, were massive and that in sixteen years of service history and over thirty-six million flight hours such a fracture had never occurred.

There is always a first time of course, but the event was deemed by the Board to be highly unlikely and was not considered. Later it was revealed that at the time of the inquiry no less than six cases of cracked actuator pistons had been reported to Boeing by Lufthansa. Separation of the actuator rod from the actuator piston seemed to the Board to be the only reasonable single failure which could have permitted an unscheduled slat operation, but this was also discounted. The Safety Board contended that the distortion of the remaining section of the broken actuator cylinder and the fact that the piston did not stay in the remnant of the cylinder indicated that the piston rod was attached to the piston when the slat extended. The problem facing the NTSB, however, was that the forward two-thirds of the actuator cylinder, the actuator piston and the actuator piston rod were missing and in their reports the investigators could only speculate as to the reason for the failure. The Safety

Typical slat section. (NTSB)

Slat Track

Slat Actuator

Track Roller

Leading Edge Slat

Board had to reach their conclusions only on the limited evidence available and it seemed a firm dismissal of any mechanical failures, especially the only single failure which was considered reasonable, when the suspect parts were never recovered.

Over the years, a large number of 'service difficulty reports' had been received by the Federal Aviation Administration (FAA) outlining slat problems, most of them minor, but some significant. Whether the 727 involved in the incident, N840TW, was the subject of such reports is not known, but it was an old aircraft and was TWA's first 727-100 in service. Up to 1973, there had been approximately fifteen reported cases of uncommanded single leading edge slat extensions at low level with the slat separating in flight. To resolve the situation, in 1973 Boeing issued an Airworthiness Directive requiring a stronger actuator piston rod end, and the problem was assumed to be solved. In the five years preceding Gibson's upset, only two instances of importance were reported. One notable event arose in 1976 when an unscheduled extension of a leading edge slat occurred. Significantly, the extension resulted from the failure of a slat actuator support fitting. The slat remained attached and the aircraft upset was contained.

In 1978, one B727 operator declared that in cruise at 25,000 ft (7,620 m) the numbers six and seven leading edge slats had been unintentionally extended by the crew. The captain stated that he believed the trailing edge flaps were partially extended and when he attempted to retract them the leading edge devices were accidentally operated. The captain immediately retracted the leading edge slats, but the numbers six and seven slats remained extended. The roll to the right was contained, and when the aircraft slowed the slats retracted. Whether rumours of flight crew tampering with the flap controls surrounded this upset was not revealed, but the NTSB appeared to be drawing comparisons between this event and Captain Gibson's. Since the investigators had discarded the likelihood of mechanical malfunction, the Safety Board were forced to consider that Flight 841's crew, in spite of their statements, had deliberately operated the flaps.

The NTSB advanced the theory, therefore, that the electrical circuit breaker for the leading edge lift devices had been pulled to prevent their extension and the trailing edge flaps had then been set to 2° to improve aircraft performance. The Board then tried to imagine a scenario in which the number seven slat could have been inadvertently extended and were aided in their quest by what appeared to be an unusual source: Captain Gibson himself. In an unofficial interview given shortly after the incident, an FAA representative had asked Gibson if all the crew members had been in their places when the upset occurred. The captain replied in the positive, adding that the flight engineer had just returned to his seat. The FAA representative assumed from the statement, incorrectly, that Banks had actually left the cockpit and, unknown to Gibson, the NTSB were informed accordingly. The suspicions of the Safety Board were corroborated by a female passenger in economy class who stated that she saw a male crew member carry trays back to the galley from the forward end of the aircraft. The unidentified man was wearing epaulets and was assumed by her to be one of the flight crew. Later it appeared that one of the stewards, who also wore epaulets at that time, had carried the cockpit crew's meal trays back from the flight deck. The Board, therefore, attempted in secret to build a scenario around an erroneous premise and surmised that the setting of the flaps might have occurred with Second Officer Banks absent from the flight deck. The relevant circuit breaker was to be found aft of the flight engineer's station and, on his return, it was suggested, he may have found it tripped. Unaware of the circumstances, Banks may have simply pushed it home, resulting in extension of the leading edge devices. The captain would then have selected the flap lever to up but, in something similar to the previous case, the number seven slat remained extended. An examination of the offending slat mechanism seemed to support the theory. A sheared bolt was shown by metallurgical tests to have been weakened by fatigue and had probably broken before the event. The failure would have resulted in sagging of the inboard end of the slat, which seemed to be confirmed by slat wear. The number seven slat would, in this condition, have extended misaligned and aerodynamic loads would have prevented its retraction.

A broken bolt was also found on the outboard aileron's mechanism which had been weakened similarly by fatigue. It was not possible to determine when the bolt had failed but, if it had sheared before the barrel rolls, the free play in the mechanism would have permitted the aileron to float upwards about one inch (twenty-five millimetres). This would have induced a roll to the right which would have been noticeable to the pilot and would not have helped in controlling the gross upset. All the events could, of course, have occurred simultaneously, but the NTSB investigators concluded that, even had the broken aileron bolt existed at the moment of the upset, it would not have contributed to the loss of control of the aircraft. There were those who disagreed. The US Air Line Pilots' Association (ALPA) were also participating in the investigation and they were becoming increasingly disturbed by the trend of the inquiry. ALPA instigated its own study and claimed that in the five years before the incident no less than 400 'service difficulty reports' of B727 slat problems had been submitted to the FAA.

'ALPA is concerned that this incident is not limited to a single aircraft on a single airline. Rather it appears to be symptomatic of the fatigue problem that has not been properly addressed by the aircraft industry. Recent emphasis on this aging problem associated with the older jets through-out the world underlines ALPA's concern.'

The Pilots' Association felt that the large number of slat problems which had been reported tended to support the mechanical failure theory. The Safety Board's suggestion of malpractice, therefore, appeared hasty and their rejection of the only single failure considered reasonable seemed open to argument, especially since the relevant parts were missing. The only previously reported incident of an unscheduled slat extension also related to problems with the actuator, although in that case it was failure of the actuator mount fitting.

'We believe,' reported ALPA 'that pre-existing fatigue, corrosion and component failures within the number seven slat and right outboard aileron mechanisms caused the slat to extend. We further believe that free play in the right outboard aileron played a significant part in the controllability of the aircraft and initiation of the manoeuvre.'

Flight tests were conducted by Boeing in October 1980 to examine the effects of slat extension in conditions as close as practicable to N840TW's incident, but these also resulted in discrepancies. The NTSB noted that the decrease in airspeed which accompanied the selection of numbers 2, 3, 6 and 7 slats on the test aircraft compared with the airspeed decrease indicated by Flight 841's flight data recorder in the moments preceding the upset. This, the investigator claimed, was evidence that the relevant leading edge devices had originally extended before the number seven slat had become isolated and was conclusive proof of their theory. Captain Gibson's control deflections of elevator, aileron and rudder in an attempt to maintain level flight, however, could, likewise, have caused a similar reduction in speed. There were also significant differences in other areas, namely the 'g' forces at the onset of buffet. The effect of selecting leading edge slats in the test in fact produced more than moderate buffeting, while Captain Gibson had testified that only light buffeting was experienced. The 'g' traces supported the captain's statement. Gibson's colleagues on the flight deck were not at first aware of the developing situation before the spiral dive, a fact which also seemed to be in keeping with the buffeting being light. If the buffeting had been moderate their attention would have been more readily drawn to the circumstances. No passengers aboard TW 841 reported any shaking of the aircraft prior to the upset. Light buffeting, however, pointed to extension of only the number seven slat, but no test was conducted with the aircraft in that condition.

On 29 January 1980, almost ten months after the upset, the three flight crew were interviewed for the first time by NTSB investigators in Kansas City, Missouri. The line of questioning was directed at the single issue of the location of the second officer at the time of the incident and clearly indicated the train of thought of the investigators. Demands to be questioned on all aspects of the case by Gibson and the FAA were ignored. Captain Gibson and his crew once again gave testimony but, on this occcasion, only regarding the position of the flight engineer, and no other depositions were made.

The US ALPA, with increasing concern at the direction of the inquiry, issued a statement to the NTSB.

'It has been alleged during the investigation that the crew, through some unorthodox procedure, inadvertently extended the leading edge slats, recognised their mistake, and took action to retract them. This allegation further assumes that due to pre-existing damage to the number seven slat it did not retract, but went to the fully extended position. The crew members vehemently deny that this happened. TWA undertook a flight test to determine the effect of extending the leading edge slats at the same height and airspeed. According to the pilot of this flight, Captain George Andre, the aircraft experienced moderate buffet. This statement contradicts any possible extension of other than the number seven slat as the initial onset of this incident.'

At no time during the investigation, or at any other time, were the crew confronted with the evidence upon which the Board based its findings: the analysis of the flight data recorder, the results of the simulator exercises and the outcome of the flight tests. Captain Gibson and his colleagues had to await the publication of the official report before such details were revealed. It was to be June of the following year, 1981, and a further sixteen months of anxiety for the crew, before the NTSB's findings were released.

'The Safety Board determines that the probable cause of this accident was the isolation of the No 7 leading slat in the fully or partially extended position after an extension of the Nos 2, 3, 6 and 7 leading edge slats and the subsequent retraction of the Nos 2, 3 and 6 slats, and the captain's untimely flight control inputs to counter the roll resulting from the slat asymmetry. Contributing to the cause was a pre-existing misalignment of the No 7 slat which, when combined with the cruise condition airloads, precluded retraction of that slat. After eliminating all probable individual or combined mechanical failures or malfunctions which could lead to slat extension, the Safety Board determined that the extension of the slats was the result of the flight crew's manipulation of the flat/slat controls. Contributing to the captain's untimely use of the flight controls was distraction due probably to his efforts to rectify the source of the control problem.'

It was a tremendous blow to Flight 841's crew and one that was followed by vociferous denials from the three concerned, as well as hostile reaction from ALPA. But there was more. The report had been signed by three NTSB members, one of whom was Francis McAdams, the only pilot and aviation professional on the Board. McAdams was unhappy with some aspects of the case, especially the fact that neither he nor anyone else on the Board had seen or interviewed any of the accused, and he appended his own statement to the report.

'Although I voted to approve the Board's report which concluded that the extension of the leading edge slat was due to flight crew action, I do so reluctantly.

'The report as written, based on the available evidence . . . appears to support the Board's conclusion. However, I am troubled by the fact that the Board has categorically rejected the crew's sworn testimony without the crew having had the opportunity to be confronted with all of the evidence upon which the Board was basing its findings. At the time of the first deposition . . . no evidence was available to the crew or to the Board. Although the crew was deposed a second time, their testimony was limited to one issue, i.e. the physical location of the flight engineer at the time of the incident. I had recommended that since the Board was ordering a second deposition it be conducted *de novo* so that the crew would have been aware of all the evidence. The Board did not agree.

'Furthermore, I do not agree that a probable cause of this accident, as stated by the Board, was "the captain's untimely flight control inputs to counter the roll resulting from the slat asymmetry." In my opinion, the captain acted expeditiously and reasonably in attempting to correct for the severe right roll condition induced by the extended slat.'

The report, although firm in its conclusions, remained unconvincing, and the crew was left with a 'not proven' verdict. Under a cloud of uncertainty the three continued their duties with TWA, still proclaiming their innocence. The strain, however, proved too much for the second officer and Banks retired early to become a college lecturer.

As time went by the struggle to clear their names did not diminish and much information was gathered by ALPA in support of their cause.

At the beginning of the inquiry, suspicions of malpractice were initially aroused by what appeared to the investigators to be the deliberate erasure of the cockpit voice recorder (CVR) by Captain Gibson. The crew, the Board surmised, must have had something to hide. Erasure of the tape by Gibson, however, was clearly shown to be impossible. The CVR can be erased by the pilot only when the aircraft is safely on the ground with the parking brake set. Squat switches on the landing gears contact when the oleos compress with weight, closing circuits which confirm the machine is on the ground. The high speed lowering of the landing gear during the upset resulted in damage which tore the squat switches and circuitry from the structure and the 727 landed with both main gear lights glowing red. The CVR erasure circuit was incomplete and, even if the captain had pressed the button on the flight deck, nothing would have happened. Gibson could *not* have deliberately erased the tape and the Board's initial suspicion that he did so because he had something to hide was unjustified. What is more, this was known and understood by the investigators early in the inquiry. Also after erasure, the tape recycled and a further nine minutes of conversation, including statements relating to the incident, were recorded. If it had been Gibson's intention to erase the tape, and it had been physically possible to do so, it is most unlikely that any evidence would have remained. So how was the tape erased? *Popular Mechanics* magazine interviewed a CVR technical expert and revealed that on a slow transfer of electrical power from the 727 engine to the auxiliary power unit (APU), which Banks accomplished on this occasion, erasure of the CVR is possible. This is the only way in which erasure of the CVR could have occurred. The timing of the tape recycling and the moment of slow power transfer also corresponded, as did the ending of the recording, nine minutes later, and the shut down of the APU.

The question of whether the flight engineer had left the flight deck was also suitably resolved. Gibson and his colleagues denied that Banks had left the cockpit and it was established that shortly after top of climb the flight engineer had risen only momentarily from his position to place finished meal trays at the back of the flight deck for collection. The flight attendants, when interviewed, supported the flight crew's statements and fourteen passengers, including four to five first class travellers who were in a good position to view movement from the flight deck, were also questioned. All swore that Second Officer Banks did not leave the flight deck near the time of the incident. The NTSB refused to consider this evidence and the statements were ignored. During the investigation, Captain Gibson kept hearing that someone had told the Board of Banks' absence, although the informer's identity could not be revealed, and it was realised only much later that it was Gibson's own comment which had led to the misunderstanding. The FAA representative who had spoken unofficially to the captain immediately after the accident, in spite of claiming that 'he was not wired for sound and wouldn't take notes', did write down in pencil the next day his recollections of the interview. It was the FAA representative's mistaken belief that Banks had left the flight deck, unwittingly reported to the NTSB, which had started the Board's 'what if the flight engineer had left the cockpit' scenario. With Banks on the flight deck the NTSB had no case.

The Board's version of the slat extension also did not stand up to scrutiny and when examined closely seemed absurd. The NTSB imagined the 727 levelling off at 39,000 ft (11,890 m), the power being set and Banks leaving the flight deck for a brief spell. Since all on board, except one lady passenger in economy class, testified to not having noticed his departure, his absence must have been short indeed. One of the pilots was then imagined jumping from his seat and in the darkness moving aside the crew's coats and swiftly finding and pulling the relevant circuit breaker. Very quickly, and in secret, the trailing edge flaps are set to 2°. Almost immediately Banks is imagined returning and noticing in the darkness, *beside* the crew's coats, that the circuit breaker is pulled and, *without saying anything*, pushing it back in again. According to the NTSB, half the leading edge slats then fully extend causing, by their own admission, moderate buffeting, and the three crew members are imagined sitting doing nothing for six seconds as they watch the leading edge flap lights sequencing. Then, with the leading edge slats fully extended, someone realises the error of their ways and is imagined selecting the flap lever up, thereby retracting all the lift devices except the number seven slat which inadvertently remains fully extended. This account, unfortunately, fails to appreciate the fact that if the pilots had just set the flaps they would have been highly aware of the circumstances and at the first sign of buffet one of them would have selected the flap lever to up long before full leading edge slat extension had occurred. It also fails to appreciate that modern airline crews do not operate in this manner and that in any usual situation, circumstances are discussed fully before action is taken. And, if the practice of selecting two degrees of flap had been widespread, as alleged, Banks, had he noticed the popped circuit breaker, would have known exactly what was going on and that would have been the last thing he would have touched. The NTSB scenario did not fit the facts and, even if the crew had deliberately set 2° of flap, an action not entertained here, the extension of number seven leading edge slat was highly unlikely to have happened in this manner.

There were also a number of other factors relating to the investigation which were disturbing. One hundred and eighteen simulator tests were undertaken by Boeing and the NTSB in order to resolve the situation but all tests were conducted according to the flight data recorder (FDR) and not one trial was performed in the manner described by the flight crew. The scientific officers analysing the accident data accepted only the scientific details as revealed by the FDR, even though it was known the equipment could be unreliable after being subjected to such a violent manoeuvre. The recorder indicated, for example, a rapid heading change of about five degrees to the right in less than a second at the start of the upset which was identified as a sharp roll. The flight crew denied that the wings rolled, stating that the upset was preceded by a fierce yaw to the right. The flight attendants also stated that they noticed no rocking of the wings and the passengers interviewed said the same. Not one simulator exercise was conducted with yaw as described by Gibson. All tests were performed in a 727-200 series simulator whereas Captain Gibson's machine was a 727-100, a shorter version which was considered by pilots to be less stable at high altitude. Having taken the decision to fly at the unusually lofty level for a 727-100 of 39,000 ft (11,890 m), the crew were then highly unlikely to jeopardise further the aircraft's stability by deploying the trailing edge flaps. As Captain Gibson commented, 'It is very difficult to get three crew members to agree to take a 727-100 to 39,000 ft. I seriously doubt that the three most stupid pilots in the industry would ever consider experimenting with flaps at 39,000 ft in a 727-100.'

All NTSB trials were restricted to the suspected Board scenario and all fault analysis was confined to calculated problems which could have resulted in the extension of a slat. The most improbable cases were simply discarded. The U.S. Air Line Pilots' Association (ALPA) demonstrated that 'a fracture of the actuator piston circumferentially through the lock key hole', no matter how unlikely, could have resulted in unscheduled extension of only the number seven slat. Although the NTSB and Boeing pointed out that the piston design strength negated the possibility of this failure and that it was claimed no record of such an occurrence existed, it was still possible, especially since the number seven slat mechanism had been damaged previous to the upset. The aileron hinge bolt that had also failed had a design strength which, likewise, negated the possibility of its shearing, and there was also no record of such a fracture existing, yet the bolt had failed. If one component which was deemed impossible to fail had done so, it was surely possible that another on the same aircraft could have suffered a similar fate.

The passengers were also asked if they had heard any unusual noises during the flight. The investigators hoped that some might have mentioned the unmistakable, high pitched, shrill scream of the hydraulic motors operating which would have indicated extension of the trailing edge flaps. In the quietness of the cruise at 39,000 ft (11,890 m) the hydraulic motor noise would have been quite piercing, much louder than at the lower altitudes when flaps are normally operated after take-off or before landing. No-one, however, noticed any high pitched scream although many mentioned the light buffet and hearing the bangs of the compressor stall. This, alone, seemed conclusive proof that the crew did *not* operate the flaps.

The NTSB's accusations regarding untimely control inputs at the moment of the upset, disagreed by Francis McAdams, the only pilot on the Board, were also disputed. As early as 1975, Boeing had conducted a 727-100 flight test 'to investigate stability and control characteristics at high speed with one leading edge slat extended.' It is interesting to note that the test was ordered two years after the slat problem was assumed to have been solved by the issuing of the Airworthiness Directive in 1973, which required strengthening of the actuator piston rod ends. The aircraft took off with the number two slat bolted in the extended position and climbed in that condition to the required altitude. The test was abandoned at 33,400 ft and Mach 0.80 because of severe control difficulties resulting from heavy outboard aileron vibration. The test engineer at the time, D. L. Mahon, wrote on the flight log, as much in alarm as in jest, that the trial was curtailed 'due to several cases of extreme cowardice'. The aircraft, therefore, was never tested in this condition throughout its entire flight envelope. Captain Gibson's upset had occurred at 39,000 ft and Mach 0.81. Later it was demonstrated that the control forces at high altitude were not sufficiently effective to recover from a gross upset and that the more dense air at lower levels was required for full control effectiveness. The performance of the simulator during the trials was based on wind tunnel testing which had not been verified by flight test at high altitude. In fact, the analytical data for flap extension at lower altitudes had had to be adjusted significantly to match flight test results. As a note, the severe roll to the left experienced by Gibson after selection of the remaining slats at about 13,000 ft

(3,960 m) on the approach to Detroit could not be explained by Boeing. At slow speeds with the number seven slat missing and all other slats set, the aircraft should have rolled to the right.

During the Boeing 727-100 flight tests in October, 1980, while checking performance in cruise with slats retracted and 2° of trailing edge flap extended, it was discovered, to everyone's surprise, that the configuration rapidly deteriorated performance. If the practice of selecting this configuration had been as widespread as alleged, crews would have been aware of the poorer performance; the corollary being, of course, that once the crews had discovered the deteriorated performance the practice would not have been widespread. Something, somewhere was wrong.

The entire investigation was conducted without the assistance of Captain Gibson and his colleagues and, after the initial testimony taken under the glare of publicity about one week after the incident, the flight crew were denied due process. At no time after the first deposition, during the whole two and a half years of the investigation, the longest ever, were the flight crew consulted, cross examined or questioned by any investigator, except to answer 'no' to the question of whether or not Banks left the flight deck near the time of the incident. All of Gibson's phone calls to the NTSB were either refused, or never returned, and all notorised statements were ignored. The flight crew were also denied admission to the first hearing, which ended inconclusively, although the press and other interested parties were permitted to attend. Captain Gibson and First Officer Kennedy were admitted to the second hearing but they were not allowed to take part and they weren't even recognized by the investigators.

An appeal against the verdict was launched but it was to be eight years later before it reached the Supreme Court, the highest authority in the land. Unfortunately, Gibson's case was not one of those selected for review and the situation was never resolved.

In 1983, a few of the passengers who had suffered minor injuries in the upset took TWA and Boeing to court in pursuit of compensation. Judgement was found in the plaintiffs' favour and sums of money were paid by both companies.

In spite of the result, however, Gibson and his crew, according to Donald Mark Chance Jnr., the lawyer representing TWA, came out of the proceedings well.

Captain Gibson and his colleagues attempted to take their case against the NTSB and Boeing to court but were denied due process of the law. A federal judge declared Gibson a 'public person' and, because of other legal difficulties at the time, action by the flight crew through the civil courts was refused. A documentary, entitled 'The Plane that Fell from the Sky', was made by Paul and Holly Fine for CBS's 60 Minutes programme and was sympathetic to Captain Gibson's case, but was all to no avail.

The crux of the matter in this entire case lay in the statement of the original hearing officer, Les Kampschror, that if the crew were not found in error then the airworthiness of the 727 would be cast in doubt. Since, in the minds of the investigators, no mechanical fault of the 727 appeared feasible, they left themselves little choice but to blame the flight crew. The majority of the NTSB were satisfied with the decision. The publicity surrounding the case and the verdict against the crew, it was reasoned, would eradicate the alleged widespread practice of tampering with the flaps in the cruise and further inadvertent slat extensions would be prevented.

On 28 August 1982, a 727-100 of International Air Service Company Ltd experienced an uncommanded number seven leading edge slat extension, after slat and flap retraction, while climbing through 4,000 ft (1,220 m) *en route* from Tulsa to St. Louis. Substantial aileron inputs were required to maintain control. Inspection revealed that the number seven slat actuator had malfunctioned and extended the slat.

On 17 November 1984, once again on the climb out with flaps and slats retracted, an unwanted extension of the number eight leading edge slat occurred to an American Airlines 727-200 whilst flying from Las Vegas to Los Angeles. A large lateral control input was required to control the aircraft.

In the cruise, on leaving 31,000 ft (9,450 m) for 29,000 ft

(8,840 m), a partial and momentary extension of number two leading edge slat occured to a United Airlines 727 on 10 September 1985. The aircraft pitched and yawed moderately. No cause of the unscheduled flap extension was discovered. Remarked the captain later, 'I know Boeing says it can't happen, but it did.'

On 8 January 1986, a TWA 727-100 outbound from St. Louis with flaps and slats retracted, experienced an unscheduled extension of the number seven leading edge slat whilst climbing through 6,000 ft (1,830 m). The aircraft rolled to the left with moderate buffeting and the captain decided to return to St. Louis. On the ground the number seven slat remained extended when the flaps and slats were selected up. Inspection revealed that the inboard number seven slat track extend stops were missing.

Whilst climbing out from Detroit on 22 February 1987, with flaps and slats retracted, an unscheduled extension of the number two leading edge slat occurred to a North West 727. The captain reduced the speed to 210 knots, selected two degrees of flap (which also extended slats 3, 6 and 7 giving a symmetrical slat condition) and continued to destination, Cleveland.

Another incident occurred on 24 August 1987 to a TWA 727 *en route* to St. Louis. At a speed of 300 knots, and climbing through 10,000 ft (3,050 m), with the flaps and slats retracted, an unscheduled extension of the number seven slat began. The captain reduced speed and the number seven slat retracted of its own accord. Later, the number seven slat actuator was replaced.

In none of these incidents were the crew accused of tampering with the flaps. To this day, over a decade later, the NTSB's verdict of guilty on Captain Gibson, First Officer Kennedy and Second Officer Banks, still stands. It is time the judgement was reviewed.

**Note:** 'Hoot' Gibson flew as captain on L1011s for three years after the upset, then transferred to the Boeing 747 as a first officer in 1982. In 1983, the litigation in which he became involved took its toll and in January 1984 Gibson retired early on medical grounds, with review after five years, and went back to his farm in Costa Rica. After only two years of farming 'Hoot' Gibson returned to flying duties with TWA in January 1986 and is now a 747 captain. Jess Kennedy remained in service with TWA and gained his command, but Gary Banks never returned to flying.

# Chapter 9
# Strange Encounter

The Islamic Festival of Ramadan falls in the ninth month of the lunar calendar and celebrates the first revelation of the Koran to Mohammed. The event begins with the new moon and ends with the old, and marks a month of daylight fasting for the Muslim faithful.

In 1982, 24 June fell on the second day of Ramadan and the night was moonless and dark. At just after 20:00 local time a British Airways Boeing 747, en route from the United Kingdom to New Zealand, took off from the Malaysian capital of Kuala Lumpur into the clear, black night. A quick five-hour hop to Perth in Western Australia lay ahead. For the passengers enduring the twenty-nine-hour journey from London to Auckland, Kuala Lumpur marked the halfway stage of the flight. The travellers from Europe destined for Perth were joined by a tour group of about thirty returning to that city who had been on holiday in Malaysia. Of the 247 total on board, therefore, about a hundred were due to disembark in Perth, the first Australian stop. The flight was then scheduled to continue via Melbourne to Auckland.

In 1982, British Airways won the 'Airline of the Year' award, being voted number one by regular business travellers, but the accolade had not been achieved without difficulty. Industrial and security problems at Heathrow had disrupted many departures and British Airways' Flight BA 009 from London to Auckland on 23-25 June was no exception. As the Boeing 747, named *City of Edinburgh*, registration *G-BDXH*, known phonetically as X-ray Hotel, lifed off from Kuala Lumpur's runway 15, the flight was running about one-and-a-half hours late. The aircraft's weight at take-off was about 304 tonnes, which for the short journey was well inside the maximum structural take-off weight of 371 tonnes. The ninety tonnes of fuel carried was more than sufficient for the flight to Perth, which would consume about fifty-five tonnes, but with the Western Australian metropolis being one of the most isolated cities in the world more was needed in case of diversion. The designated second choice in case the destination airport was closed because of weather, or some other unforeseen circumstance, was the remote military base of Learmonth lying on the coast 600 nm north of Perth. With the high fuel load, however, BA 009 could, if necessary easily overfly Perth to Adelaide, a somewhat less isolated alternative. The briefing in Kuala Lumpur attended by the flight crew, Captain Eric Moody, Senior First Officer (SFO) Roger Greaves and Senior Engineer Officer (SEO) Barry Townley-Freeman, had given no indication of any adverse weather conditions en route, or in Perth, but the extra fuel carried was a sensible precaution. All expected a smooth, pleasant and routine flight.

On boarding in Kuala Lumpur, the passengers made themselves comfortable for the journey which lay ahead, but those travelling from London were becoming overtired and found it difficult to settle. Of the Australian tour group bound for Perth from Kuala Lumpur many were unhappy at being kept waiting for so long at the terminal before the late departure. Unconcerned with the problems at Heathrow the general feeling was that the Poms had let them down again. The big jet roared down the runway and after a long run because of the hot air became airborne at 20:09 local time (12:09 GMT). At 500 ft (150 m) in the darkness X-ray Hotel banked slightly left in the smooth air to turn towards Singapore and the route to Perth. Captain Moody established the aircraft on airway G79, flying towards the Johor Bahru VOR (very high frequency omnidirectional radio range beacon) which lay in the south of Malaysia at a distance of 150 nm. The climb continued steadily to the cruising altitude of 37,000 ft (11,280 m) and the aircraft was accelerated to the normal climb speed of 320 knots. The autopilot was now engaged and would remain so until approaching Perth. Passing 11,000 ft (3,350 m) the altimeters were adjusted to the standard pressure setting of 1013.2 millibars.

In the cabin drinks were served. At the request of the tired passengers the bar service was to be followed immediately by a light meal and then afterwards the lights were to be dimmed. In the quietness the weary travellers hoped to get some rest before arrival. As the journey progressed it soon became apparent to the passengers that they were being looked after by very able flight attendants, and they began to relax and make themselves at ease. Captain Moody's entire crew of sixteen, consisting of himself and the other two on the flight deck, plus thirteen in the cabin, led by Cabin Services Officer (CSO) Graham Skinner, had been together since they left London five days earlier. On this trip they had already been as far east as Jakarta, the Indonesian capital. The previous day the crew had then passengered out of Jakarta's International Airport, Halim, to position to Kuala Lumpur to pick up the BA 009 which they now operated down to Perth. The rapport enjoyed by the crew was reflected in the comments of their passengers, many of whom remarked that they seemed a 'happy band'. Little could any of these travellers have guessed at the time that before the flight was out they would be more than grateful for the professionalism of Captain Moody and his gregarious team.

As the climb continued the captain lifted the PA handset to say a few words to the passengers before they settled down for the night. He described the route the aircraft would follow as it flew over the Indonesian archipelago, explaining that from Singapore they would fly down the coast of Sumatra and across the Java Sea to overhead Jakarta,

A British Airways 747. (British Airways)

then from there they would proceed over the Indian Ocean to Carnarvon on the Australian coast, and on down to Perth. The remaining flight time of just under five hours gave them an estimated time of arrival of 01:30 local time in Perth, the time there being the same as in Kuala Lumpur. There was little or no cloud expected en route so flying conditions would be smooth, and the forecast for Perth was fine. The captain concluded by saying that he would leave them in peace now in the hope they might get some rest and he would talk to them again on the descent into Perth.

Approaching the Johor Bahru VOR beacon, X-ray Hotel levelled off at 37,000 ft (11,280 m) and accelerated to the cruise speed of Mach 0.85. The buffet speed of 265 knots the lowest cruise speed for that flight level and weight, was bugged on the airspeed indicator (ASI), and the three engine drift-down cruise level of 27,000 ft (8,230 m) was also noted. If an engine failed suddenly at 37,000 ft X-ray Hotel would be unable to maintain its altitude with reduced thrust and would have to descend to the more dense atmosphere at 27,000 ft to maintain level flight. As the aircraft weight reduced with fuel consumption the three engine drift-down level would, of course, rise and would eventually reach the actual cruise altitude if the aircraft remained level.

Over Johor Bahru, air traffic control (ATC) changed to Singapore, and BA 009 was cleared to proceed by airway B69 out of the Sinjon VOR beacon which lay just south of Singapore Airport. Airway B69 led all the way to Perth via Jakarta. Only the odd cumulonimbus (Cb) cloud could be seen flashing intermittently in the darkness below and the flight was proving to be as smooth and pleasant as expected. Captain Moody, SFO Greaves and SEO Townley-Freeman were being looked after by Stewardess Fiona Wright who had been assigned to duties in the first class upper deck area. The few first class passengers on board had all been accommodated in the main deck below and, with more than sufficient staff to cater for their needs, Stewardess Wright was free to attend to the flight crew. Normally they would have had to wait until after the passengers had been served but this evening they were able to eat right away. As the cockpit crew dined they remained strapped in their seats eating from trays on their laps. Duties were continued as usual with navigation and performance being monitored and communications being maintained en route.

Approaching Singkep radio beacon, situated on one of the outer Indonesian Islands, BA 009 was instructed by Singapore to call Jakarta on the HF long range radio frequency of 6556 KHz. Meanwhile, in the cabin, the trays were quickly cleared away and within one hour of departure, as the aircraft passed abeam Palembang in southern Sumatra, most were quietly asleep in the dimmed light. A few minutes later X-ray Hotel entered the Jakarta upper control area and SFO Greaves established VHF short range radio contact with Jakarta on 120.9 MHz. BA 009's progress was now monitored by radar, although position reports were still expected along the way. The crew were also monitoring their own radar sets, checking the small screens for any tell-tale signs of cloud activity lying in their path. A scanner in the nose was tilted down one degree to detect any weather ahead by reflecting transmitted signals from the large water droplets suspended in thunderclouds. The clouds would show up as small 'blips' on the pilots' radar displays. To avoid the Cb cloud it was simply a matter of engaging heading mode on the autopilot and steering round them. A faint outline of the northern coast of Java could be seen painted on the weather radar screen, but no large clouds were indicated on track.

An occasional flash of lightning appeared far to the east in the black night, and to the west lights on the coast of Sumatra were clearly visible. In the distance a low overcast obscured the brightness of the Indonesian capital. The Jakarta VOR was selected and the needles of the indicator pointed steadfastly ahead indicating that the inertial navigation system (INS) was accurately flying the south-east airway track of 157° magnetic towards the beacon. At 126 nm north of Jakarta X-ray Hotel crossed position Bidak, an important reporting point which lay on the Indonesian air defence identification zone. The wind blew from the north-east at about thirty knots giving a ground speed of 490 knots. The time was 13:17 GMT and it was estimated that X-ray Hotel would be overhead Jakarta in sixteen minutes' time.

'Jakarta, Speedbird 9,' called Greaves on the radio.

Captain Eric Moody.

'Go ahead.'

'Speedbird 9 was Bidak at 1317, level 370, Jakarta 1333.'

With the flight crew's meals finished the trays were removed and Stewardess Wright now took time to prepare her own fare. In the cockpit the relaxed progress of the flight left the crew at ease. In just under four hours they would be landing at Perth and after a short ride to the hotel some would be enjoying a few beers at a room party.

At 13:33 GMT BA 009 passed over the Jakarta VOR beacon, situated in a large bay to the north of the city, and from there the aircraft turned towards Halim VOR, lying only seventeen nm away. Its position six miles (9.6 kilometres) south-east of Jakarta marked the international airport from which the crew had departed northbound only the day before. At 13:35 GMT X-ray Hotel flew over Halim, still level at 37,000 ft, and Greaves once more radioed details of their progress to ATC.

'Speedbird 9, Halim at 35, level 370, Topar 52.'

The flight had been airborne now for almost one-and-a-half hours and Captain Moody felt it was time to stretch his legs. On long-haul journeys flight crew are encouraged to take short breaks from the cockpit and all emergency drills and procedures are designed to be performed by only two people. SFO Roger Greaves and SEO Barry Townley-Freeman were both very able and experienced airmen, with thirteen and eighteen years' flying experience respectively, so Captain

Eric Moody, himself with 9,000 flying hours and seventeen years' experience, had no reservations about leaving his copilot in charge. Flight conditions were satisfactory and a check of the weather radar indicated a clear path ahead. On exiting the flight deck Moody found the crew toilet occupied and seeing no sign of Fiona Wright assumed it was she who was having a wash and brush up before her own meal. He went below to the main deck but at the bottom of the stairs he bumped into the first class purser, Sara de Lane Lea, and stopped to talk to her for a while. He never did get to the toilet.

On the upper deck Stewardess Wright was at last able to begin her own meal, while on the flight deck all was calm. The quiet and routine progress of the aircraft reassured the two left in the cockpit that the flight was proceeding as planned, but it was an illusion of wellbeing that was soon to be shattered. In a few short moments the crew of BA 009 were to find themselves entangled in an emergency of dire proportions; caught up in an event unprecedented in the history of civil aviation.

At about 13:40 GMT Roger Greaves leaned forward in the right-hand seat to peer into the darkness beyond. His attention had been drawn by a strange visual effect on the windscreen and what appeared to be hazy conditions outside. A quick inspection of the radar screen showed no storm cells lying ahead and they were probably just catching some thin cirrus cloud or perhaps penetrating the tops of weak isolated cumulus clouds. He switched on a landing light to check the situation. At night it is sometimes difficult to tell if cloud penetration has occurred and such a procedure is an old pilot trick to illuminate the cloud if weather is encountered. A hazy effect seemed to be apparent and as a precaution the engine igniters and anti-icing systems were switched on. Combustion is normally self-sustaining once a jet engine is running, but heavy moisture can cause it to run down. In such circumstances igniters are employed which spark to maintain the engine lit without any adverse effect. Also, water droplets suspended in cloud can freeze on impact with engine sensors and nacelles and the anti-icing systems prevent disruption of the airflow through the engine. Flashing the landing light occasionally would indicate when the aircraft was in the clear and both kept a weather eye open for any change in the circumstances. It was not long before their vigilance was rewarded.

'Hey Barry, look at this.'

SEO Townley-Freeman had also noticed a glow and was already looking at the sight. Streaks of mini forked lightning flashed across the windscreen. The electrical effect is known as St Elmo's fire, which both men had witnessed before in their careers, but it is normally associated with electrical discharges in storm clouds. The flight remained smooth, nothing could be seen ahead in the form of flashing thunder clouds and no adverse weather returns appeared on the radar. All visual indications, however, were that BA 009 was on the edge of a storm cloud of intense electrical activity. Giant Cb cloud in the region can stretch up to 50-60,000 ft (15-18,000 m) and can give an aircraft quite a shaking, but it was most unusual for such thunderstorms not to appear on radar screens. If the flight was about to penetrate a storm cell it was as well to be prepared and SFO Greaves switched on the 'fasten seat belts' sign. Both flight crew already had lap and crutch straps fastened, but each now attached his shoulder harness.

The St Elmo's fire continued to develop and the two left on the flight deck had a front row view of a spectacular kaleidoscope of streaking light. The co-pilot called Stewardess Wright on the interphone.

'Fiona, come and see this. It really is quite a sight.'

'I've been flying too long to fall for anything like that, Roger. I'll be up in a minute.'

'No, no,' he insisted, 'come now. You won't believe your eyes.'

As BA 009 approached the south coast of Java, Fiona entered the flight deck and walked forward to stand behind the captain's empty seat. She stooped to look at the windscreen and was immediately taken by the beauty of the sight. The whole aircraft seemed to be enveloped in a glow and the scene ahead was like skiing at speed through a snowstorm of bright silver sparks. Amid the recognisable flashes of St Elmo's fire, streams of light like tracer bullets streaked up the windscreen. In the half-light of the darkened cockpit their faces almost shone in the irridescent light. But there was more. A strange ionised odour, like that associated with electrical sparking, could also be detected and a thin veil of mist with a bluish hue began to shroud the flight deck. Something very odd was happening to BA Flight 009.

'I don't like the look of this,' remarked Greaves. Quickly he turned to Stewardess Wright. 'I think you'd better get the skipper back up here.'

Fiona Wright made her way down the spiral staircase with some haste and from half way down called out to Captain Moody who was still standing chatting by the galley at the foot. He had been joined by CSO Skinner.

'Captain, you're wanted on the flight deck.'

He didn't need to hear her request twice to detect the urgency in her voice. Stewardess Wright turned and hurried back to the upper deck while Moody immediately dashed for the spiral staircase, mounting the steps two at a time. CSO Skinner followed behind. As the captain's head reached the floor level of the cabin above, however, he almost stopped in his tracks. In the dim light he could see from below the seats what appeared to be puffs of smoke emanating from the low level air conditioning ducts. It reminded him of the clouds of water vapour that billow from the air conditioning vents in hot and humid climates. He, too, could detect the acrid electrical odour. 'Smells like the London underground,' he thought to himself. It could also be an indication of an electrical fire. Any fire in flight is one of the greatest hazards to be encountered and he was now not at all surprised that he had been summoned back to his post.

He rushed into the flight deck and rapidly scanned the cockpit. The engine anti-icing and igniters were checked on and the fuel panel configuration was checked as satisfactory. Although the problem seemed to lie outside nothing could be seen on the radar.

'It's quite incredible,' said Greaves.

Captain Moody stared wide-eyed at the intense and spectacular display of dancing lights. For a moment the St Elmo's fire, tracer and glowing luminescence distracted his attention from the smoke enveloping the flight deck. The two cabin crew, Stewardess Wright and CSO Skinner, stood behind almost unable to believe the beauty of the sight.

'And look at the engines,' said Roger Greaves.

The captain turned to the left and could see what appeared to be the engines lit from within by an intense white hot light, like the illumination from a magnesium flare. Shafts of light extended forward from all four engines. The powerful brightness shining through the fan blades produced a stroboscopic effect which made the fans appear to turn backwards in the engine nacelles. Barry Townley-Freeman also rose briefly from the flight engineer's seat to peek from the side window behind Greaves while the flight attendants took turns to view from the captain's side.

In spite of the impressiveness of the display, however, there was mounting concern for the 'smoke' on the flight deck which was becoming more dense. If it became any worse they would have to don oxygen masks. CSO Skinner didn't need to be told something was amiss, and he quickly left the cockpit to warn the crew to prepare the cabin in case of problems. He was met by other flight attendants reporting evidence of smoke throughout the aircraft, and the instruction was given to switch off galley electrical power and to stow equipment safely.

To SEO Townley-Freeman, the thickening acrid smoke from the air-conditioning system suggested an electrical problem, and he carefully scanned his large instrument panel for any signs of trouble. The time was now 13:45 GMT and X-ray Hotel was crossing the Java coast and heading out over the Indian Ocean on Airway B69. As Townley-Freeman continued with his scrutiny, he carefully opened the check list at the drill for removal of air conditioning smoke. The procedure initially called for the donning of oxygen masks and goggles by the crew and for the switching off of gasper and recirculation fans. On the captain's command he would be ready for action. Suddenly the flicker of a light from an unexpected source caught his eye. The intermittent flashing was from a pneumatic valve light which was designed to illuminate when the valve was closed. The valve supplied compressed air direct from the engine compressors to feed air driven equipment and air conditioning and pressurisation systems. It was designed to close automatically when an engine ran down to prevent reverse flow, and its movement towards the shut position indicated more of an engine problem than trouble with the air conditioning system. Quickly Townley-Freeman glanced forward to check the main engine instruments situated in the centre of the pilot's panel. Number four engine on the outer right side was running down! Something had disturbed the flow of air through the compressors and the engine had surged, i.e. had suffered a giant hiccup, and the power was dropping. By contrast the exhaust gas temperature (EGT) was soaring and the indicator pointer was racing off the clock. The amber EGT warning light illuminated.

'Engine failure,' shouted Townley-Freeman, 'number four.'

The three flight crew: SFO Roger Greaves (left), Captain Eric Moody (centre) and SEO Barry Townley-Freeman (right) stand before *G-BDXH*'s number one engine.

The pilots also felt a slight swing of the nose as power dropped on one side and rudder was applied to hold the aircraft straight.

'Engine fire drill number four engine,' responded Captain Moody.

Greaves and Townley-Freeman carried out the fire drill from memory, closing the number four thrust lever, shutting off the fuel supply and pulling the fire handle to isolate services from the failed engine. As they completed the drill and confirmed their actions from the check list, the captain monitored the flying, holding on a little left rudder with his foot to balance the aircraft. The entire procedure had taken about thirty seconds. Some fairly quick thinking was now required, for on three engines X-ray Hotel was unable to maintain 37,000 ft (11,280 m). At about 280 tonnes they would need to descend down to 29,000 ft (8,840 m), the appropriate level for their weight and flight direction. Permission would be required from Jakarta and would have to be obtained promptly. It would also be unwise to commence a journey over the ocean on three engines, for if a second engine failed in mid-crossing BA 009 would be in a serious situation. Jakarta lay about ninety nm to the north and, with flight easily sustainable at the lower level on three engines, the sensible approach would be to turn back and land at Halim to have the engine checked. A rerouteing, however, would also require clearance over the radio. Before the crew could plan or even think procedures, events took a turn for the worse. Number two engine surged and began to run down. Once again the power drop was accompanied by a rising exhaust gas temperature.

'Number two's gone,' called the flight engineer.

Almost immediately Townley-Freeman saw to his horror that numbers one and three engines had also surged and were running down.

'They've all gone!' he shouted with disbelief.

If there was alarm on the flight deck at the situation, in the cabin the passengers, unaware of the problem, were becoming increasingly distressed. Although the main cabin lights were dimmed, the acrid 'smoke' in their midst was quite obvious and the thumping of the surging engines could be heard and felt through the structure. The glow from the engines could be clearly seen in the black night and huge sheets of flame could be seen shooting from the jet effluxes illuminating the interior of the cabin. To those by the windows it seemed as if the whole aircraft was on fire. Suddenly, for a reason they could not comprehend, those at the rear of the aircraft noticed a drop in the noise level and they could sense the cabin being engulfed in an eerie silence.

In the cockpit the initial reaction of the flight crew was one of total disbelief. Four engines don't just stop; what have we done wrong, was their first thought. Engine intakes can freeze up causing run down, but the engine anti-icing had been checked on. So, too, had the igniters to sustain combustion. Fuel mismanagement can also cause problems: it had been known on the rare occasion for all four engines to be run from one fuel tank for balancing purposes and for inattention to have caused the tank to run dry, stopping the engines. Moody and Townley-Freeman had both confirmed the fuel configuration as satisfactory. The engine indicator pointers were all over the place, causing confusion, but there was no doubt that, for whatever reason, all engines had failed.

Crew training, of course, covers every contingency, no matter how remote, and total engine failure was no exception. Only a few months earlier Captain Moody had successfully completed his biannual simulator check and had practised this very procedure. The simulator cockpit had quietened, the lights had dimmed to emergency level, the autopilot had disconnected and many instrument failure flags, including most of those on the co-pilot's side, had appeared. On X-ray Hotel's flight deck, however, the situation was quite different. The rush of air masked any reduction in engine noise, the cockpit lighting stayed on, the autopilot remained engaged and the instrumentation, apart from the engine indicators, displayed as normal. Whatever was happening to X-ray Hotel was a complete mystery. The strange storm producing the intense electrical activity also seemed to be affecting the power, and some unknown force had choked the engines into silence.

Immediately Captain Moody instructed Greaves to send

out a Mayday and Townley-Freeman commenced the 'loss of all generators' drill. The procedure assumed, of course, that primary services had been lost: pneumatics, including pressurisation and air conditioning, normally supplied by bleeds from the engine compressors, and electrics, normally supplied by the engine-driven generators. With total engine failure, however, no attempt to restart could begin without standby electrical power from the batteries to supply essential engine controls: fuel valves, start levers, standby ignition and some engine indicators. The 'loss of all generator' drill, therefore, began by checking that the battery switch was on and that the standby electrical busbars were powered. DC power from the battery was changed by an inverter into AC to supply the standby AC busbar. The combination of DC and AC buses also fed the captain's flight instruments, number one VHF radio, the interphone and the PA system. Having checked these items Townley-Freeman then opened the fuel cross-feed valves. In a matter of seconds he had reached the point at which the drill split: loss of electrical power caused by a massive short which had tripped all the generators, or the loss of all generators caused by total engine failure. In this case the course of action was obvious, and he prepared for in-flight starting of the engines. The air was too thin at cruising altitude for an engine start to be recommended, but under the circumstances there was little point in waiting and it seemed worth a try.

'Mayday, Mayday, Mayday,' shouted Greaves over the radio. He called on the Jakarta control frequency of 120.9 MHz, having set the emergency code of A7700 on the transponder. If there was no reply he would transmit on the emergency frequency of 121.5 MHz. 'Speedbird 9, our position is 100 miles south of Halim. We have lost all four engines. We're descending and we're out of level 370.'

Silence, and then a few moments later: 'Jakarta, Speedbird 9, have you got a problem?'

The electrical static produced by the storm was distorting transmissions and making communications difficult.

'Jakarta, Speedbird 9,' repeated Greaves carefully, 'we have lost all four engines. We are descending and we are now out of level 360.'

Another short pause followed, then Jakarta replied. 'Speedbird 9, understand you have lost number four engine?'

Greaves turned in frustration to his Captain. 'The fuckwit doesn't understand.'

'Negative, Jakarta, Speedbird 9,' spoke Greaves slowly and distinctly, trying to control his frustration. 'We have lost all four engines, repeat all four engines. Now descending through level 350.'

The Jakarta controller was still unable to understand but fortunately a Garuda Indonesian Airways flight on the frequency interrupted the exchange.

'Jakarta, Garuda 875, Speedbird 9 has lost all four engines, he's lost *all* his engines, and he's out of level 370.

At last Jakarta got the message and understood the full force of the problem. Greaves requested radar assistance for return to Jakarta but the conditions prevented the controller from identifying X-ray Hotel. In the end the first officer simply told the controller they were turning back for a landing at Halim Airport. As Greaves battled with the radio, Townley-Freeman fought to bring the engines back to life. The number four engine had been fully shut down so the fire handle was reset and the thrust lever was placed in line with the others. Although it was not advisable to relight an engine after a non-recoverable stall unless a greater emergency occurred, this occasion surely qualified. It seemed common sense to Captain Moody and the crew to attempt to restart any one out of four engines instead of any one out of three. For the flight crew, however, the mental action of reading the check lists and performing the drills in such a desperate situation was, in Barry Townley-Freeman's own words, like trying to think through treacle. In such circumstances it is the man who can use his common sense who will win the day. The reinstating of number four engine may have seemed like a simple act but it was to prove significant at a later stage.

To begin the start sequence the start levers were selected to cut-off to reschedule the fuel control units. The standby ignition was switched on to power the igniters and the start levers were selected back to idle. The crew looked in hope to see the instrument readings rising indicating light up.

Nothing. Not even a hint that at least one engine was going to start.

In the meantime, the captain had exchanged height for speed and had commenced descent to stop the speed dropping further. Using the autopilot he had set 500 ft (150 m) per minute descent and the speed had settled on the airspeed indicator at 270 knots, which was close to the speed for minimum drag for the present all-up weight. He now turned the autopilot knob to bank left, clear of the airway, and although X-ray Hotel was descending over the sea he set the safety height for the return to Jakarta over Java of 11,500 ft (3,500 m) in the altitude select window. It is normal in such reports of aviation emergencies to read of aircraft plummetting to the ground, but in this case it was far from true. Normal descent procedures approaching destination include closure of the throttles to idle power at top of descent and the aircraft literally glides to the lower levels before power is re-applied for the approach to land. The aircraft's sleek aerodynamic lines reduce air resistances to a minimum and even slowing down without power at level flight takes time.

In X-ray Hotel's situation the lack of any residual thrust from idling engines and the drag from the big engine fans windmilling in the airstream would increase the rate of descent, but it would only be marginal. The windmilling engines, however, were a distinct advantage in this emergency, for even at speeds as low as 160 knots they could still turn the hydraulic pumps sufficiently to pressurise the system for operation of the aircraft's flying controls. Also, unknown to the crew at the time, in spite of complete engine failure number three generator had stayed on line, supplying electrical power. It was being driven by the windmilling engine and was the reason the autopilot had remained engaged and the cockpit lighting and instrumentation displays had stayed normal. The generator would not remain on line for long, however, but when it tripped electrical power would be supplied by the batteries for thirty minutes.

Meanwhile the captain could use the autopilot to control the aircraft in the descent and leave himself more free to concentrate on the problems in hand. The cabin was normally pressurised by the engine compressors to a pressure equivalent to 6,000 ft (1,830 m), but with power loss, even though the outflow valves had automatically run closed, the cabin pressure was beginning to drop.

In spite of total engine failure, therefore, the aircraft was under control. Hydraulic pressure was sufficient to operate the flying controls, electrical power, although fluctuating, was still available from number three generator, and the cabin pressure, although reducing, was still sufficient for normal breathing. X-ray Hotel was descending at around 2,000 ft (610 m) per minute and was now out of 35,000 ft (10,670 m). In its clean condition, i.e. no flaps or gear lowered, it could remain airborne without power for about a further twenty minutes, covering a ground distance of approximately 140 nm. Although the aircraft was in dire straits the problems were compounding gradually and the crew were able to gather their senses. The initial alarm had subsided and with the adrenalin flowing the three worked well together as a team. Even the early failures to start the engines did not leave the flight crew in complete despair. Engine start required conditions to be within certain para-meters: indicated airspeed 250-270 knots, altitude below 28,000 ft (8,530 m), and windmilling engine compressor rotations within tolerance. Once they had descended to lower altitudes they were sure the engines would fire up again. After all, the same had happened in the simulator check; once below 28,000 ft the engines had relit. And X-ray Hotel was also a Rolls-Royce aircraft: American-built but fitted with good reliable British Rolls-Royce engines. Of course they would start.

Turning the aircraft back to Jakarta brought BA 009 closer to a suitable airport where the captain could land once the engines had been restored, but attempting a dead stick landing, i.e. touching down without power, could not be considered. Judging such a landing in the darkness would be almost impossible and the chances of success negligible. There was also a tall mountain range lying across Java which resulted in the safety height being as high as 11,500 ft. X-ray Hotel could not clear the high ground without power.

Many of the mountains were volcanoes and some of them were very active. In the Sunda Strait which separates the Indonesian islands of Java and Sumatra was once situated the then volcanic island of Krakatoa which erupted on 27 August 1883. The explosion was equivalent to a force of 50,000 H-bombs and blew the island completely off the map. The bang went on record as the loudest produced on earth and was heard halfway round the world. Almost one hundred years later, another mountain of the chain, Mount Galunggung, situated 100 miles (160 kilometres) south-east of Jakarta on the Java coast and one of sixty-seven currently active volcanoes in Indonesia, had recently been belching fumes into the atmosphere. It was considered the most dangerous and a major eruption was expected.

A map showing BA 009's routeing on B69. Also shown is the position of Mount Galunggung and the area of volcanic ash.

If the crew were unable to start the engines they would be forced to ditch in the black sea, but that was some way off. There was still about eighteen minutes to save the situation and all their efforts and thoughts could be concentrated on the single aim of getting the engines going again. They had no opportunity to think beyond their immediate tasks and they had not reached the point of assuming the worst. At that stage they were too busy to be afraid, but they were not to realise then that shortly the situation would turn much worse. Later they would know fear.

Once more the three scanned the flight deck for clues as to their predicament: engine anti-icing on; standby igniters on when required; fuel panel checked, all main boost pumps on; circuit breakers checked, all confirmed set. The thrust levers were simply left in the positions they were in at the time of failure. Again the start levers were selected to cut-off, fuel shut-off valves were checked open, standby ignition was selected and the start levers were set to idle. Still no response.

By now the crew had exhausted all their options and it was simply a matter of selecting the start levers to cut-off, switching on standby ignition, and reselecting the start levers to idle. Standard procedures in an emergency, requiring the captain to fly the aircraft and the other two to perform the drills, were abandoned in the circumstances. With the autopilot still engaged and the radio work completed for the moment, both pilots found themselves free to lend a hand and all three took turns at trying to start the engines. If persistence alone could have achieved results the four engines should have roared into life, but it was not to be. They remained ominously silent. In the cabin the initial alarm had subsided, but there was mounting apprehension at their plight. The captain had been too busy to make an announcement and the passengers were ignorant of the circumstances. Those at the rear of the cabin by the windows could witness, without realising what they saw, the crew's attempts to get the engines going. On each occasion when fuel was introduced and the engine failed to light-up, the kerosine ignited in a huge flame which shot from the jet efflux. The process shook and vibrated the aircraft.

The number three generator was still being driven by the slowly rotating windmilling engine via a constant speed drive which was unable properly to perform its task. The resulting fluctuating frequency made the cabin lights cycle on and off, brighter one moment then dim the next. At the back of the cabin the eerie silence also persisted and they could hear each other breathe. Under the circumstances it would not have been surprising if the passengers had panicked, but they remained remarkably calm. The cabin crew did a wonderful job in reassuring the travellers and moved about the cabin comforting those in greatest distress.

At this stage BA 009 was only a few minutes into the emergency and the crew seemed to have exhausted all their options except the hope of starting the engines at a lower altitude. Amazingly, most of the captain's and first officer's flight instruments remained powered and displayed normal indications and the cockpit lighting remained illuminated. Only occasionally did some engine instrument failure flags appear. The engine indicators were a mix of Smiths and General Electrics and the former gauges froze where they stood with power loss while the latter gauges ran to zero. It made it almost impossible to monitor properly the engine start sequence and difficult to know whether or not light-up was occurring. To add to the difficulties, the electrical storm still danced magnificently before their eyes and their headsets crackled loudly from static interference.

X-ray Hotel was now descending through 30,000 ft (9,144 m) out over the ocean at a rate of 2,000 ft per minute, in a gentle turn back towards Jakarta. If the engines failed to relight Captain Moody would simply turn back southbound away from the mountains and remain over the flat sea. Townley-Freeman continued with the start attempts and with the approach of 28,000 ft (8,530 m) all were confident of a recovery. Still nothing happened.

With time, the bluish mist in the cabin began to disperse as the inert compressors of the failed engines no longer pumped contaminated air, or any air at all for that matter, into the aircraft. Oxygen masks were not needed as a protection against the 'smoke', but they would shortly be required for another reason. As X-ray Hotel descended through 28,000 ft (8,535 m), an intermittent warning horn sounded in the cockpit: *beep, beep, beep*. Although the aircraft was descending the cabin was, in a sense, ascending, as the pressurised air within leaked to the atmosphere. On 'climbing' through 10,000 ft (3,050 m) the cabin pressurisation warning horn sounded and the flight crew were obliged to use oxygen. It was a moment that those in the cockpit did not relish for the masks were uncomfortable to wear, but what happened next took them all by surprise.

To begin with the flight engineer's mask stowage had been incorrectly installed and it was impossible to reach while seated. At a time when seconds were precious he had to undo his seat belt and stand up before stretching backwards to reach his mask. As the pilots pulled their oxygen mask harnesses over their heads, the supply hose of Greaves's mask came away in his hand and the connecting pieces fell apart in his lap. He was now without oxygen in the 'climbing' cabin and as the altitude increased he was in danger, if the situation continued, of suffering from anoxia. The effect induces a feeling of wellbeing in the victim although performance is akin to being drunk. Unconsciousness eventually results.

Standard procedure for the failure of pressurisation in the cruise is for a steep descent to be initiated immediately. The throttles are closed, speed brakes are deployed, the gear is lowered and the nose is pushed down to attain maximum speed. Descent rates of 10,000 to 12,000 ft (3-3,600 m) per minute can be achieved and the aircraft can quickly be brought to safety at a lower level. In X-ray Hotel's case it was pointless to throw away precious height if, for the time being, the crew could breathe normally, but with the threat of incapacitation to his co-pilot, the captain had little choice but to get down quickly. Captain Moody disconnected the autopilot to hand fly the aircraft and lowered the nose.

It was an agonising process for Moody to throw away height, the one commodity which could both buy them time and save everyone's life. The landing gear could be lowered by using the alternate system which simply released up-latches to allow the wheels to drop by gravity. Once lowered in such a manner, however, it could not be raised. If a ditching became necessary, touching down on the sea with the landing gear extended could place the aircraft in danger. Moody compromised on procedures by pulling only the speed brake lever, but even so the aircraft dropped at an alarming 6,000 ft (1,830 m) per minute. The passengers could feel a rumble through the cabin with the speed brakes deployed. As height tumbled from the altimeters, Greaves fought desperately to refit the hose attachment. With nimble fingers and cool nerves he managed to fit the pieces together and to place the mask on his face. By now the aircraft had descended to about 20,000 ft (6,100 m) and Moody retracted the speed brakes to resume the glide.

'I've got 320 knots,' said Greaves. 'We are going too fast.'

A speed of 250-270 knots was required for engine start but his airspeed indicator displayed a higher speed. The captain quickly glanced across.

'That's strange, I've got 270 knots.'

The discrepancy of fifty knots was a mystery, but could be the cause of the engines failing to relight at the lower altitude. Captain Moody varied the speed using the co-pilot's airspeed indicator and then his own while the flight engineer repeated the start sequence, but to no avail. In the cabin, to add to the passengers' discomfort, the aircraft now seemed inexplicably to climb and descend at varying rates and they could feel the heaving in the pits of their stomachs. There was still no time for the captain to explain the predicament, even if he knew what was happening, so in more ways than one the passengers were left in the dark.

The cabin continued to 'climb' in spite of the aircraft descending and, as X-ray Hotel passed 18,000 ft (5,485 m), the cabin height rose through 14,000 ft (4,270 m). Passenger oxygen masks dropped from their overhead stowages. The appearance of the masks added to the distress of the travellers who had just felt what seemed to be the aircraft plummetting out of control. The cabin crew donned portable oxygen equipment and performed a marvellous job in calming the more disturbed passengers and helping to fit masks as they walked round the cabin. Unbelievable as it may seem some travellers were still asleep. The emergency announcement explaining how to use the masks had failed to function and CSO Skinner found he was unable to operate the PA system from the cabin stations. He pulled a megaphone from one of the overhead lockers and attracted the attention of the passengers to give them instructions.

'Can you hear me, mother?' he called, imitating a northern English accent. It brought a moment of light relief that was greatly needed.

On the flight deck attempts to start the engines continued without success as Moody hand-flew the aircraft. The fifty knot discrepancy in the airspeed indicators was still evident and once again he varied the speed. X-ray Hotel was now running out of height although mysteriously descent was not as fast as expected. The outside air temperature was much higher than normal and the hot rising air was also producing an uplift to help keep BA 009 airborne, not unlike that experienced by a glider in an updraught. X-ray Hotel was still losing the race against time, however, and the flight crew were under a lot of pressure. The dim cockpit lighting, the wearing of uncomfortable oxygen masks, the flashing electrical discharges, and the loud headphone static did not make their tasks any easier. The electrical activity in the atmosphere also seemed to be playing some very strange tricks on the aircraft's electrical systems. The inertial navigation system displayed random digits and patterns, with nothing making sense, the VOR needles spun round in circles and the distance measuring equipment (DME) was blank. The dark night made visual flying impossible and the captain had to fly solely on instruments.

It was now that nagging doubts began to invade their minds and thoughts that the engines might not start entered their heads. Townley-Freeman surmised that water contamination in the fuel tanks could be causing the problem and if that was so there was no way the engines were going to light up again. There would be no choice but to ditch. Captain Moody had already decided that he would fly towards Jakarta until approaching 12,000 ft (3,660 m) just above the Java safety height, and then he would turn southbound to land on the sea. It was not a prospect any of them relished. The pilots understood the principles of ditching: landing along the line of the primary or predominant swell and upwind and into the secondary swell, or downwind and down the secondary swell. That was the theory, of course, but landing on a shark-infested ocean in a black night with a heavy sea running was a different matter.

The captain had watched flying boats as a boy and knew that they didn't operate at night because of the difficulty in judging height in the darkness. On X-ray Hotel, if only battery power was available for ditching, there would be no radio altimeter for precise height indication and there would be no landing lights available. The landing gear would remain retracted and the underside of the aircraft would present a smooth surface to the sea on touchdown, but it would not be possible to lower flaps and the ditching would be fast. The aircraft stall speed at sea level was 179 knots, so to achieve a safe margin a speed of 190-200 knots would be required. The engines would almost certainly break off on impact and the wings and structure might be damaged. Once stopped the aircraft would probably remain afloat for a reasonable time, but launching the life rafts in the heavy swell would be extremely difficult. There would also be a very real danger of sharks. X-ray Hotel was now descending through 16,000 ft (4,880 m) and if the engines didn't start soon they were going to be in trouble. Strangely, the flight crew as yet felt no great fear, but there was certainly growing apprehension.

In the cockpit the captain now felt they had caught up with events but there seemed little more they could do. Townley-Freeman had not rested in his attempts to start the engines and he continued to try. He would still be having a go when they touched the sea, if it came to that. Greaves repeated requests for radar assistance from Jakarta, but the electrical storm was making contact difficult. There was still no range or bearing information from Halim VOR, but one of the three inertial navigation sets suddenly made some sense and true track and distance were observed and transmitted to Jakarta.

'We're out of level 150 now, descending,' radioed Greaves, giving the position information at the same time.

'Roger, Speedbird 9, if possible maintain not lower than 12,000.'

It was a useful reminder of the safety height.

In these dire circumstances the captain felt the need to speak to CSO Skinner and to ensure that he understood the predicament, but Moody was unable to contact him on the interphone. The captain also felt that, in spite of the situation, he had some spare thinking capacity and now seemed an appropriate moment to talk to the passengers. He could also request Skinner's presence at the same time. Moody took a deep breath and spoke into the oxygen mask: there was little he could do but tell the truth.

'Ladies and gentlemen, this is your captain speaking. We have a small problem. All four engines have stopped. We are doing our damndest to get them going again. I trust you are not in too much distress.' There was a short pause in which the message took effect, then he added, 'Would the CSO come to the flight deck immediately, please.'

The last statement was not only a summons to Skinner, but was also a signal to the cabin crew in an emergency to stow their equipment and to move to their respective stations. No-one was now left in any doubt as to their predicament. As CSO Skinner made his way towards the flight deck, Captain Moody's mind flashed to a scene from a training film depicting a moment of great emergency. He could recall the amateurish screen captain delivering his instructions to his senior flight attendant in stilted but impeccable English.

'It seems it's not our day. I'm afraid we're going to have to ditch.'

It was not Moody's way. As Skinner entered the flight deck carrying his portable oxygen set the captain turned briefly to glance at his CSO.

'Got the picture?' he shouted with difficulty through his mask.

Skinner only heard a muffled sound, but didn't press the matter. He could guess from the activity on the flight deck that a forced landing, probably on the sea, was imminent. He gave a quick thumbs up to his captain and when no further direction was forthcoming he returned to the cabin.

The flight crew now began to feel more than concern for the height being lost. As the aircraft descended through

14,000 ft (4,270 m), about one minute remained before Captain Moody planned to turn southbound again and back out to sea. Once heading away from Java, approximately five minutes — no more — would be left for some further endeavour at starting the engines, then the flight would be over. The time was now 13:57 GMT, and X-ray Hotel had been without engine power for over twelve minutes. The crew had lost count of the number of failed attempts and it was unlikely at this stage that their efforts would bear fruit. It did not stop them trying, but a ditching seemed inevitable. Now they knew fear.

At that moment X-ray Hotel appeared to break from the hazy cloud of the electrical storm, and the aircraft flew into clear air. The dancing lights vanished from the windscreen and the glow from the engines dimmed. Suddenly Townley-Freeman let out a cry.

'Number four's started!'

The three watched with bated breath as the engine gauges rose steadily and the power settled. Gingerly Moody advanced the thrust lever and the engine ran successfully at normal power. It was only one relit, but they were on the road to recovery. In the cabin the roar of the engine was music to the passengers' ears. If they now turned out to sea and descended to a lower altitude, quickly dumping fuel at the same time to lose weight, they may just be able to remain airborne. If they couldn't hold height the power would at least slow the rate of descent. More importantly, the vital services of electrics, hydraulics and pneumatics could now be supplied from this one engine, and, if necessary, compressed air could be tapped from the engine to help turn the others and give a better chance of starting them. Number four engine had been shut down early in the emergency and it had been the least affected by whatever had caused the damage. It now seemed to have saved the day. The crew could also now remove their rather uncomfortable oxygen masks. X-ray Hotel's rate of descent eased to 300 ft (ninety m) per minute, but the aircraft continued inexorably downwards. Approaching 12,500 ft (3,810 m) there was little margin to clear the mountains for an emergency landing at Jakarta. As the seconds ticked by the initial relief abated, for all efforts to get the others going proved to be in vain. One minute passed in what seemed like an eternity, and still the moments slipped away. A further twenty seconds went by without success, then Townley-Freeman called out again.

'Number three's lighting up.'

Soon number three was restored to life and with two engines running at sufficient power to arrest the rate of descent, the aircraft was held level at 12,000 ft (3,660 m). X-ray Hotel could now remain safely at altitude if only the engines, which were probably damaged, could sustain power. They could then cross the mountains and execute a two-engine landing at Jakarta. Almost immediately numbers one and two engines relit in sequence and, from a situation of great danger only a few moments earlier, they now found themselves with all four engines running normally.

'Jakarta, Speedbird 9,' called a relieved Greaves, 'we're back in business, all four engines running, back at 12,000.'

Unfortunately the controllers were still unable to establish radar contact because of X-ray Hotel's proximity to the mountains, and a request was made for climb to 15,000 ft (4,570 m). As the aircraft levelled off at the new height, Greaves relayed their position giving bearing and distance from Halim VOR and radar contact was confirmed. The airspeed indicators had settled down and were reading in agreement but 'A' autopilot would not re-engage. 'B' was selected instead. They now seemed home and dry with their troubles over, but there was more to come. In the meantime the captain took advantage of this quiet moment to speak to the passengers.

'Ladies and gentlemen, we seem to have overcome our problems and have managed to start all the engines. We are diverting to Jakarta and expect to land in about fifteen minutes.'

Captain Moody had no sooner replaced the PA handset when they found themselves in the hazy conditions again. Once more the St Elmo's fire danced on the windscreen and their headsets crackled loudly with the static. There was no doubt that X-ray Hotel had climbed back into danger and Moody's first thought was to descend out of it as quickly as possible.

'Christ, we're not staying here.'

Moody slammed the throttles closed and lowered the nose for descent to 12,000 ft. Suddenly number two engine surged violently. It auto-recovered and surged again. The bangs from the engine were so loud they could be heard on the flight deck and the entire aircraft shook. Having lost all four earlier the crew were reluctant to shut one down again themselves, but they had little choice.

'Shut down drill number two engine,' shouted Moody.

The other two performed the drill and, with the fuel cut, engine power ceased. X-ray Hotel was now back on three engines. The failure of the number two engine for a second time gave the crew quite a shock, for it indicated that the damage sustained was worse than previously realised. Would another engine fail again?

'Speedbird 9,' radioed Greaves, 'we've lost another engine. We're now on three and we're descending to 12,000 feet.

Jakarta Control approved the lower level and issued radar vectors for their prompt return to Halim.

'Ladies and Gentlemen,' spoke the captain again on the PA, 'I have had to shut down number two engine as it was rough running. We shall be landing in Jakarta in about ten minutes.'

The general feeling aboard BA 009 was the sooner on the ground the better, but it was now obvious that some gentle nursing of the aircraft was going to be required to ensure a safe landing. Rather than adjust the power and risk further upsets, Moody used the speedbrakes to control aircraft speed, and once over the mountains began a shallow descent with speedbrakes deployed. Fortunately, Jakarta weather was fine with a calm wind, little cloud and good visibility. Runway 24 was in use and the temperature was 26°C. A few minutes later, Control instructed Greaves to call Jakarta Approach on 119.7 MHz.

X-ray Hotel now approached Halim Airport from the south-east but the aircraft was too high for landing and some height needed to be lost. Moody decided to overfly the 'AL' non-directional beacon, situated on the approach to the landing runway, at about 10,000 ft (3,050 m) and then to proceed initially to the north-west before banking right in a shallow descending turn out over the sea. He would complete the let-down by flying all the way round to land to the south-west. It was a non-standard approach which suited their purposes, and they would be guided on the way by radar which would direct them onto the instrument landing system (ILS). Fortunately, the crew had been into Halim in the daylight only the previous day, so they had recent experience of the airport. They knew there was a lot of high ground in the area.

X-ray Hotel was cleared initially to 2,500 ft (760 m), but as descent continued Captain Moody was informed of another difficulty. Normally the ILS displays both runway centre line and descent path guidance, but at Halim only runway direction guidance was available. On a big jet, judging the correct descent profile for the approach to land without radio aids is difficult at the best of times, but after a major emergency it was the last thing the captain wanted. Fortunately, visual approach slope indicators (VASIs) were available, if they could see them, for in spite of the clear visibility indicated by the controller, the conditions were very misty. It was more like dust haze, in fact, and there was a sulphurous odour in the air.

As X-ray Hotel completed the turn and approached the airport from the north, heading 210° under radar control, the flight was further instructed to descend to 1,500 ft (457 m) and was cleared to pick up the ILS extended runway centre line. Halim lay to the crew's right, about eight miles (13 kilometres) away, but the view through the first officer's number two window still appeared hazy.

'Can you turn up the runway lights?' requested Greaves over the radio.

Moody turned the 747 on to final approach and suddenly, from a dark area on the ground ahead, the brightened runway lights could be seen, but the view was very blurred. It was as if there was oil on the windscreen but the wipers and washers had no effect. Unknown to the crew, the 'cloud' which had choked the power from the engines had also sandblasted the windscreens. As BA 009 got nearer the brightness of the runway lights on the opaque windscreen blinded their vision and they had to be turned down a little.

A landing light window showing the opaque effect of the sandblasting. The 747 windshields were similarly affected. (British Airways)

The central and inboard sections of the pilot's windows were worst affected, but Moody managed to catch sight of the left side of the runway through a relatively clear three or four inch wide outer strip. Leaning sideways he established on the runway centre line and gingerly commenced descent on the final approach.

Greaves retained the distance measuring equipment on his side and called out the recommended descent profile of 300 ft per mile (fifty-seven m/kilometre): distance four miles, height 1,200 ft; distance three miles, height 900 ft; etc. He switched on the landing lights but their covers were also opaque and they gave almost no illumination. Greaves then called the Tower on 118.3 MHz and was given the clearance to land.

Captain Moody's view was not very clear but at least he could pick out the VASIs and had some descent slope indication. Sitting in this bent position, however, made it difficult to scane the instruments at the same time, an essential part of flying a large aircraft. As an aid, Greaves called out the heights every twenty-five feet (7.6 metres) from the radio altimeter. Townley-Freeman called the speed and the engine power settings. Cautiously X-ray Hotel groped towards the runway. On three engines, with visibility curtailed, difficulty in reading the flight instruments and no radio descent path indication, Moody had his work cut out. It was, in the immortal words of the Hampshire captain, like trying to negotiate your way up a badger's arse. The cabin crew had been instructed to prepare for an emergency landing and they waited anxiously at their stations.

BA 009 finally crossed the threshold of runway 24 at 150 knots but, as Moody prepared for touchdown, he still found his forward vision severely reduced. The lack of landing lights did not help. Normally pilots look far down the runway to judge height on landing but Moody could view only the hazy outline of the left-hand runway lights closest to him. Using all his experience he eased back gently on the control column and the wheels kissed the ground. It was a perfect touchdown. In the cabin the passengers spontaneously applauded. The time was 14:10 GMT and the emergency had lasted twenty-five minutes, thirteen of which had been totally without engine power. In a period of less than a quarter of an hour they had been to the edge of great danger and back again. Moody ran the aircraft right to the end of the 9,800 ft (2,990 m) runway then, with Greaves's help, managed to feel his way round the turning pad and to back-track towards the terminal. Eventually they groped their way to a turn off but as they approached the stand area the bright lights completely obscured their view.

'That's it,' said Moody. 'We're stopping here.'

Greaves called the tower to say they were unable to taxy further and asked for a towing truck to pull them to the arrival gate. Townley-Freeman then fired up the auxiliary power unit and shut down the engines. It was all over. The tension drained from their bodies and they were flooded with relief. There was no doubt it had been a close-run affair, but the cause of their predicament remained a mystery. As the arrival of the tow truck was awaited the flight crew had time to reflect on their experience. Black dust seemed to lie everywhere on the flight deck. Barry Townley-Freeman wiped his hand across a surface and rubbed the substance he picked up between his thumb and fingers. It was gritty, sooty and had a sulphurous smell.

'I reckon that's volcanic ash, you know.'

No-one believed him at the time, but the next day he was proved right.

On the evening of 24 June, Mount Galunggung, the active volcano situated on the south Java coast 100 miles (160 kilometres) south-east of Jakarta, had erupted violently. Giant plumes of ash and grit had been hurled eight miles (thirteen kilometres) into the air. The explosion had created a vast volcanic storm of thick, hot sulphurous gases and high electrical activity. No aviation warning was given. North-easterly winds aloft at twenty-five to thirty knots had blown the plume across the path of BA 009 and it had been engulfed in ash. Flying through the hot grit at speed had the effect of sandblasting X-ray Hotel's leading edges and had stripped paint and caused the opaque surface on the windscreens and landing light covers. The dust had pen-etrated aircraft sensors such as pitot tubes which sense dynamic pressure to measure airspeed. The discrepancy in the airspeeds was the result. The engine nacelles, intakes and fans were shot-blasted and stripped clean. Erosion of the compressor blades had occurred and the ash, which was of a silicate material, had fused in contact with the hot metal of the combustion chambers and turbines. Deposits of fused volcanic ash up to half an inch in diameter were later discovered in all the engine tailpipes. The effect was sufficient to disrupt the airflow and was similar to dampening a blaze with sand. As a result the engines had flamed-out and all power had been lost. At 13,500 ft (4,115 m), X-ray Hotel had broken into clean air and the least damaged engine, number four, had roared into life. Subsequent climb to 15,000 ft (4,570 m) had taken them back into the ash cloud. It was a close escape which might have ended

Fused volcanic ash on the number two engine high pressure nozzle guide vane. (Rolls-Royce Ltd)

tragically had not the skill, coolness and persistence of the flight crew won the day. But the passengers and crew of BA 009 were lucky, too, for the aircraft only just emerged from the volcanic storm in the nick of time.

'If the base of the ash cloud had dropped to the sea,' said Moody, 'so would we.'

Captain Moody was awarded the Queen's Commendation for Valuable Service in the Air, plus the British Airline Pilots Association Gold Medal, the Guild of Air Pilots and Navigators Hugh Gordon Burge Memorial Air Safety Award, British Airways Board Certificate of Commendation, Award as one of the twelve 'Men of the Year' in Britain, and Lloyds of London presentation set of crystal decanters. SFO Roger Greaves was awarded the British Airline Pilots Association Gold Medal and Lloyds of London presentation silver tray. SEO Barry Townley-Freeman was awarded the Flight Engineers International Association's Frank Durkin Award and Lloyds of London presentation silver tray. CSO Skinner

The entire crew of BA 009, with the then deputy chairman, Mr Roy Watts, at the British Airways Award presentation ceremony. (British Airways)

was awarded the Queen's Commendation for Valuable Service in the Air, the British Airways Board Certificate of Commendation and Lloyds of London presentation silver tray. Those mentioned above also received, together with the remainder of the crew, the British Airways Customer Service Award.

Of all the awards, accolades and applause received by the captain and crew of BA 009, however, no praise was more heartfelt than that offered by one of the Australian passengers. With great emotion she sobbed, 'I'll never rubbish the Poms again.'

# Epilogue

*Emergency* proved to be a most enjoyable book to write and during its production many interesting and gracious people were met along the way. Much kindness and help was willingly given. The fact that most participants were quite humble about their experiences, in spite of the heroic endeavours involved, served only to increase their stature. On some occasions help was forthcoming under the most extraordinary pressure, as in the case of Captain Pat Levix, who still found the strength to offer assistance only shortly after his son Jim was discovered murdered by persons unknown in 1987. Such men are gracious indeed.

The author managed to contact, sometimes with great difficulty, at least one flight crew member from each of the major events outlined in the chapters of the book. The search was conducted from Anchorage to Auckland and from Ottawa to Miami and involved some time-consuming 'detective' work. Fortunately, some lucky breaks during the process contributed to success. A few gentlemen, such as Harry Orlady of the San Francisco office of NASA's Aviation Safety Reporting System, were able to furnish information which proved invaluable to the completion of the book and the tracing of individuals. Without such help *Emergency* could not have been written.

All the participants contacted were interviewed either by letter, telephone or in person and each was given the opportunity to read the manuscript. Advice was freely given on improving and correcting the texts and the assistance was gratefully received. The final drafts, without exception, were accepted and approved by all concerned, giving *Emergency* an accuracy and authenticity not always found in aviation publications. It is hoped that the reader has been given a refreshing insight into the drills and procedures of modern flight crew members, not only during difficult and unusual circumstances, but also in the day-to-day operation of an aircraft. It is seldom as simple a task as it seems.

In all the incidents recounted in this book, in spite of the seriousness of some of the situations, not a single life was lost, and this in itself is a great credit to the aircrew involved. The accolades received by the participants in these events are not only a testament to their skills, but also to the abilities of pilots and flight engineers everywhere. The problems outlined in *Emergency* are but a sample of the difficulties, some more critical than others, faced on rare occasions by crew members in the execution of their duties. Few of these incidents are heard outside the profession and, of those who perform their tasks so successfully, most remain unknown and unsung heroes.

The men and women of the airlines who fly their machines throughout the world give of their best at all times and are ready for any contingency. When the completely unexpected arises, as in some of the stories of this book, crews are known to respond with ingenuity and resourcefulness. And, in the everyday operation of an aircraft, the expertise and professionalism exercised daily by crews during flights contribute significantly to making air travel routine, commonplace and, most importantly, safe. The travelling public can feel comfortable with the knowledge that aircrews, like all other personnel within the aviation industry, are doing their utmost to maintain standards. It is hoped that *Emergency* has increased the general awareness of the capability of aircrews and that it inspires confidence. Above all, it is intended to reassure.

# Abbreviations and Glossary

| | |
|---|---|
| AC | alternating current |
| ADF | automatic direction finder |
| Aileron | wing turn control |
| AINS | area inertial navigation system |
| ALPA | Airline Pilots' Association (US) |
| Alternate | diversion airport |
| APU | auxiliary power unit |
| ASI | airspeed indicator |
| ATC | air traffic control |
| ATCC | air traffic control centre |
| ATIS | automatic terminal information service |
| Attitude | aircraft orientation relative to the horizontal e.g. nose up attitude |
| | |
| CAT | clear air turbulence |
| Cb | cumulonimbus cloud |
| circuit breaker | breaks electrical circuit |
| CSD | cabin services director |
| CVR | cockpit voice recorder |
| | |
| DC | direct current |
| DF | direction finding |
| DME | distance measuring equipment |
| Drag | air resistance to motion |
| Drift | wind effect |
| | |
| EGT | exhaust gas temperature |
| Elevators | tailplane climb and descent control |
| EPR | engine pressure ratio |
| ETA | estimated time of arrival |

| | |
|---|---|
| FAA | Federal Aviation Administration (US) |
| FDR | flight data recorder |
| F/E | flight engineer |
| FIR | flight information region |
| Flaps | wing trailing edge lift devices |
| Flare | arrest of descent on landing |
| Flight level | level expressed in hundreds of feet, e.g. FL 390 = 39,000 ft |
| FMC | flight management computer |
| FMS | flight management system |
| F/O | first officer |
| | |
| 'g' | effect of gravity |
| Gear | undercarriage |
| Glide path | approach descent profile |
| GMT | Greenwich Mean Time |
| Go-around | missed approach procedure |
| Graduated take-off | reduced power take-off |
| | |
| HF | high frequency (long range radio) |
| Hold | holding area before approach to land |
| | |
| IAS | indicated airspeed |
| ILS | instrument landing system (runway centre line and glide path radio guidance) |
| INS | inertial navigation system |
| | |
| KHz | kiloHertz |
| Knot | nautical miles per hour |
| | |
| Mach number | aircraft speed relative to local speed of sound |
| Mayday | radio distress call |
| mb | millibar |
| MEL | minimum equipment list |
| MHz | megaHertz |
| | |
| NDB | non-directional radio beacon |
| nm | nautical miles |
| NTSB | National Transport Safety Board (US) |

| | |
|---|---|
| PA | public address system |
| psi | pounds per square inch |
| | |
| RMI | radio magnetic indicator |
| rpm | revolutions per minute |
| Rudder | tail fin yaw control |
| RVR | runway visual range |
| | |
| SEO | senior engineer officer |
| SFO | senior first officer |
| Slats | wing leading edge lift devices |
| sm | statute mile |
| S/O | second officer |
| Spoilers | speed brakes used to spoil lift |
| Squawk | radar transponder coded transmission |
| Squawk code | aircraft transponder code |
| Squawk ident | press aircraft identification button |
| Stabiliser | variable incidence tailplane |
| Stack | hold |
| Stall | loss of lift |
| | |
| TAS | true airspeed |
| Transponder | airborne equipment which receives a ground radar signal and responds by transmitting back a coded signal |
| | |
| V1 | take-off go or no-go decision speed |
| VR | rotation or lift-off speed |
| V2 | initial safe climb out speed |
| VASI | visual approach slope indicator |
| VHF | very high frequency (short range radio) |
| VOR | VHF omni-directional range radio beacon |
| | |
| Yaw | aircraft nose movement, left or right, in horizontal plane |

# Bibliography

**Chapter One — Pacific Search**
> *Air New Zealand Staff Magazine*

**Chapter Two — Bermuda Tangle**
> National Transport Safety Board Report, NTSB-AA4-84/04

**Chapter Three — To Take-off or Not to Take-off**
> National Transport Safety Board Report, NTSB-AAR-72/17

**Chapter Four — The Windsor Incident**
> National Transport Safety Board Report, NTSB-AAR/73/2
>
> Eddy, Paul; Potter, Elaine and Page, Bruce, *Destination Disaster*, Hart, Davies, McGibbon, 1976
>
> Godson, John, *The Rise and Fall of the DC-10*, New English Library, 1975

**Chapter Five — Don't be Fuelish**
> Pan Am Incident Report
>
> Canadian Air Safety Board Report, T22-64/1985E

**Chapter Six — The Blackest Day**
> Arey, James A., *The Sky Pirates*, Charles, Scribners' Sons, 1972, Ian Allen, UK, 1973
>
> Redfield, Holland L., *Thirty-five years at the outer marker*, Pitot Publishing Co., 1981

**Chapter Seven — Ice Cool**
> National Transport Safety Board Report, NTSB-AAR-82/4

**Chapter Eight — Roll Out the Barrel**
> National Transport Safety Board Report, NTSB-AAB-86/3
>
> National Transport Safety Board Report, NTSB-AAR-81/8
>
> AL PA Report, 1981

**Chapter Nine — Strange Encounter**
> Tootell, Betty, *All Four Engines Have Failed*, André Deutsch, 1985
>
> Diamond, Captain Jack, 'Down to a sunless sea', BALPA 'Log' article, April, 1986